MW01061416

THE AUTHOR:
ADOLF DICKFELD

ORIGINAL COVER ART

BY

LONNIE ORTEGA

We propose to offer the original cover art as a limited edition art print, numbered and signed by the author, Mr. Dickfeld and the artist, Mr. Ortega.

FOOTSTEPS

OF THE

HUNTER

ADOLF DICKFELD

Translated by David Johnston

FOOTSTEPS OF THE HUNTER

By Adolf Dickfeld
English translation by David Johnston

Copyright © 1993 by
J.J. Fedorowicz Publishing Inc.

Published by
J.J. Fedorowicz Publishing Inc.
267 Whitegates Crescent
Winnipeg, Manitoba
Canada R3K 1L2
(204) 837-6080

Printed in the USA
ISBN 0-921991-17-7

Typeset by The JADA Group
Printed by Publishers Press

PUBLISHER'S ACKNOWLEDGEMENTS

We wish to thank the following individuals who have contributed to the publishing of this book.

David Johntson --- Translation
Lonnie Ortega --- Cover Art
Brian Molloy --- Signing Box

We also wish to thank you the reader for purchasing this book, and all those of you who have written us with your kind words of praise and encouragement. It gives us the impetus to continue to publish both translations of the best German books available as well as specially commissioned books. More excellent books are either being prepared or negotiated, thanks to your helpful proposals. These will be announced as they near completion.

John Fedorowicz and Mike Olive

Books published by J.J. Fedorowicz Publishing

THE LEIBSTANDARTE (1 SS Panzer Division) volumes I, II, III, and IV/1
EUROPEAN VOLUNTEERS (5 SS Panzer Division)
DAS REICH I (2 SS Panzer Division)
OTTO WEIDINGER
OTTO KUMM
MANHAY, THE ARDENNES; CHRISTMAS 1944
ARMOR BATTLES OF THE WAFFEN-SS 1943-45
TIGER; THE HISTORY OF A LEGENDARY WEAPON 1942-45
HITLER MOVES EAST
PANZER ACES
TIGERS IN THE MUD
FIELD UNIFORMS OF THE GERMAN ARMY PANZER FORCES IN
    WORLD WAR 2

In preparation for publication in 1994
HISTORY OF THE 12 SS PANZER DIVISION HITLERJUGEND
DAS REICH II
INFANTERIE ACES
GRENADIER
LUFTWAFFE ACES

J.J. Fedorowicz Publishing Inc.

Table of Contents

FOOTSTEPS
OF
THE HUNTER

by

ADOLF DICKFELD

Adolf Dickfeld was born on 20 February 1910 in Jüterbog, Mark Brandenburg. As a student he demonstrated his technical gifts by establishing a radio link between a ship in the Arctic and one in the Anarctic, and by setting up Europe's highest radio station on Mont Blanc. As well, in 1928, he played a leading role in the rescuing of the crew of the downed airship "Italia", commanded by Admiral Noble, after receiving the ship's SOS. After graduating he took up flying and was later trained as a fighter pilot while a reservist.

At the outbreak of war Dickfeld was assigned to III/JG 52 and flew missions over France, England, Greece and Crete before his unit was transferred to Rumania.

With the outbreak of war against the Soviet Union, Adolf Dickfeld soon became a well-known fighter pilot because of his numerous victories achieved in a short period of time. In 1942 he scored an amazing series of victories (11 on the 8th of May, 9 on the 14th and 10 on the 18th) which resulted in the awarding of the Knight's Cross with Oak Leaves.

Soon afterward, Dickfeld was named "Gruppenkommandeur" of II/JG 2, which was immediately transferred to North Africa. He achieved further victories in Tunisia before being injured in a takeoff accident.

After recovering from his injuries, Dickfeld was appointed "Gruppenkommandeur" of II/JG 11, a Reich Defense unit based in the Bremen-Helgoland area of northern Germany. He scored further kills against the Anglo-American air forces before being appointed to the position of "General of the Replacement Luftwaffe" in the RLM in Berlin.

Dickfeld once again flew operational sorties shortly before the end of the war, against advancing Soviet forces in the Lansberg-Küstrin area.

Finally, Dickfeld was charged by Göring with the formation of a fighter unit equipped with the Heinkel He 162 jet fighter. He flew a number of sorties in the He 162, scoring one victory.

During the Second World War Adolf Dickfeld flew a total of 1,072 combat missions and scored 151 victories, 136 of which were confirmed.

The Military Career of Adolf Dickfeld

Entry into the Luftwaffe:
1 March 1937 with *Aufklärungsgeschwader 7.*

Promotions:
Leutnant: 11 December 1939
Oberleutnant: 21 May 1942
Hauptmann: 7 January 1943
Major: 18 May 1943
Oberstleutnant: 21 June 1944
Oberst: 22 February 1945

Decorations:
Iron Cross, Second Class: 13 December 1939
German Cross in Gold: 3 May 1941
Iron Cross, First Class: 12 January 1942
Knight's Cross: 19 March 1942
Knight's Cross with Oak Leaves: 19 May 1942
Honour Goblet: 15 December 1943
Mentioned in the Armed Forces Communique: 5 May 1941

Victories:
18 August 1941 victory number 10
24 October 1941 victories number 16-20
29 April 1942 victory number 56
08 May 1942 victories number 63-73
14 May 1942 victories number 82-90
18 May 1942 victories number 91-100
19 May 1942 victory number 101
Further victories in North Africa and in the Defence of the Reich.

Total of 151, of which 136 were confirmed, in 1,072 combat missions

FOREWORD

Almost half a century has passed since I laid down my weapons, weapons which I believed I had to use to protect my homeland against enemies who had been hammered into my head since my childhood.

Out of the shambles of the First World War, as the son of a General, I knew nothing else but to wait for the day when I could avenge my dead father, who was killed at Verdun in 1917.

Hitler came and took us all into his arms, we who felt ourselves surrounded by enemies. We gladly followed his slogans, for the outside world was an unknown for us, a hellish conspiracy against our existence, against our mothers and fathers who sought to protect us.

No, we were not a will-less tool in Hitler's hands, but we were a generation bent on revenge.

Not until today do we see how blind we were, how naively we followed slogans such as: The traditional enemy sits on the other side of the Rhine, the enemy is the Jew, the enemy is the Russian, the Pole, the American and so on and so on.

Fate followed its course and sucked me into a maelstrom of misery and hopelessness. Gradually, however, I learned to value the things I had not known earlier, things like tolerance, the acknowledgement of other mentalities, other races, religions, ways of thinking and the good in other men. Oh but it was so late in life that I learned to honour these values and to adopt them as my own. But it was not in vain and I am thankful for that.

INTRODUCTION

It is best that you put this book down if you are expecting sweet tales of May nights and silver clouds gliding by, or something equally lyric or asthetic, for the war knew nothing of lyricism or asthetics, not even of pity. All that it knew was terror, force, hate, sweat, blood and tears. This is a book about a war which witnessed the pitiless destruction of peoples, races, existances, and the lives of men like you and I. Put it down if you do not wish to see events as they really were. Keep your beliefs in the holy, just world until reality overtakes you. Just don't suffer the same fate as I, who, believing with child-like naievete in those who were supposed to be our role models, placed his life in the balance and in the end was forced to pay, empty handed, for the crimes of others until the end of his days.

It has taken a long time for me to decide to write from my soul; not of "Deutschland, Deutschland über alles", of heroism, blood and earth, of the nordic elite or of other things which were given to us as slogans. Actually I intended to take it all with me to the grave, hidden away from all those who came after me; I no longer wished to be confronted with the terrible memories and experiences to which one had been exposed in a time which was later to be called the Second World War, a war which followed years of a shamefully unsuccessful democracy associated with bitter distress, and lack of work. Senior statesmen from Great Britain and France, indeed from the whole world, vied with one another for HItler's favour without recognizing his goals. As Brecht said so tellingly in his work "Galilei"; "He who does not know the truth but nevertheless suppresses it in spite of knowing better, or who even calls it a lie, is a detestable criminal!"

Today the Prime Ministers of Great Britain and France shed crocodile tears as they excuse themselves for their predecessors, Chamberlain and Daladier, having concluded the Munich Agreement with Hitler in 1938. How were we then, completely inexperienced and unsuspecting in political matters as we were (we were after all still children), supposed to distinguish between king and charlatan and realise what game was really afoot? But later it was we who were supposed to shoulder the entire burden for what had taken place, a burden which we could not and were unwilling to bear. No we were not ready to bear the guilt unto the third and fourth generations, no matter how much some might have liked it. Right up to the present day human history contains numerous such examples and it will remain so long as those in power are capable of the most terrible crimes. Whether called Attila, Alexander, Nero, Cortez, King Gustav of Sweden, Napoleon, Hitler, Churchill, Harris, Stalin, Pol Pot, Brezhnev, Khomeni, Ghaddafi, Xiaoping, Ceaucescu, Ulbricht, Honecker, or Hussein of Iraq, who has just lost the war there is always another ready to cause his neighbors and us so much trouble.

I could easily add another dozen names guilty of similar terror.

And let us not forget Lebanon, where there is fighting between Moslems and Christians, Moslems and Jews, or vice versa, and what about Ireland, where Catholics and Protestant murder in the name of God, and this is in the middle of Europe? In South Africa the black followers of Mandela of the ANC and Buthelezi of Inkatha kill each other instead of fighting together against the hated apartheid regime. What of the acts of cruelty of a Milosevic or a Karadsic in Yugoslavia and in the same context the scandalous, pitiful failure of the European Community, to say nothing of the United Nations and its questionable "Blue Helmet Operations"?

One sees helpless "world personnel" running here and there in Yugoslavia, driven to flight, begging and praying at the sides of the roads and at the roadblocks.

As well one could name Cambodia, Haiti, Zaire, Togo, Angola, Afghanistan, Azerbaizhan, Tadzhikistan, Armenia, Georgia, the Far East and so on and so on. Oh what an unendingly tragic history of humanity! What was it that a certain Max Liebermann, who was also quite a good painter by the way, once said: "I couldn't possibly eat enough to throw up as much as I'd like in the face of such madness!"

Everyone has blood on his hands, the blood of millions of innocent people — men, women and children. Even as a soldier who intended to serve his fatherland, one is not free of it. But it is well known that in war each side has its own truth. I suffer as a result of it and can no longer explain what might have once driven me to do what I did. But whatever it is, it still stands behind me and looks over my shoulder with its long shadow. Long a stranger to me, a someone whom I believe I scarcely know but whom I must know, I am inextricably bound to him until my last hour on this spaceship we call the earth.

Only hypocrites are free of guilt and God knows we have enough of those, especially in our land, always ready to wash their hands in innocence. Often I ask myself, "Were you perhaps born in the wrong century as a result of a tiny mistake by the "great computer", which others once called "providence". There is no pity for being born too soon or too late.

Times change men, times change cultures, religions, the climate, the environment, the solar system, indeed the entire universe in every second we breathe. I myself will do no more than attempt to illustrate the horror and the cruelty of the war, with only a few happy moments, for it was a war which knew no pity, especially by the victors toward the vanquished. "Vaehe Victus"! Where have I read that before?

War has become practical again, one need look no farther than the Gulf War. But obviously it has always been so and will always remain that way as long as human feeble-mindedness can rule unpredictable minds. More than 200 conflicts have been waged since th end of the Second World War alone, claiming more victims than the First and Second World Wars combined. More than 50 conflicts are currently being waged, leaving behind mass graves, broken families, raped women, streams of refugees, unending suffering, hunger, and destroyed cultures, to say nothing of nature. It is becoming increasingly obvious that war is no way to settle problems in our highly integrated community, but who, even in our enlightened century, has held true to such a notion, following the maxims of the United Nations, the European Community, or other equally complacent, self-serving organisations?

A Learning Experience

Kraussen-Guterfeld, who'd ever heard of the damned place? It was way up in the East where even the foxes didn't say good night. The first time I heard of it was when a completely overtaxed *Feldwebel* in Berlin catapulted me up into that part of East Prussia. On my arrival I saw a few scattered shacks and not much else, but far on the horizon, scarcely visible to the eye, there was an air base with huge hangars and several runways. A Kübelwagen drove me there. This was to be my home for the next few months. People talked of war, of the impudent Poles who had attacked a radio transmitter in Upper Silesia and killed some people. There was also talk of teaching them a lesson as quickly as possible. It made little difference to me; my fighter pilot training would take some time and by the time it was over Poland would have been long forgotten.

We were a thrown-together group of pilots from every conceivable field, from Lufthansa drivers to survey specialists, and in the midst of it all me, a blind flying instructor on the Ju 52. The course didn't involve much theory; we were familiarized with the latest types, the bomber pilots with the Ju 88, which was later to become so famous, and we fighter pilots with the Messerschmitt Bf 109. There were nine of us budding fighter pilots, all ready to serve Führer, Volk, and Fatherland. I had never seen one of these fast birds before, while the other eight already knew all about

5

the Bf 109. Just seeing one caused my heart to drop into my trousers, but what could I do? It was my own doing after all. When the pasty-faced *Feldwebel* in Berlin asked whether I had flown the Bf 109 before, I had replied: "I've done more than 100 takeoffs in the bird!"

It was of course a boldfaced lie, which was a capital offence, but I was willing to do anything to become a fighter pilot. The ruse had worked and I kept my secret to myself while waiting to see how things turned out. I did let my good friend Fritz Simon, a test pilot with the Mauser works, in on the secret. He provided encouragement and in the evenings gave me a private theoretical course on how to fly the Bf 109.

Finally he said to me, "If you're not too stupid you'll soon have both aerobatics certificates to go with all your flying licences. Stay on your toes or you'll crack up for sure, in which case the Fatherland will have to do without your services. Oh, before I forget, where do you wish to be buried?"

He had the nature of a butcher's dog, that fellow. And so my only hope for the coming day was luck, for the Me was a single-seater and there was no instructor in back to help out. I slept fitfully. Since my name began with the letter D, I was to be first out of the gate the next morning right after breakfast. I was scared to death as I climbed into the cockpit and strapped in. Simon was at my side. He spoke to me calmly, and we quickly went over the controls and possible problems once more. Then he closed the canopy. The motor was running. I opened the throttle and the bird raced off with me as if it had been shot from a pistol. It felt as if a regiment of sparrows were flying out my rear end. Knees shaking, I held the rudder, and after a few seconds the beast lifted off by itself. I soon had the bird in hand, however, nothing could go wrong now. I made a butter-smooth landing right in front of the instructor. Soaked in sweat, I clambered out of the cockpit.

Simon came over to me and said, "You idiot, that went quite well, what were you on about?"

The following weeks were filled with various exercises. In the meantime our armed forces had overrun Poland and everything seemed quiet on the Western Front.

Then came a day I'll not soon forget and one which comes back to me even today. We were sitting at breakfast, Ebbinghaus, Kraus, and I. Kraus smeared an extra-thick layer of cheese on his bread, and as he ate his creation said, "You'll have the room all to yourself tonight. On our return from the channel we're going to land in Hamburg and then tie one on in the Reeperbahn. But don't squeal on us! It's a shame that you have to stay here!"

The two of them were making their first long-distance flight that day, to the English Channel and back. They had planned it well, staying up late into the night studying maps. It was just after eight, and I had to get out onto the airfield, the "old man" was waiting. There was just time for a quick handshake; I wished them good luck and said, "see you tonight." These were to be the last words I ever spoke to them.

I saw their Ju 88 begin its takeoff roll. The aircraft lifted off, climbed about 50 metres, and then suddenly rolled onto its back before crashing at the end of the runway in a tremendous explosion. Fire trucks and ambulances raced across the airfield. Paralysed, we sat at the takeoff point. It was impossible to tell whether anyone had survived, as the crash site was too far away.

Our flying activities went on as usual. About midday we heard the news: Walter Ebbinghaus and Karl Kraus were no more. Killed as a result of human error was the simple explanation given.

The next morning, following a sleepless night, I was summoned by the CO. Without further ado he said to me, "You're off flying duties for today. A Kübel will take you to Königsberg where you are to go to the hospital to identify the bodies of your two roommates."

I was dumbstruck. Before I could say a word the Major had gone out the door and I was left with my orders, as pale as the walls. It was 0900. If I hurried I could be in Königsberg by 1100. Bright sunshine accompanied me into the city on the Pregel. I reached the main entrance of the hospital. More than anything I would liked to have turned round and left, but what could I do, orders were orders! I identified myself to the doorman.

"You'll probably have difficulty finding the autopsy theatre quickly," he said candidly, "So come with me."

We walked down many corridors and around numerous corners and finally ended up in front of a white door. The good man opened it and the scene that greeted me almost boggled my mind. Lying on two large cement tables were two human bodies, face down. Two young doctors had obviously removed the backbones of both. The gutters were full of blood and excrement.

One of the two looked at me and said, "Ah, you've come for the identification. Step closer."

As he said this he grasped one of the corpses by the hair on the back of the head, turned it around, and sprayed it with water so that I could see the features. It was Ebbinghaus' face, or what was left of it. My stomach turned and I threw up, grasping a chair.

"Now young man, don't be so squeamish," said the other anatomist. "You'll soon see worse than this in the war."

He turned the other body towards me. Without doubt it had to be Kraus, but the once proud face was now little more than a mess of blood and brains.

I must have fallen from the stool, because when I came to I was lying on a cot in the hall. A nurse was standing beside me with smelling salts.

7

"He's coming to," I heard her say.

Then an older doctor helped me to my feet and took me into his office.

"Were you able to identify both of them?" he asked sullenly.

"Yes, I believe it's Ebbinghaus and Kraus."

"Sign the certificate here and then you may go."

I did what he asked. A voice inside screamed at me to just get away, away from this perversion of blood, brains, entrails, brutality, and indifference. When I finally stepped out into the bright sunshine it was as if I had awakened from a terrible dream. These scenes were to haunt me for a long time. Back at the airfield Simon came into my room.

"How was it?" he asked incidentally, as if he had just come from a party. "Oh before I forget, you're to go and see the 'old man,' he's asked for you several times already."

I didn't wait around for an explanation and soon I was standing in the room of the *Oberleutnant*.

"Good that you're here," he began. "I have news. Because of your good flying evaluations you're to be the first to be sent to an active fighter wing. Congratulations. Tomorrow morning you'll travel to Laachen-Speyerdorf on the Western Front, I think it's somewhere on the Wine Road. All the best and good luck!"

He shook my hand and I was dismissed. That evening Simon and the others threw me a little party in my room. Quite drunk, I fell into bed, and I had a rather difficult time getting up the next morning.

. . .And It All Began So Innocently!

Dead tired from the long train ride, I found myself standing in my light sky-blue uniform (I had been hastily kitted out by the stores sergeant), at the temporary end of what was likely to be a long journey. The tiny city on the wine road was still sound asleep, far and wide there was no one I could ask for directions. Even the station master appeared to be still dozing, so I trotted on foot to the market place, my heavy kit bag over my shoulder. Finally I encountered the first sign of human habitation, an old woman.

"Dear lady, could you possibly tell me the best way to the airfield?"

Looking me up and down she replied, "You must want the fighters out at Laachen-Speyerdorf."

"Yes, yes," I replied, somewhat astonished.

"The best way is to take the bus which will be leaving in a few minutes from right here in front of the town hall."

I thanked her politely. The kindly woman went on her way. She turned to look at me several times, shaking her head. What must she think of me, I thought to myself. Then the bus arrived and soon it dropped me off at the front gate of an airfield. There was a surprise waiting for me in the office; they weren't expecting me and were rather uncertain what they should do with me. Then a *Hauptmann* blew in. I saluted and reported my arrival from Kraussen-Gutenfeld, transferred to JG 52, and produced my transfer papers.

The *Hauptmann* also seemed to be at a loss at first, but in the end he said good-naturedly, "Well, since you're already here we don't want to send you right back, quite apart from the fact that it would mean a long train ride back up to East Prussia. I'll assign you to *Oberleutnant* Keidel's 3 *Staffel*. You can work out everything else with him."

The *Hauptmann* disappeared as quickly as he had come. I heaved my kit bag onto my back again and made my way to the "Third." After passing some brand-new "Me's" I finally arrived in a smoke-filled barracks where a lively game of skat was in progress. A rather young *Oberleutnant* threw down his cards and came over to me.

"Ah, you're the new one. *Hauptmann* Graf Peil has already told me about you."

He told me to sit and began leafing through my papers and asking me questions.

"So you've already flown the Me, hmm, hmm, also gunnery practice on ground targets, target sleeve, dogfighting, and so on?" he asked slightly sceptically. "And how old you are, already 29 and married, two children. Man, that makes you the Methuselah of our *Gruppe*. I don't think we'll be going into business together. It's your age and limited experience on the Me, but Plunser will take you up tomorrow morning and then we'll see."

Then he abruptly turned his back on me and picked up his cards again. The game resumed: "Eighteen, twenty, two, zero, pass."

The next thing I knew I was outside on the airfield again in front of the barracks belonging to the "Third." I felt ashamed, and more than anything I would liked to have bundled up my things and headed back to East Prussia straight away. Then someone called to me in an Austrian dialect. I snapped to attention and saluted.

The man introduced himself: "I'm *Oberleutnant* Plunser, tomorrow morning we'll be going up together. If what you've told the *Staffelkapitän* is true you'll have no problems. But come into the mess now, you've surely not eaten yet."

And so we walked into the main building, where French pilots may well have dined right after the First World War. We got to know one another while we ate. He was from Innsbruck and had only recently been taken into the *Luftwaffe* from the former Austrian Air Force, along with a number of other Austrians as I learned later. He told me that I shouldn't take Oblt. Keidel's gruff manner too seriously, as he was otherwise quite an affable man who had already seen combat in Spain with the Condor Legion. Afterward I was assigned my quarters, which I shared with two other pilots. That evening I fell dead tired into the quilts and didn't come to until I was awakened by the sound of running feet in the corridor. It was exactly six A.M. I heard someone shout for the coffee orderlies to fall out. As I turned over I thought: thank God you don't have to get up! However my two roommates had already jumped out of their beds. "Inspection is at 7 o'clock and the pilots have to fall in as well, so you'd better get your rear end out of bed otherwise you won't be in the mess in time for breakfast. That won't impress the old man!"

I raced into the washroom where I ran into Plunser. As he washed he told me that we were to begin our aerial circus at nine. I was to meet him in front of the "Third"'s barracks.

I showed up punctually, my parachute on my back, and there they were, the two Messerschmitts. The mechanics were sitting on the wings of the aircraft, waiting for "my" Oberleutnant. The weather couldn't have been better, a clear blue sky and not a cloud to be seen. Then he arrived, my "examiner."

"I'm sure you're familiar with the new Me 109 Dora. It has a few more horsepower than the Berta you've flown, but that shouldn't bother you. You know how the circus works: you stick to me and don't lose sight of me. We will fly various maneuvers and after half an hour or so we'll come back for a second breakfast in the mess. Alright, let's go then."

When he had finished speaking, Plunser swung himself into the cockpit of his aircraft.

I climbed into my machine. Radio check: all in order. Canopy shut. The mechanic turned the crank and in a few seconds the engine was purring smoothly. But something kept my heart in my trousers. What if the lad in front of me was a better pilot than I. What if he lost me and I, being unfamiliar with this area from the air, couldn't find my way back to the airfield? It was a feeling worse than homesickness. We taxied out for takeoff and Plunser opened his throttle. I did the same. We lifted off and the fellow began a snap roll barely 50 meters above the ground. What could I do but follow? Nice prospects indeed! Then he began to climb. Our machines hung in the sky like flour sacks. I was thinking that he would never stop climbing when suddenly he tipped forward with me behind right him. It was at this point that I lost my breakfast. For a second Plunser was only visible through an evil-smelling "fog bank," but I stayed close behind him. Meanwhile he had pulled up again. We climbed and climbed.

"Oxygen mask on," he ordered over the radio.

It was just as well that everything had come up, otherwise wearing the mask would have been much less pleasant. I felt relieved. The fellow in front could do what he liked: loop, roll, half-roll and dive, it didn't matter, I stayed on his heels. Then he dived toward the airfield from a good 9,000 meters. I adjusted the propeller pitch, selected flaps and landing gear down, and in no time we were back on the soft, grass-covered surface of Laachen-Speyerdorf, he in good condition, I covered with vomit from top to bottom. I opened the canopy and climbed out of my crate. I walked over to report.

Plunser began to laugh, and said, "Don't feel bad, I did the same thing on my first aerial circus. Meet me in the mess when you've cleaned up, or have you no appetite for a decent coffee?"

But nothing came of the invitation. As soon as I had washed up for the second time that morning I was summoned by the *Staffelkapitän*.

"I watched you with Plunser. Not bad the way you stayed with him. I think we might go into business yet. Anyway stay with us for now. If you can play skat then our good fortune will be complete," he said, not without a trace of irony. (I would later play many great hands with him as part of a foursome!)

Meanwhile the battle of all battles was growing in intensity. At the *Westwall*, which we were supposed to protect, the French had been reinforced by the arrival of the English. The climate became noticeably more raw. Our opponents were French Morane fighters. During my first contact with the enemy I froze. I was seized by a terrible fear and when the first Morane came toward me with its guns blazing I reported that I had engine trouble and headed for home. Morally destroyed inside, I landed alone and gave my "damage report" to the technical officer. He looked at me sceptically for some time, and then went into his barracks without a word. Reeling, I walked to the command post, where I could hear the excited voices of my comrades, who were still engaged in the air battle. I didn't know what to do: should I go to my quarters and put a bullet through my head for cowardice in the face of the enemy? What would happen to Liesel and the children? Then the first 109s landed and our pilots jumped out, still gripped by hunting fever. One reported shooting down an enemy aircraft. I crawled into my room, ready to pack my bundle again and flee far, far away to peaceful East Prussia. Then the door flew open and Oblt. Plunser was standing before me. He came over and sat on my bed.

"I would rather have a pilot back on the ground again following 'engine trouble,' with whom I can discuss everything calmly, than a dare-devil who gets himself shot down and ends up burnt up somewhere. I'll see you at supper."

Then he left again. I had no idea how grateful I was to be in the coming years for this advice.

Outside the weather was awful. Fog, fog, and more fog. I had overcome my "cowardice phase." For days we sat in the mess playing skat and drinking beer, with "Löwenbräu Export" being our favourite brand. Our meteorologist said this was typical weather for this area just before Christmas. It was only three days until Christmas Eve, what was it to bring us? Then the chief blew in and we jumped to our feet.

"As you were!" said Oblt Keidel cheerfully, "I have news for you. We will be celebrating Christmas Eve tonight. We've had to move the date up slightly, you'll see why soon enough!"

Then he disappeared as quickly as he had come. We looked at one another in bewilderment, probably also a little stupidly, but everyone in the circle thought, that's the air force for you, and went back to playing cards again.

It was just three o'clock in the afternoon. Outside it was already dark, but none of us was in the mood for "Silent Night" or "Oh Tannenbaum." A few kilometers away in the *Westwall* sat the infantry, like us waiting for orders, orders to strike out, to achieve victory over an enemy who wanted to destroy our home, our fatherland, whether it be France, England, Poland or anyone else who wished us ill. Well-camouflaged, our Messerschmitts sat round the dispersal, fuelled, armed, and ready to "tear the arm" off the enemy. There had been a few skirmishes with French reconnaissance aircraft in the past few days but for the most part there wasn't much going on. Then Oblt. Lewald burst in.

"The mess must be cleared as the orderlies have to set the tables for the Christmas celebration; please go to your rooms and be back here punctually at 9 o'clock. I may assume that you will consider the dignity of this evening and dress accordingly."

The poor fellow, he didn't have an easy time with us, we pulled every practical joke in the book on him. Two days earlier one of our number had secretly placed a sun lamp to shine on his balding forehead while he slept. He subsequently sought out the "assassin" responsible for his bright red, badly-burned pate. Only two days later he took his revenge on us in an even more common fashion.

The hours passed quickly. It was exactly 9 o'clock and each of us stood "booted and spurred" at his seat in front of one of the festively decorated tables. The chief entered and we came to attention. Then he invited us to sit down. There was tension in his face. We weren't used to seeing him like this. Then the large folding doors of the mess opened and in walked the supreme commander in person, Adolf Hitler, surrounded by a staff. He was as we knew him from photographs in the press, only he seemed pale and weary, his face frozen like a mask. Hptm. Graf Peil jumped up and presented himself.

"*Mein Führer*", he said, his voice trembling slightly, "II *Gruppe* of *Jagdgeschwader* 52 present for the Christmas celebration."

Hitler had us sit down and then seated himself at the end of the table. The orderlies served supper and the room was deathly still except for the rattling of knives and forks. One could have heard the famous pin drop. Each of us in turn risked a quick glance toward the end of the table to make sure that it really was the *Führer* and not a double. Many of us pinched ourselves and at the same time wondered why this honour should have fallen to an unknown fighter unit such as ours.

Then the *Führer* stood up and began to speak softly, his voice barely audible. I heard words such as: home, fatherland, family, women and children, defense against an enemy who wants only one thing, namely the destruction of the *Reich*. There was something striking, something demanding about the voice, and for the first time I sensed what bound, captivated, and yes, even compelled the masses to this man. He told us that we are very lucky to stand in the front lines in defense of a unique empire, a unique nation. What the fatherland asked of us was no more or no less than what each of our wives risked in childbirth, namely our own lives. We were impressed, and before we could fully comprehend everything he had said, Hitler and his staff had gone again, leaving us full of foreboding, doubt, and yes, even dismay. Each of us was lost in his own thoughts. This was how I had always imagined the people's tribunes in ancient Rome or Greece, who purposely drove a people into battle. There was no singing of "Silent Night" or "Oh Tannenbaum" that evening. The same night we were moved north. The ground personnel left immediately while we pilots prepared to depart at dawn.

First Disillusionment

For some days now the unit had been back on the outskirts of Trier, that old and venerable cathedral city, and to please us pilots we'd been quartered in the Jesuit monastery high above the city. The view of the Mosel Valley and the surrounding vineyards was breathtaking. *Leutnant* Hölzel arrived with our rations, and in addition to the usual tins of meat and cheese and the awful service bread he had organized a large quantity of wine. The wine made the rounds for several hours and soon the sound of singing and laughter could be heard from the monastery. *Leutnant* Schulz, a tall Saxon, was scarcely able to stay on his feet. It was still not too late, just before midnight I would guess. Suddenly there was a din and loud cheering! In came *Leutnant* Waldner, his arms full of crucifixes he had gathered as he staggered from room to room. He obviously intended to throw them from a window.

"Man," he shouted, belching loudly, "Look at all the 'tree observers,' I've never seen so many and that's only the fourth floor. How many do you think there are in this entire prayer shack? They should all go in the trash, I say all the 'tree observers' out of this lousy monastery!"

I felt sick, but before I could react *Leutnant* Fermer, a stocky East Prussian, stood up, swung, and hit the man right in the mouth. Waldner fell and the crucifixes tumbled loudly onto the stone floor. It had become quiet. Waldner spat blood. Stunned, we left the scene of this perversion. I felt a chill. Who knew what the next day would bring us?

So far the war had been anything but exciting, at least for us fighter pilots. There was scarcely any action. Apparently our bombers were letting the French have it, but without us. Occasionally a battered He 111 came staggering back from the West at low altitude to attempt a crash-landing on the grass field. One day one such bomber neared our airfield. It fired

red flares as it approached, letting those on the ground know that it was in serious trouble and needed help. The bomber touched down and for a few minutes a huge dust cloud shrouded the drama. We raced to the crash site in our car. The scene we found was horrible. The pilot was slumped over the control column, bleeding from the mouth. The observer, his face chalk-white, showed no signs of life. His lower body was torn and intestines welled out. The gunner dropped down out of the bomb-bay. He had been wounded in the thigh but stood up at once.

"We got hit while making a low-level attack," was all he could say before a deep unconsciousness mercifully took him into its arms.

None of us remained unaffected by this awful scene. I'm sure many wondered if one day they might not end up looking the same, or perhaps even worse. But what was there to worry about? The *Führer* had promised a speedy victory and perhaps we wouldn't even see action. It would be a pity if we came home from the war after so short a time without having fired a shot or at least having smelled powder! What would we say to your children or even grandchildren when they asked: "Tell me grandpa, what was it really like in France back then? Did you kill many Frenchmen?" And we'd have won no Iron Cross for bravery, to say nothing of the Knight's Cross or other high decoration.

The unit was moved farther west. We landed at an airfield at a place called Sissonne. The French campaign seemed to be progressing smoothly. I had time to indulge my curiosity and have a look around. Infantry and artillery battles had left terrible scars on this blessed patch of earth, with awful consequences for the population. I stopped at the first barn I come to. It had been completely destroyed. The swelling cadavers of dozens of horses and pigs lay in the pitiless sun. A bestial stench hung in the air. Nearby, at the likewise destroyed farmhouse, lay the bodies of two French soldiers. I moved closer and saw that they were negroes. Their bodies, too, had swelled to bursting in the heat; only the uniforms kept the corpses together. I was about to move on when I hear something. Was that a voice? It sounded like someone groaning in pain beneath the wreckage of the house. There was no doubt about it: the voice was French and was coming from inside. I went closer and saw a human hand. Drawing upon my schoolboy French, I called: "Can I help you?"

The hand moved a little. I began digging like mad with my bare hands, and after a good half-hour I had freed the man, a French soldier. He was unconscious. I fetched a can of water from the well and poured it over his head. He came to and looked at me in surprise. I could almost sense what he was thinking: A Boche! He's going to liquidate me now." His eyes told it all.

"Don't be afraid," I said to the man, "I'll take you to a hospital. They'll help you there."

I'm not sure how I got the heavy man into my car. All I know is that I got him to the hospital tent where Dr. Sander looked at the man, who had a stomach wound, and assured me that he'd pull through. (Back then I couldn't imagine that I would one day run into this very Frenchman again in Tahiti, where he was an appointed notary.)

We're still in the Champagne, and who wouldn't roll his eyes and click his tongue, to say nothing of his palate, on hearing this name.

"Go out and see if you can't get some red wine," suggested *Hauptmann* Döring, who was always finding fault with me. "This area is supposed to be one big wine keg. It would be a shame if we couldn't supplement our rations with a few bottles of such delicacies."

So once again I climbed into the Kübel and headed out into the countryside past the destroyed farmhouse from the day before. The corpses and carcasses were still there. When was someone going to bury them? At the entrance to the next village I passed a winery. Take a look inside and see what's to be done there, I thought to myself as I drove into the courtyard. The house appeared to be deserted. I called but no one answered. In the living room on the raised first floor there was a freshly-set table, but the food, now swarming with flies, had apparently not been touched. The occupants must have fled their home in panic and left everything behind. Out back a stairway led into an open wine cellar. I encountered a wine mist while I was still outside. I went down the few stairs quickly, and what I found almost took my breath away. The cellar was filled with wine. The red liquid was still pouring out of holes in the huge casks, obviously caused by rifle and pistol bullets. In the half darkness I saw the bodies of two German soldiers floating in this pool. I was horrified. Already nearly overcome by the wine mist, I stumbled up the steps to get some fresh air. How could they have ended up here? Did they just want to get drunk or was it curiosity? I simply didn't have the nerve to recover the dead men. The infantry could pull their comrades from this disgusting lake themselves. How would they write to their parents: "Fallen for *Führer*, Volk, and Fatherland?" Will their names one day be chiselled in marble at a military cemetery? I drove back to the *Staffel*, silent and lost in thought. I was met there by *Hauptmann* Döring.

"And where's the wine," he growled. "What did you waste our precious fuel on? Were you at the brothel? We'll certainly never win the war with the likes of you!" (The man had no idea how right he was!)

How I would have loved to have punched him in that repugnant face of his! But what would have been the point?

"ALARM!!!"

Drugged with sleep, I dove out of my tent. The mechanics were already at the Messerschmitts, cranking for all they were worth to get the engines going. I raced to my "Me" dressed as I was, in my pyjamas. The mechanic was already cranking like mad. Canopy closed, helmet on. Through the headset I heard: "Enemy bombers approaching the airfield!"

The first of our machines were already racing across the field. I rammed the throttle forward and seconds later I was hanging in the air beside the *Staffelkapitän*. Then I heard a loud, rasping voice in my ears:

"We'll climb to 4,500 meters. Bristol Blenheims approaching from 320 degrees at 2,500!"

At once we formed up into four-aircraft formations. There they were below us, the enemy twin-engined bombers! I quickly realized that this wasn't going to end well for them. The British roundels shone brightly. In my headset I hear the signal to attack: "*Pauke, Pauke!*"

The *Staffelkapitän* rolled his Me onto its back. The rest of us followed and we dove toward the trailing Bristols at terrific speed. There was a fat "plop" as I cocked my weapons. Now the enemy was in my reflector sight, as big as a barn door. I pressed all the firing buttons but nothing happened. My weapons had failed. There was a terrific mix-up in the innocent sky over France's Champagne region, with Messerschmitts hanging above and below the Tommies. Everywhere I looked there were burning machines, fluttering parachutes, and fires on the ground from crashed aircraft, in short all hell had been let loose.

Suddenly my motor began to clatter; had I been hit? Biting smoke entered the cockpit. "Make sure you get home," I said to myself, "Otherwise you'll end up pushing up the daisies!"

I had to jettison the canopy in order to see. The propeller was already stationary. I still had 100 meters to go. Flaps down, and then I crashed through a fence. Pickets went flying every which way. The ailerons sailed away and the propeller blades twisted themselves into corkscrews. The aircraft slid to a stop in front of a herd of cows. The cattle ran for their lives. Blood trickled down my face, I had probably banged my head on the instrument panel. Some Frenchmen arrived, intending to help. They got out the packet dressings and one of them skilfully applied one of the bandages. It was a good thing that my last mark in French at school had been an "A." They told me that I was only 10 kilometers from my base. A motorcycle took me home. *Hauptmann* Döring greeted me.

"I have good and bad news for you, which would you like first?"

"The bad, if I might," I replied.

He looked at me underhandedly for a while and then said:

"Effective immediately you are being transferred to a test *Gruppe*. That is the bad news if you like. The good news is that the unit is based on the Channel; you'll have a chance to score some kills there. There's not much going on here anyway!"

I was stunned. I was ready for anything, but to have to leave "my" unit, where I felt comfortable, was a bit much. I turned round and left the command post barracks without saluting. I had to digest what had happened, so I went to the mess and poured down one beer after another. Some time later Hannes Zimmermann joined me.

He looked at the empty beer bottles and asked, "Now then, what's wrong with you—love sick?"

"No, not at all," I mumbled, "But that idiot Döring has transferred me to the Channel, to a totally strange unit! Testing unit it calls itself; I ask myself, who's supposed to test whom there?"

Zimmermann was stunned too. "He never liked you from the start and wanted to be rid of you long ago. Now he's done it and hopes to see you sent packing as quickly as possible. What's the name of the *Gruppe* and where exactly is it located?"

"He didn't say what it's called, but it's supposed to be based in the Calais area!"

That night I packed my few things and the next morning reported to the "old man" right after breakfast. There was no chance to say farewell to my comrades as the morning alert had sent them all into the sky. I picked up my papers plus movement orders in the office and only then learned where I was being "shoved off" to. The unit was unknown to me, but it was in fact based at Calais. A *Kuübel* took me to the station and that was that. I could have killed the "old man."

A Hard Road!

Following a two-day journey I finally arrived, dog-tired and in a sour mood, at a small village not far from Calais. I reported immediately to the *Kommandeur*, a young, dynamic-looking *Hauptmann*.

"So, there you are, I was expecting you yesterday. Something happen in the meantime?" he asked with a grin.

I sized him up as a not unsympathetic man, but we would see.

"Now tell me where and what you've flown up to now," he said.

In a few words I described to him my flying career, not forgetting to emphasize that I would gladly have stayed with my former unit.

"You're familiar with the 109 Emil already, we have nothing better to offer here. Oh, before I forget, early tomorrow morning Fw. Hörtel can give you an initial briefing on our sector. But first let *Leutnant* Müller show you to your quarters. We'll see each other at supper."

I was dismissed. Muüller, who as I learned later was a former reservist, as well as a Doctor of Philosophy and a drummer, took me to a small but nicely-decorated chateau in which the pilots were billeted. After unpacking my few things, which took only a few minutes, I went back to the command post with Müller. I was interested in the situation on the Channel and a few other things. *Staffelkapitän* Steiner of the "Second" was just reporting to the "old man" following his return from a combat mission.

"Had contact with eleven Spitfires at 3,500 meters, south of Dunbridge Wells. No victories. Fw. Arling hit by flak and forced to bail out, made it down to the ground safely. He may have been captured."

The *Kommandeur* frowned: "We would have to lose Arling, one of our most capable pilots. I'll write to his parents this evening."

Then he turned to me: "Oblt. Steiner can fill you in on how we do things here. Oh, and before I forget, you're assigned to the *Gruppenstab* and will fly as my wingman for the first few weeks. Are you sure you're ready? Hunting over the Channel is rather different than cruising around above the Westwall! You'll be surprised to learn that the English just aren't the same as the French."

I was dismissed, and the CO turned his attention to Steiner again. Outside in front of the command post barracks I met the other pilots. All the faces are young and dynamic, but the strain of the recent days and weeks was plainly visible in them. I introduced myself. One pilot towered above the rest, his name was Lt. Weller. He had hands like frying pans and had to be almost two meters tall. I wondered how he could possibly squeeze himself into an Me.

Then the "old man" called me into the command post: "Get ready for action at once and take my machine. You'll fly along the coast to Dunkirk with Oblt. Steiner. That way you'll get to know our area of operations today. My crew chief will give you your helmet, oxygen mask, parachute, and the rest."

I replied "*Jawohl, Herr Hauptmann!*" and slipped out of the barracks. Actually I was about to have lunch with Müller, but like a good Prussian I pulled my belt tighter, clenched my jaw, and replaced the hunger with grim determination. Steiner, too, came out of the barracks. Just back from a sortie, he had no desire to climb into his crate again straight away.

"We'll meet at the aircraft in half an hour, shall we say 1230?"

Just then sirens began to blare.

"Alarm!!"

Everyone raced out of the barracks and into the slit trenches, and in the next instant all hell was let loose. I dove into the trench too. Beside me lay *Leutnant* Müller. Soon Weller threw himself into the trench, almost squashing me. Spitfires and Bristol Blenheims were attacking the airfield at low level. Fragmentation bombs rained down on us while cannon shells tore up the turf. Bomb splinters raced overhead, howling crazily. Lumps of earth rained down on us. I pressed my head firmly against the bottom of the trench, my hands scratching into the damp earth. A few moments later the entire affair was over, but on getting out of the trench we grasped the full extent of the destruction. Of the twenty-one Me's standing about the field, seven were burning and splinter damage had left some of the others, including the one I was supposed to fly, unserviceable. The chaos was complete. The alert *Schwarm*, which was actually supposed to protect us from such surprises, hadn't got off the ground! The pilots and their ground personnel were in the trenches too. Where was the quadruple flak which had been watching over us? The crew must have been sleeping, because the gun hadn't fired a shot.

There was smoke and explosions everywhere. Ammunition from burning and exploding machines was still whizzing across the field, so I jumped back into the trench. It would have been idiotic to die a hero's death here on the airfield, killed by one's own ammunition. *Hauptmann* Kiefer was of the same opinion and quickly jumped in with us. After what seemed like an eternity we climbed out of the trench. We looked around with shocked faces, that of our "old man" probably the most shocked of all. His unit had been wiped out and it would surely take weeks before it was even relatively close to being complete again. By the grace of God we had suffered no personnel losses. With the exception of several minor wounds, which were handled by our unit medical officer, everyone was OK.

"Your flight to Dunkirk is postponed for the time being," observed the *Kommandeur* sarcastically.

That evening, as we licked our wounds, we learned the extent of the damage caused by the attack. There were only seven aircraft still operational, to say nothing of destroyed refuelling trucks, technical equipment, barracks, tents, and ammunition. As a result we were placed under the command of a unit at Le Touquet, but we remained at our former base.

Late in the afternoon a *Schwarm* led by Fw. Bach roared off in the direction of Dover. The orders came from Le Touquet. After nearly two hours we slowly began to get uneasy. Our radio operator listened intently, but after three hours there was nothing, absolutely nothing. Dejected, our CO had to come to terms with the fact that the four weren't coming back. Three machines, that's all that was left of the once so proud test *Gruppe*. The atmosphere in the mess that night was appropriately subdued.

Before leaving the mess the CO said to me, "You're flying to Dunkirk with Steiner tomorrow morning. The command post already knows about it. I've given orders for an 0700 takeoff. I hope that's alright with you," he added ironically.

What could I say? Then I, too, went to bed. The night passed quietly, apart from the soft droning of a reconnaissance aircraft at high altitude. Steiner woke me at about six and we ate breakfast together. Our aircraft were ready to go and we took off at precisely 0700.

There wasn't a cloud in the sky, visibility was more than 100 kilometres, in short excellent weather for heroics. We climbed quickly to 7,000 metres. We had agreed beforehand to maintain radio silence, and we had only hand signals with which to communicate. The Tommies monitored our radio frequencies and they were very well informed, with some help from the French population. (Who could blame them, we were after all uninvited guests in that land.) I hung to the left of Steiner, and as the air was rather turbulent I had to be careful not to ram him. Consequently I had little opportunity to scan the area beneath us. We flew along the coast and I was thinking to myself that we must be getting close to Dunkirk, when Steiner pointed down with his thumb, rolled his Me onto its back, and dove away. I stayed right behind him. "What's he doing?" I asked myself. Then I saw them. Below us, at about 3,500 metres, was a formation of 18 Blenheims and 22 Spitfires. They were flying toward the British coast and home. Is he crazy, I thought, taking on so many? But he was already behind the trailing Blenheim and soon opened fire. I had just cocked my guns when tracer flashed past my cockpit. There was a Spitfire about 50 metres behind me, blazing away. I pulled up sharply to the right and lost him. Rolling onto my back and then descending, I ended up behind the enemy aircraft. He hadn't noticed me yet. I pressed the triggers as my Me bounced around in his propwash, but to my horror I realized that my guns weren't working. I rolled my Messerschmitt onto its back again and dove away toward the grey water of the Channel. My only thought was to get away from that hell. I couldn't worry about Steiner, he'd have to extricate himself, after all this situation was his doing. Flying low over the water, in a few minutes I reached the mainland just west of Dunkirk. There was nothing I could do without Steiner so I flew home. I landed and reported my return immediately.

"Where did you leave Steiner?" asked the "old man," wearing a look of concern.

When I told him what had happened he just shook his head, apparently he also considered Steiner's decision to have been a risky one. A search effort now began, the like of which I had never seen. A *Schwarm* of 109s took off. Although it was already late in the afternoon, patrol boats and the vital air-sea rescue service were called into action. I was able to give them the precise quadrant in which I had last seen Steiner, which ought to have made their task somewhat easier. The four search aircraft returned after more than 90 minutes without results. The patrol boats also reported no luck. However the crew of an air-sea rescue *Weihe* thought they had spotted a floating object about 12 kilometres north of Gravelines long after sundown. They had to call off the search, however, as fog was moving in. We still held out hope for the coming morning, when I was to take part in the search effort. That evening in the mess was more or less cheerless. The "old man" was very curt and it was obvious that he was avoiding contact with me. I wasn't sure why. Was he blaming himself or blaming me? Although my front-line experience was meagre, there was no way I would have attacked the Tommies. In view of the numbers involved there was no chance of success. I went over it again in my mind: 40 to 2 were the odds, and I, a mere small-fry, counted for less than one. I endured a restless night, reproaching myself for the loss of Steiner. Over and over again I saw him half-roll and dive on the Blenheims. At five o'clock the commander of the guard knocked on my door; I was glad that the night was over. After breakfast there was a briefing in the command post. The "old man" himself was leading the search *Schwarm*, with me as his wingman. We took off at dawn and were soon over the Channel. The CO had ordered radio silence. We steered toward the quadrant where I had last seen Steiner, flying about 500 metres above the green-grey water, which rolled beneath us in long swells. If Steiner had come down in the water uninjured we should be able to find him in his brilliant yellow life-raft. Then we spotted the *Weihe*, searching low over the water. The pilot waggled the aircraft's wings and began circling. As he did so I spotted a tiny, yellow something. That had to be him.

At this point the "old man" broke radio silence: "We have him, that must be Steiner!"

The four of us dove on the small rubber raft and circled round it waggling our wings as the man inside waved to us. But was it Steiner? Just before we set course for home a flying boat escorted by two Bf 109s flew past below us toward the downed pilot.

"Hopefully the effort to rescue you will be as efficient if you ever come down in the drink," I thought to myself. But then we were over our base and we approached to land one after another. That evening the "old man" bet Lt. Breuer a case of Munich Löwenbräu beer that Steiner would be back with us by morning at the latest. But he lost the bet. The air-sea rescue *Staffel* called the next morning. It turned out that the occupant of the yellow life-raft was a member of a tactical reconnaissance *Gruppe*. Steiner remained missing.

Some new machines arrived, delivered from Augsburg by young factory pilots. There were seven in all, and one was for me. It wasn't enough to bring the *Gruppe* back up to authorized strength, but in any case it was better than nothing. With the arrival of replacement aircraft it didn't take long for the CO to decide to have another go at the Tommies. I had just come from my quarters into the command post when *Hauptmann* Kiefer said, "Ah, Dickfeld, as a matter of fact you can come along in my *Schwarm* today. We're going to strafe the airfield at Maidstone. We take off at 1630. Lt. Weller will be leading the other *Schwarm*."

My heart fell into my trousers. Strafing attack: that meant English anti-aircraft guns and they were nothing to sneeze at. All too many pilots had failed to return from previous operations of this sort. But I didn't let my feelings show. I strolled over to my new aircraft and had a long talk with the mechanic. The new bird had 200 more horsepower and cannon as well as machine-guns. At 1500 there was a briefing in the command post. There on the General Staff map was Maidstone, located south of London.

"If all goes well, it will take us about 20 minutes to get there. We'll fly low over the Channel, pull up at the coastal cliffs, and remain at treetop height to the target. Approaching from the south, we'll make just one attack and then turn towards Folkstone where we will reassemble if necessary. There are plenty of barrage balloons in the area, but we'll have to live with them."

21

We went out to our aircraft. Our orders were to maintain radio silence until the attack. It was 1630. We took off in two formations of four aircraft each. I flew to the left of the CO. We soon crossed the coast and were over the Channel. Visibility was poor, I estimate only 5 kilometres, with a ceiling of no more than 300 metres. Quite restricted, I thought to myself. We hung low over the grimy water of the Channel. The chalk cliffs raced toward us. We leapt over them, staying close to the ground. Roads, barracks, and houses streaked past beneath us. I cocked my weapons. We dove toward the enemy airfield, where aircraft were in the process of being refuelled and rearmed. We opened up with everything we had. Then the flak found us. To my right Fw. Marquardt's Me was hit. The aircraft caught fire and Marquardt was forced to crash land. Then there was a thump, and a hole as big as a soup dish appeared in my right wing. Nevertheless I was able to maintain control of the aircraft. I had lost sight of the "old man" and the others had disappeared. I wanted to break radio silence and call, but the equipment wouldn't work. It had probably been damaged too. Where is this lousy Folkstone, I asked myself. Suddenly tracer flashed past my cockpit and to my horror I saw a Hurricane behind me and to the left. I pulled my Messerschmitt up and to the right and raced toward the coast. I dared not let myself get involved in a dogfight. The Tommy quickly fell behind. In a few minutes I was over the Channel. Ahead of me were two Me's. Thank God! It was Reuter and Niegel. They indicated that I was to follow them. Both had taken a number of hits in the wings and fuselage. In the meantime it had become almost dark. We arrived over the airfield just as the light was failing. In view of the hits I had taken, a normal landing was out of the question. I decided on a belly landing, as the hydraulics for lowering the undercarriage had been shot out. I picked out a quiet part of the airfield and, behold, it worked. The radiators, landing flaps, and propeller were damaged, but I got down safely. As I was scrambling out of the cockpit in the midst of a huge cloud of dust, the CO's Kübelwagen pulled up beside me.

"Man, where did you get to, I was worried about you. Did you see any sign of the others?"

Some time later the full extent of our losses became clear. Only four of our eight aircraft returned, all riddled like sieves, practically scrap! The following morning brought a surprise. Five more aircraft arrived from Augsburg. The "old man" breathed a sigh of relief.

"Now we can give Tommy's arm a good yank, right up to the collar if need be."

Fate was soon to cast its shadow over me too, in the guise of mission orders. Shortly after breakfast the *Hauptmann* said to me, "Dickfeld, I have a new Messerschmitt for you and I want you to try it out. How about going up on a free hunt in the first *Rotte* tomorrow morning with Lt. Weller as element leader?"

"Thank you, *Herr Hauptmann*," I replied, playing the hypocrite.

"I'll arrange it with him this evening."

Then I turned around and left the command post, which was slowly becoming uncomfortable for me. Free hunting was fine, just no more low-level attacks, they were terribly hard on my nerves. Weller, however, was enthusiastic.

"You know, this is our chance to finally get a kill. Usually they're only for the 'higher-ups.' We poor wingmen are only there to keep their tails clear."

"You're right," I thought to myself.

"Until tomorrow morning then. It would be best if you had them wake you up at about five. Good night, sleep well."

I slept fitfully until two o'clock. I woke up and heard a loud droning, as if an entire bomber stream was passing overhead, then I fell asleep again. There was a knock on my door. Someone in the hall called, "Five o'clock, *Herr Leutnant.*"

I rolled out of bed. We met in the mess. Weller looked damned tired. Had he continued drinking, or had something else gone on last night? All he said was a brief "Good morning." He munched down his army bread and then we headed out onto the airfield. Our mechanics were waiting at the aircraft.

Before climbing in, Weller said, "We'll fly at 3.5, first in the direction of Dunkirk, then north out to sea. We'll have a look at what's going on on and over the Channel, and maintain radio silence, understood?"

The mechanics were already turning the starter cranks as we closed our canopies. Almost simultaneously the two 1,200-horsepower engines came to life with a sonorous roar. We taxied out for takeoff and within a few minutes had disappeared in the morning mist. Weller climbed to 3,500 metres and soon we were over Dunkirk, which was apparently still sound asleep. The sky was cloudless, visibility about 50 kilometres. To our left was the Channel. The only indication that there was water below was a light swell, otherwise it could have been taken for a huge mirror. As planned, Weller now turned out to sea. Soon we were over the middle of the Channel. The chalk cliffs of Dover were clearly visible. The airspace around us appeared to be "clean," no one from either side, us or the Tommies, to be seen far and wide. But then we spotted something. Fast vessels, right off Dover, apparently heading for the middle of the Channel. There were six of them, obviously British. Their bow waves shone with a silvery gleam. Then Weller spotted them and broke radio silence.

"Should we have a go at them?"

I hesitated to answer, knowing that these boats had quite potent anti-aircraft defences. But before I could say anything Weller rolled his Messerschmitt onto its back and dove on the target. I had no choice but to follow him. In an instant we were doing 500 kph. The motor torpedo boats raced towards us and in fractions of a second they were as big as barn doors. Weller had selected the last two boats and now he opened fire. But they had spotted us a long way back and greeted us with a wall of fire which soon made itself felt. Before I could open fire there was a thump and a crash, and boiling glycol vapour sprayed me in the face. I turned away from the vessels, jettisoned my canopy to avoid suffocating, and tried to gain altitude. But then, after climbing to about 1,000 metres, the propeller froze. I placed the propeller blades in the gliding position and switched off the ignition. Then I began gliding in the direction of Calais. Where Weller was I had no idea. What was more I had lost sight of the enemy boats as well; only the devil knew where they were. I had enough on my hands as it was. I was still a good ten kilometres from the coast at Gravelines and I couldn't make it. My altitude dropped to 100 metres, then 50. I touched down on surface of the water. Thank God the sea was calm. My Messerschmitt submerged before I could loosen my straps. I swallowed water: salty, filthy, sickening Channel water. Then my machine resurfaced. I jumped out and seconds later my proud ship disappeared beneath the surface for good. In the meantime I had inflated my life jacket. Then I removed the small inflatable raft which lay flat about my hips like a cummerbund. A turn of the CO_2 bottle and in an instant a bright yellow rubber sausage lay beside me. I had no difficulty climbing in. The coast, which a few moments ago had seemed near enough to touch, had disappeared. There was only water and horizon about me. But no, there was something in the water not far away, rocking gently in the swells. It looked like an inner tube or perhaps a green tarpaulin. I paddled over to it with my hands and recognized it as a piece from a barrage balloon, which the Tommies had hung in the skies of England by the thousands. But it was of no use to me. I ripped open my packet of dye and in an instant found myself floating in a brilliant yellow, fluorescent circle, hoping that someone would find me and get me out of there as quickly as possible. By my wristwatch it was exactly 0615, therefore there was plenty of time to rescue me before the sun went down. There was no trace of Weller. Had he failed to notice my disaster or had he been shot down himself? Thoughts circled in my head like a swarm of hornets. What sort of spot had Weller got himself, and me, into with his lust for victories?

It was beginning to get cold. Thanks to the drag anchor, the small rubber raft held bravely against the rising swell. 1300, still nothing. There were many aircraft high above me, circling wildly. Then I heard cannon and machine-gun fire. A burning Spitfire came down and crashed into the sea not far away. Behind it swung a parachute. It came down in the sea close by, but I was unable to help the pilot. Suddenly a *Schwarm* of 109s appeared from out of the sun. They waggled their wings, dove toward me, pulled up, and flew away. It all happened so quickly that I had no time to draw my flare pistol. At least they knew that I was still alive and would hopefully send an air-sea rescue aircraft. It was already 1500 and day was slowly drawing to a close. If they didn't come by 1700 I would have to prepare for a night in the awful Channel water. If only it hadn't been so cold. Strangely I was neither hungry nor thirsty, but my teeth were chattering. Then they came, a Dornier "*Wal*" flying boat escorted by four Bf 109s. The huge machine turned and set down beside me, producing a considerable swell. The bow wave struck me and tipped over my raft. I fell into the water, but it didn't matter now. I had been saved. I can't remember how I got into the flying boat or how I was unloaded at Le Touquet, but I did learn later that they had also fished the Tommy out of the Channel. That evening I got drunk. Lt. Weller had been posted missing, which hit me hard. Surely one of the British torpedo boats had him on its conscience. But what of conscience? There certainly was none at the front, and which of us there still had one? In any case I had to prove myself all over again each day. Feeling rather beaten, we stayed in the mess until late into the night.

The End of My Battle of Britain

Our unit struggled on. Losses were enormous and each of us knew what might happen, namely disbandment and transfers to other fighter units. Three days later it all came true.

"Dickfeld," began the CO, "I have good news. You are being transferred effective immediately. Your new base is called Olmtz. You've been assigned there as a company officer in a Luftwaffe training battalion. It's a regular life insurance policy. Your wife and children will be happy. The war will have been won in a few months anyway."

The news hit me hard. Is this it, I asked myself? Farewell to being a fighter pilot, farewell channel coast, farewell fame and glory, farewell Knight's Cross, and so on. You've had it, Old Father Christmas. You're a washout, you have no kills, on the contrary the enemy has shot you down. All you've done for the Fatherland is wreck its aircraft, and not just one! This self-recrimination went on and on. They simply don't need such a failure. Like Rumpelstiltskin I could have snapped.

Where was this lousy place Olmtz anyway? I thought it must be in Czechoslovakia. I'd heard of a cheese made there, or something like it. Taking my leave of commander and comrades was brief and painless. Each was engrossed with his own future. The next day I was back on the familiar train and on day two I arrived at Olmtz. My quarters were in an old, bug-infested barracks from the time of Maria-Theresia. What came next just about finished me: my company commander was a dyed-in-the-wool Prussian. Our routine consisted of drill, firing practice, locker checks, cleaning the barracks, marching, and so on. Occasionally we went to a tavern in the evenings, but the hostile attitude of the Czech population soon led us to abandon such pleasures. Luckily my wife and children were allowed to join me. I had already been in the God-forsaken place for four weeks and if my family hadn't been there I'd have surely hung myself. Time dragged on and I had resigned myself to my fate, when one day I was ordered to the office.

"Dickfeld," began *Hauptmann* Engelke, "You have been transferred to JG 52 effective immediately. Report to *Gruppe* headquarters at Berlin-Schönefeld the day after tomorrow."

I could have hugged the man. Not long afterward he was killed in Crete while serving as a paratrooper. I wanted to get away from this stupid battalion as quickly as I could, and the same day saw me and my family aboard a train bound for Berlin. The "Führer" granted me a day at home with my wife and family, but the next morning the strong hand of pitiless fate grasped me once again. I soon arrived at Schönefeld, an airfield which was to play a macabre role in my future. I moved into new barracks and was soon a part of my old *Jagdgruppe* once again.

On the Road to Paradise!

"Mamatschi, buy me a pony," bawled the aging "Chansonette." She was lolling on the slightly-curved grand piano, which helped conceal her plumpness. The air in the lovely cellar bar on the Kurfurstendamm was thick. Outside there was a roar as the anti-aircraft guns began their usual evening concert. The target was almost certainly another English reconnaissance aircraft. Several officers and their ladies hurried down the long set of stairs, completely filling the place. Seated beside me was Kurt Kunze, the meteorologist.

What had become of "my" JG 52? Many of my old comrades were dead. *Leutnant* Fermer, the East Prussian, Keidel, my *Staffelkapitän* and constant tormentor, also Waldner of the crucifixes, Schulz, and the nice Hölzl, *Hauptmann* von Houwald, who always wore glasses when he flew. The Spitfires had made quite a job of it. How many of my former comrades were now lying at the bottom of the English Channel, waiting for Judgement Day? (I recently flew across the channel to London in a Lufthansa aircraft. It was a strange feeling to fly over the scene of so much suffering and horror after so many years. I kept thinking that but for kind fate I might have been one of those lying on the sea bed awaiting Judgement Day.)

It was clear that one ought to, indeed had to, forget such things if he was to remain unaffected by the great conflict which had just properly got under way, and so we lived for the day.

Gerd Ritter's face suddenly turned green. He tipped off the bar stool and began to vomit. A champagne cooler full of ice water over his face and neck helped get him back on his feet faster than a few aspirin. By now the anti-aircraft barrage had died down to an occasional burst of fire in the distance. Not bad, this Blitzkrieg, I thought to myself. The tooting of the three-piece band and the voice of the singer were scarcely audible above the babble of voices, thank God. The old lady and her "Mamatschi" were beginning to get on my nerves.

But soon it was time for us to leave if we were to reach the airfield by midnight. It was a good hour's drive to Schönefeld, what with our rickety Kübel and the total blackout. By now Ritter was wide awake again, while Kunze and Hannes Zimmermann snored softly to themselves. As the most sober of the group, I once again had to play the role of "rag picker." The cool breeze in the open car soon turned me into a block of ice. It was a relief when we finally landed back at the barracks. How I got into bed I no longer know.

A whistle and a distant shout that sounded something like "Alarm!" brought me back to semi-consciousness. From the hall came the sound of running feet and voices; I couldn't explain the din for the life of me. Then suddenly my door was yanked open and there before me, looking like "Old Nick" himself, stood no less a personage than the Major, my CO. Why is he shouting at me so, I thought to myself. Then I realized that I was the last one still in bed. Outside my window was the entire unit, ready to take off. The first word to come into my head was in French: *merde*! The old man slammed the door behind him and I knew I was in for it. How I managed to get dressed and into my aircraft in time I cannot say. An angel must have been pushing me along.

The unit taxied out for takeoff led by the Major, destination unknown. We took off and formed up. The formation flew over the Mark Brandenburg in an innocent blue sky; on my left was Hannes Zimmermann and to my right the Major, who had cooled off by now. At this point I must have looked as bad as my two companions from the previous night and I certainly had the same headache. Some consolation! I heard the CO's voice over the radio:

"Our initial destination is Vienna-Schwechat. We will refuel there and take off again immediately. Base course 170 degrees."

Soon we were over Vienna. My God, it certainly took a lot of time to get a fighter unit on the ground and refuelled. But soon the whole circus was in the air again, 36 machines, Bf 109s, all brand new, the very best. We maintained radio silence, the only sound in my headset was a soft crackling and clicking now and then. Soon, however, the old man had to break the silence to update us on the heading and so on. My 1,200 horsepower Daimler engine roared reassuringly. Below us was Lake Neusiedler. We were headed for Hungary, no doubt about it. Then there was the CO again, with the voice of a raped capon:

"Next landing at Kecskemet. 2 Staffel close up and don't spread out the unit so," he hissed into the microphone.

Kecskemet, that brought to mind Pussta, gypsy music, Julischka, Piroschka, and so on. But were we staying there? That certainly wouldn't be bad. But wine, women and song again? No, I'd had enough of that to last me a week. To our left we caught sight of Budapest, but it soon disappeared again behind a cumulus cloud. A look at the map, that must be Kecskemet ahead. From 5,000 meters the place looked damned small. A tiny, straight line in the burnt, yellow steppe appeared to be the runway. Then the "chief" broke in: "Prepare for landing."

We taxied to a halt on the grass-covered runway. Hungarian soldiers helped us from our aircraft. There was a briefing while our aircraft were refuelled:

"Our next and final destination is Bucharest."

Just as I had suspected. We taxied out for takeoff, but 3 Staffel was delayed. Two aircraft refused to start. In our headsets we heard the old man grumble:

"Ritter, follow with the Third."

"We'll follow as quickly as possible," I heard him reply.

Soon we were in the sky above the land of the Magyars. I began thinking that we ought to be near Bucharest, because before long we would be in darkness, fatal for day fighters with no night landing instruments! Finally, in the fading light of day, we spotted the brightly-lit metropolis, the little Paris of the Balkans. Through the headset came the familiar voice:

"Form up for landing, beneath us is Pipera airfield."

The old man sounded damned tired and annoyed. But where was Ritter with the Third? We taxied in and parked our aircraft at the edge of the airfield. This was followed by a debriefing. The major berated us: our formations had been too loose and we lacked discipline, but he assured us that he was going to change that in the coming weeks. What did the stinker want? With the exception of 3 Staffel we had arrived safe and sound, with no mechanical problems, absolutely nothing. But he always acted that way when something was bothering him. It was all the same to me, I soon had a bed under me and that was all I cared about.

In the Vestibule of Ecstasy

After much discussion we pilots were taken into the glittering, shining city by bus and deposited at an average-looking hotel. "Baneasa" was the barn's name. It was to be our quarters for the next weeks and months, well hello then. Behind the reception counter, lolling more than sitting there, was a buxom, red-haired "promise." She gave each of us a suggestive side-glance as she passed us our room keys.

"Hey, she's as obvious as a mailbox," Hannes whispered to me quickly.

Our barn had eight floors. The redhead informed us apologetically that the elevator was out of order. I had to carry my heavy "assault pack" up six flights of stairs. I finally arrived, snorting and cursing, and threw myself down on the unmade bed. It stank of the cheap perfume worn by the previous occupant, man or woman I wasn't sure. I picked up the telephone but it was stone dead. I went back down to reception. The redhead understood only Romanian and sign language, but I was able to make it quite clear to her that something was wrong upstairs. A few minutes later she appeared with fresh linen and began, slowly but surely, to undress me with her pitch-black, languid eyes. At that point the last thing I had in mind was joining her. Luckily there was an energetic knock on the door at that very moment. A man with a walrus moustache, a muscular gypsy type, strode into the room and began screaming at her (in Romanian of course). Red-faced, the "temptress" fled from my room. The fellow never even glanced my way. Nevertheless, as a precaution, I quickly felt in my pants pocket for my 7.65mm pistol. I was reassured to feel its warmth in my hand. How often in the past had a jealous Othello killed someone much more harmless than me with little cause? I finished the rest of my so abruptly-started beginning alone, making the bed myself. "My God Walter," I thought, that was a close one. Soon, however, I was fast asleep. The next day began as the last one had ended, with a fuss. There was a briefing following our rather paltry hotel breakfast.

We learned for the first time what our role was to be here. We were to act as an instructional unit, teaching the Rumanians to fly and shoot. In addition to my flying duties I was made military welfare officer. What this involved was at first a mystery, but it wasn't long before I found out what I'd let myself in for. After the briefing we were taken by bus to the airfield. The place was called Pipera. There were some horrid looking barracks and in the middle of the field the takeoff and landing strip. It consisted of grass, nothing more. Our ground elements had still not arrived, nor had 3 Staffel, which we had left at Kecskemet the day before. Soon we learned that it wouldn't be coming for some time. It was a sad story. Ritter had become a victim of false reasoning. In Rumania the sun sets almost two hours earlier than in Berlin. Ritter forgot this when he took off after us from Kecskemet some time later. He and his twelve aircraft were caught by the approaching darkness long before they reached Bucharest, but instead of turning back they continued on. As a result he was forced to attempt a landing in the countryside in the blackness. The site he chose was near a brightly-lit country fair. The result: 18 dead, civilians and soldiers, 12 severely injured, only Ritter and an *Unteroffizier* unhurt, all machines lost. For Ritter it meant a court martial. Quite a beginning!

The Unusual Profession of "Herr D"

Our ground personnel finally arrived. They had taken the overland route. Without them there was no flying. They moved into the Romanian barracks and right out again! The Romanian quarters were so bug-ridden that the beds seemed almost to move by themselves. The only choice left to them was to pitch tents and move in. Their motto was: Better to have a sore rear end from sleeping on straw then to be chewed up by bedbugs and lice. They were all quite cheerful, our soldiers, and that evening, apart from those on guard duty, they all disappeared into the milling throng of the big city. Disappeared, that is, until reveille. The object of their desires: "Stone Cross," the Balkan bordello quarter of that francophile city. The next morning the CO counted his "lambs" to make sure none were missing. This went on night after night. Then one morning the medical officer, Hans Sander, called me over and said:

"Do you think our soldiers might have caught something in Bucharest?"

"What do you mean by 'caught,' " I asked back, naive as I was.

"I've just examined several of them and if I'm not mistaken they've bent their watering cans, gonorrhoea for sure, possibly syphilis or hard chancre as well. This is how they live and love in the Balkans. Welcome to this lovely place!"

I must confess that I was speechless at first, as I had never had the honour of such "acquisitions."

"You," continued the medical officer, "must report this to the old man, because if they continue to expose themselves to infection, that's the limit, your flying activities will soon be over!"

The man's right, I thought to myself. To report or not to report was the question.

"You know what, we'll go together and break this latest bad news to him slowly; after all I've been assigned to safeguard the 'welfare of the military.' "

The CO wasn't in a good mood when the doctor brought him the news. He hadn't yet dealt with what had happened to the Third and the many dead and injured. He was outwardly calm as he listened to the doctor's report, but there was obviously plenty going on behind his high forehead.

Then, as if he had awakened from a deep unconsciousness, he cried out, "These God-damned women, these swine in human form, I was warned, but I didn't want to believe it! These miserable Balkans, this lousy Bucharest, everything is infected. We'll make those places off-limits effective immediately. Everyone confined to base! Sander, I want you to report to me in writing immediately how many men are affected." Then he turned to me: "Organize a brothel!"

I was thunderstruck. I had never even been in such an establishment, to say nothing of organizing one. I summoned my courage and replied, "*Herr Major*, I've never even seen the outside of such a place, how am I supposed to set up something like that?"

"I don't give a damn how you do it," he shouted at me. "I want a brothel in two weeks, and I only want tarts who are clean, absolutely clean, is that understood? Sander, what are you medical officer for anyway?"

He couldn't regain his composure, the old man, and neither could I. What sort of mess did I, as military welfare officer, have to deal with? For the first time I began to appreciate the real meaning of "military welfare." War is war, but what did this have to do with it, I asked myself? I was a pilot. I wanted to fly and, if necessary, fight, but setting up a bordello and perhaps playing the role of house father? No, not me! Mutely I raised my hand to my cap, made an about face, and left the barracks.

All this required some digesting. That evening I sat in the "Baneasa" with Doctor Sander, perplexed and despondent. I was in a sour mood as we discussed the situation.

"Some cheek, actually, pawning something like this off on me," I said to Hans. But he had a solution. Our Romanian interpreter, Captain Stanescu, a charmer and jack of all trades, knew a way around it.

"Setting up a brothel? No problem!"

He said that the three of us could tackle the job the next day. I felt as if a great weight had been lifted from my shoulders and, dog tired, I slipped between the sheets, following the axiom: "Good night dear worries, kiss my hand until morning."

Unfortunately the night was all too short. In the distance I heard rifle fire. Could it be that the "Iron Guard" was carrying out a putsch against General Antonescu and the young king. There had been rumours of it for days. However there was no trouble and we were able to drive to the airfield without being bothered. Captain Stanescu was already there and he immediately picked up the theme from the previous evening.

He clicked his tongue and said, "I know a small city, not far from Bucharest, which has the best tarts far and wide. Ploesti is close to the Carpathians. It's the center of the oil industry and the women there are clean, and prettier than those in Bucharest. Let's drive over and see what can be arranged."

I wasn't quite as enthusiastic as our good Stanescu, and Hans Sander just smiled wearily, but orders were orders. My attitude was let's get this business over with. Soon the three of us were under way in our "company car," the Kübelwagen. Stanescu, who was familiar with the area, steered us toward a restaurant in the oil metropolis. The landlord took the necessary information from him and that evening we found ourselves surrounded by a vast crowd of "ladies" of all ages, the youngest perhaps 14, the oldest about 60. We had calculated in advance that we would need about 24 prostitutes with another 6 in reserve, but more than 100 candidates showed up. Like a swarm of bees they pushed and shoved inside the cafe, each wanting to be hired on. There were single, engaged, and married women, housewives, secretaries, working women, and even cleaning ladies, all ready to surrender their honour. Dr. Sander and Stanescu had their hands full separating the wheat from the chaff, off the cuff as it were. I remained at a distance, after all I was responsible only for the organization and running of the "business." What with all the haggling, appraising, and cackling it was soon getting late. Dr. Sander and Stanescu had selected 32 of the best, taken their names, and promised to send a bus for them the following day. Then it was back to Bucharest, where we arrived late in the evening. The next morning found me hard at work. Two barracks had to be prepared for the ladies. Twelve were to ply their trade in each barracks, with the remaining six on "break." An army of soldiers pitched in to help, and within a few hours everything was ready. The eagerly awaited women arrived late in the afternoon, a bus full of joy. For social reasons they were reserved exclusively for the men and not for the officers. What a disappointment, I observed to Hans Sander with bitter irony. The doctor watched proudly as his "purchases" passed by. The women were cheerful, and after being inspected by Sander they moved into their individual rooms, singing gaily (in Romanian of course). They were given the next day off, but on Saturday the great commercial enterprise got under way. I had instructions to keep the establishment open from 1700 to 2200 hours. A ten minute "cozy chat" with one of the women cost a soldier exactly two *Reichsmarks*. The price had been calculated by Dr. Sander and Stanescu. At the entrance to "ecstacy" sat a Charge of Quarters with a yellow cord over his shoulder, ready to take in the money. Beside him sat First-Aid *Gefreiter* Neumann. Then the men lined up in front of the respective doors. A whistle and they were allowed in. Ten minutes later there was another whistle. Five minutes to get dressed and the men had to line up again. Then they were marched out of the establishment straight to the medic. Cheerfully he prepared a small injection for each man and plunged it with more or less feeling into the "honoured" urethra. There was much wailing and gnashing of teeth after this "anointing!" (Where had I heard this before? Wasn't it from the Bible?) The next group stood ready. There were always lineups of mostly young men in front of the love barracks. The middle-aged men initially held themselves back. The older fellows, however, got their fun watching and needling those waiting in line. I must say, business was good, after the motto: "The ruble rolls, the panje rumbles, the bandits smile contentedly." The question remains, who were the bandits? Each evening I received a report on the days earnings from the Charge of Quarters. Hats off to them, the women were as industrious as bees. If this continued the welfare coffers would soon be filled and we could send for something better from the Reich. Naturally out of the profits came the pay for the women, a whole *Reichsmark* per day, including pension of course. Each had one day of the week off, at which time "the six reserves" would spring into action. In this way the operation gradually worked its way upwards.

"My God, Why have You Abandoned Them?"

From the city came rumours, speculation about an impending revolution by the "Iron Guard," Rumania's Nazi Party. We had no idea how the whole thing was put together and paid it no mind. The sound of fighting could be heard in the streets when we came home in the evenings. One morning we found that two rings had been established, an inner one held by the putschists, and an outer one held by the Romanian military. The two sides fired at each other, almost like in a real war. Whenever we wanted to get to the airfield the two sides called to one another that the Germans were coming. The fighting stopped until we had passed. But scarcely were the lines behind us when the firing and dying resumed. What silly theatre, and in the midst of peace; because Rumania was still not involved in the war between the great powers. I hoped that this state of affairs would continue for some time, but fate seemed to have something else in mind. In the evenings we sat in the bar with our enemies, drinking beer with English, French, and Belgian military attaches, while beyond Rumania's borders the Second World War raged on. It is difficult to believe, but we got along. What was it one of them said one evening?

"War is when complete strangers shoot at one another on orders from people who know each other very well but who can't kill one another."

It was as simple as that. Once a week I had to go on a shopping expedition to the big market hall and the slaughterhouse with our administrative official. It is difficult to imagine how much food a fighter unit could polish off in a single week. Early in the morning, just as Inspector Hamann and I were about to leave the "Baneasa," firing erupted in the immediate vicinity. Bullets flew near the reception area, it was Romanian against Romanian. The "muscular gypsy boyfriend" had taken cover behind the reception desk, and he was shaking all over when he finally reemerged. When the ruckus was over we saddled up our sixty horsepower and went on our way. We had no problems until we came to the slaughterhouse. We could go no farther, for revolutionary guards had blocked the way. However when we got out of the car in full uniform they cleared a path for us to the slaughterhouse. Hamann pushed open the large door as usual. But we weren't prepared for what awaited us; the scene that greeted us when we entered the slaughterhouse caused us to stagger backward in horror. I threw up on the spot. Instead of sides of beef, dead, naked, slaughtered men hung head-down on the meat hooks, their throats cut. Blood still dripped from the bodies; the faces of the dead men had been so badly battered that they were unrecognizable. Hamann's face went chalk-white. We turned around, walked over to the guards, and began screaming at them, demanding answers. But they just turned away with a smile and showed us the door. I have no idea how we got back to the "Baneasa." Our report to the Romanian government went unanswered. It wasn't until much later that the word got round that the Iron Guard was in the habit of dealing with its prisoners that way. Hundreds were said to have been murdered in this bestial fashion.

Meanwhile autumn had arrived and in the city things quieted down. The revolution had been suppressed in bloody fashion; General Antonescu remained in power. But I will never forget that horrible sight at the slaughterhouse until the end of my days.

Operation "CUPREX"

It was curious, but whenever I ran into any of my comrades in those days they always seemed to have their hands in their pockets, quite in contrast to normal behaviour and etiquette, and appeared to be searching for something there. I even caught the "old man" carrying out this strange procedure on a number of occasions. Then one day I felt a biting sensation in my pubic area. Washing, soap, perfume, even "Odol," nothing helped. I simply couldn't find out what was causing it. Then one morning at breakfast I saw that all the other pilots were "kicking up a row" down there. I summoned my courage and asked in a loud, clear voice: "Men, are you being bitten as devilishly as I? I simply can't stand it any longer!"

At first there was a long silence, followed by a loud outburst of laughter. At this point the medical officer stepped in:

"You're all infested. You have crab lice, a common acquisition among the men since their arrival here in Rumania. One can catch these sweet creatures in any restaurant, taxi, or bus. The men call them 'sailors on the mast.' Actually I'm surprised you didn't catch them sooner. But I have just the right medicine for them: the cure's called CUPREX. Come see me after breakfast. The first treatment is free!"

I finished eating and made my way to his first-aid barracks. And I must say that the mess, this "curse of Bucharest," was gone after the first treatment, which burned terribly. I still chuckle when I think of it. I remember well the latin name for this infestation: "phthirus pupis." It's unusual for something like that to stay in one's memory, or is it?

"Puffi" Popescu!

The days and weeks passed. The monotony of flying, training, and firing had long since become routine. The Romanian pilots had a hard time of it. I believe they were born more for fighting on the ground, man against man. Nevertheless, several of their pilots were excellent fliers, true artists. One of these was the popular stunt pilot Puffi Popescu. (I couldn't fathom just how he got this first name.) In any case Popescu, who had joined our unit, was a naturally gifted flier. So far so good. He trained with *Staffelkapitän* König and soon became a model pupil.

One day they were in the air together. It was a typical Romanian summer day: blue sky, small cumuli, little wind: in short ideal weather for training. I was sitting in front of the command post barracks, busy with my dog. "Kreck" was this lovable animal's name. The two pilots in the air were once again involved in the routine of loops, half-rolls and dives, and steep spirals, when suddenly Popescu brushed against König's left wing. There was a crunching sound in the sky. Popescu's aircraft went into a spin.

"Jump out man!" I shouted, as if he could have heard me, "jump!"

But then he came down in a corn field, not far from the airfield, with a mighty crash. König's 109 was undamaged and he was able to land a short time later. I jumped into my car, raced through the airfield gate, and set course for the corn field. Even from a distance I could see pieces of the shattered Messerschmitt strewn among the tall corn plants. I drew nearer. A few wild dogs were already rooting among the wreckage, pulling at a long piece of intestine. At my feet lay a human torso, headless with no limbs. There was blood everywhere, and entrails, over which other dogs were fighting. The blood froze in my veins in the face of this horrible scene. I turned away, sick to my stomach. I slowly made my way back to the car and left the site of the calamity. There was state funeral for him, or better what the dogs had left of him, the following day.

Wild dogs were a major problem in Rumania. Dozens roamed about our airfield, a constant danger to landing aircraft. Consequently several of the prowling animals had to be shot each day. But they never went away. Where they came from was a mystery to me. Such a sumptuous supply of dog meat would certainly have made Chinese mouths water!

In the Eye of the Storm

Winter had arrived. It became cold, damned cold actually! Overnight the thermometer suddenly fell to minus 20 degrees and lower. It was then that the social life came into its own. One invitation followed another, many from well-situated Romanian families happy to introduce their eligible daughters to the respected Germans. Even the German embassy sent us an invitation. Visits to the theatre were very popular. In this way we slowly got around Bucharest. The stores were full of delicacies which had long been impossible to get at home: salami sausages, thick and a metre long, paté in large tins, meat of every kind, and so on and so on. In short it was a land flowing with milk and honey! We shopped like champions and sent home as much as we could afford. Difficulties at the hotel, initially with cleanliness and the food, made it advisable for us to eat with the *Jagdgruppe* at Pipera. We only went back to the "Baneasa" to sleep.

It was just after midnight. As usual I was lying in my room on the sixth floor when suddenly the bed began to tremble. I hadn't been drinking, in fact I was cold sober. I tried to switch on the night lamp but it wouldn't work. The wardrobe shook back and forth and finally began moving towards me. There was a loud hiss and hot steam shot out of the bath into the room. The next second there was an sudden crash and a piece of the outer wall as big as two hands fell away, enabling me to look down into the street. There were shouts in the hall, then a tremendous din which had to be coming from outside. Across the street the twelve-storey Carlton Hotel collapsed like a house of cards. The apocalypse. The next thing I knew a shock wave blew acrid chalk dust through the hole in the wall into my face. Out, get out, I shouted to myself, just get out, it must be an earthquake. There was chaos in the hotel corridors. Knots of people raced down the stairs. Crammed inside the elevator were screaming women with their children. Then there was another seismic shock. I found myself in the hotel basement. Candles appeared in the darkness. I looked into the chalk-white, fear-distorted faces of men, women, and children, all of them only half dressed. Then there was another shock. The oil tank in the furnace room ruptured with an explosive crash. Someone shouted, "put the candles out!"

Soon we were up to our knees in heating oil. All of a sudden there was a terrible stillness. The only sound was the whimpering of a baby in the distance. I had to get out and began climbing over bodies. Finally the rail of the basement stairs was under my hand and I pulled myself upwards. There wasn't a soul in the reception area or the foyer. Then something warm and wet licked my hand. It was "Kreck," my cocker spaniel. I had quite forgotten him in the panic. The huge entrance door hung at an angle and from outside I could hear the crying of those buried in the rubble of the Carlton Hotel. What had once been twelve proud stories had been compressed into the height of a single storey and inside were people, living and dead. There must have been hundreds buried under the rubble. There was no sign of the fire brigades or rescue parties anywhere. Now and then bright flashes lit the inferno. At this point I realized that I was still in my pyjamas and that my teeth were chattering. There was no feeling in my oil-soaked legs. Finally some soldiers from my unit, who had managed to make the long trek from the airfield, came scrambling over the huge pile of rubble in front of our hotel. They had clothing and blankets with them and they set about rescuing people from the basement. Immediately afterward the basement stairs collapsed, burying those who hadn't been quick enough, especially the children. It was difficult to grasp the enormity of this disaster. Returning to my hotel room would have been madness, as there were frequent aftershocks. It was morning or perhaps even noon, I wasn't sure. The area was shrouded in a diffuse light. The silence was broken now and then by the groaning and crunching of collapsing houses. Finally, late in the afternoon, I was able to escape the scene of the terror and crawl away into a tent on our airfield.

I never found out how many people lost their lives that night. The Romanian authorities shrouded themselves in silence. I learned from our rescue teams that 400 had died in the Carlton alone. But life went on. The "Baneasa" was unlikely to survive another shock and I wasn't overly eager to take up quarters in a tent, so I was soon on the hunt for a room.

"Silent Night, Holy Night"

Christmas, the celebration of love and joy, was at hand, and an invitation arrived for my comrades and me to spend Christmas Eve with the staff of the German Embassy, dress uniforms requested. Polished and scrubbed, I climbed into my Kübelwagen. The site was a restaurant at the edge of the city. It was hard to find, but the stream of well-dressed men and women entering the place told me this was the spot. The embassy people had gone all out. White, linen-covered tables and a place card for each guest. Curious, I looked at the cards to my left and right. The place to my right was reserved for a woman. "M. Wilson, Mrs." I read. Sounded damned English. She hadn't been seated yet. Let's hope it's not a fiasco, I thought. Then from the direction of the bar came a breathtaking woman, or should I say lady, middle-aged, about 35, dark hair, beautiful face, and lovely teeth. She was stunning.

The woman spoke perfect German and said to me quite ingenuously: "*Herr Leutnant*, you must be my partner at table, I'm pleased to meet you."

My knees were shaking, she certainly had eyes! The evening got under way. There were the usual speeches, followed by Christmas carols like "From Heaven On High" and "Oh Tannenbaum." She knew them all. Then she told me something that almost knocked me from my chair: until the arrival of the Germans her husband had been the representative in the Balkans for a well-known firm and had fled to Cairo at the last minute. She, his wife, an ethnic German, was to follow soon. The gypsy band, the dance, and the hot rhythms soon made me putty in her hands. When the evening ended she invited me to her home for a cup of coffee. I was about to pack her into my Kübel, but then she waved to her chauffeur. I left the "company car" and instead drove with her in a brand-new Jaguar to the residential district. Her house was brightly lit and we were met at the door by a young, sturdy chambermaid wearing a white cap. Soon I was standing before a beautifully-set table. I was speechless. Then the inevitable happened.

I awoke in a large four-poster bed. Mrs. Wilson was kneeling beside it holding a breakfast tray. I didn't know what to say. I glanced at my watch. Damn! I was late again. I was supposed to go on duty at Pipera at 0800 and it was already ten o'clock! I pushed madame aside, jumped into my clothes, and was about to leave.

"But what's the big hurry," she said, stroking my neck softly. "I called Major Hinrichs earlier and told him that you'd be late. You should know that General Nastasse is my cousin and that the German instructional troops are under his command. He has arranged everything, you don't have to be at the airfield until 12 o'clock."

I was at a loss for words; an Englishwoman had the power to get me time off from duty. I thought to myself: what kind of a situation have you got yourself into, you idiot; it will be a miracle if there's no fallout from this. And the consequences were to come, sooner than later! But until then everything went quite normally. I moved in with Mrs. Wilson, whose first name was Margret by the way. The CO authorized it and I would gladly have spent the rest of the war there had not fate, in the form of a German Major, intervened one day.

A Lousy Game

The man's name was Castor and he had a job for me. One morning, quite mysteriously, a car arrived for me unexpectedly. My "chief" informed me that someone from the *Abwehr*, from Berlin, was in Bucharest and very much wanted to speak with me. "What have I got to do with the Abwehr," I asked, "I thought I was here to fly." He had no more information, he told me harmlessly, but I should go along and see what he wanted of me. So far so good. I climbed into the Wehrmacht vehicle. Soon we were in the city centre. The *Obergefreiter* stopped in front of an apartment house and led me into the first floor. There I was met by Major Castor, a thick-set, homely, unsympathetic type. He came right to the point. By chance he had learned that I had taken up quarters with an Englishwoman.

Then he said, "Can you find out when Mrs. Wilson intends to leave Rumania and to where? This would be of great significance to us. We suspect that she may go to Cairo where her husband has surely been waiting for her since his hasty departure."

"What have I got to do with that," I replied, "in any case she has never said anything to me about leaving."

"What is your personal relationship with Mrs. Wilson?" he asked maliciously.

I could almost imagine what this fool was thinking and replied brusquely: "We like each other. But if you suspect more you're on the wrong track, *Herr Major*."

Never before had I been so rude to a superior officer, but the man got on my nerves. Nevertheless, I had to play along with the as yet unknown game. He soon realized that he wasn't going to get anywhere with that kind of approach and I was dismissed. He invited Mrs. Wilson and me to supper at the Athenei Palace Hotel, the finest in Bucharest. Margret, who was highly intelligent, smelled a rat right away when I told her of my conversation with Castor.

Amused, she said, "Let's go and see what he's offering. Perhaps the whole thing's even to my advantage. If he wants me for the Abwehr, why not? As an ethnic German perhaps I can be of service to my Fatherland and in doing so may get to Cairo quicker than my husband would like."

I had intentionally avoided speaking of her marriage to the Englishman and had never asked her about it. It was none of my business. The next evening found Margret and me at the bar of the "Athenei." The English military attache greeted her with a kiss while totally ignoring my presence. It was all the same to me. Major Castor arrived sooner than expected and with him was a civilian who presented himself as the general representative of a major German shipping firm, Schenker I believe his name was, or something similar. What did he have to do with the *Abwehr* I asked myself. Then the Major asked us to dinner. Margret sat on his right, with me and the shipping fellow opposite them. At first the conversation centred on the earthquake, the lousy winter, the advance of the German forces on all fronts, but not a word about his request. The food was excellent, the wine delicious. The gypsy music slowly eased the tense atmosphere.

Suddenly Castor said: "My dear lady, when are you going to Cairo?" Now it was out. He had spoken to Margret tactlessly and clumsily.

She replied with an elegant riposte: "If you're paying for the trip, the day after tomorrow, even better tomorrow. Is there a steamer leaving?"

Castor was rather taken aback and placed all his cards on the table.

"We'll talk about it tomorrow in all seriousness, I have an idea."

Margret pinned them both down: "Come to my house for supper tomorrow evening, I would love to have the shipping director come too, of course."

Greatly amused, we drove home. The next morning saw me at Pipera right on time. An icy wind swept over the airfield, and I was glad to be sitting in a warm barracks. Outside the gypsy children hung on the fence, barefoot and frozen blue, reaching through the wire with their skinny arms. We tossed dozens of loaves of army bread to them. However the more we gave the more of them there were. Soon they were accompanied by their mothers, babies in their arms, begging for warm clothing. There was no end to it. We simply looked past them, ignoring our consciences. Then the old man called to me.

"Get ready. You're flying to Constanta in an hour. Courier mail."

"Can't someone else fly," I replied, "I have an appointment with Major Castor this evening."

"Why didn't you say so," he grumbled back.

A great weight fell from my shoulders. To Constanta in such bad weather, when the birds themselves were walking, no thank you. It got dark early there at that time of year. It was barely 1500 and already one could barely see the hand in front of his face, an indication that we were far to the east. When I got "home" I found that Margret had prepared everything for the evening. Castor and the shipping agent were punctual. The lady of the house received flowers, while I got a hostile side-glance from Castor. What was wrong with him? Jealousy? The conversation was bubbly and rambled from one subject to another until, over cognac, the Major came to the point.

"Dear lady," said the fellow with the charm of a cockroach, "We would consider it a great honour if you could do us several small favours."

"What sort of favours, *Herr Major*?" asked Margret.

39

"You see, we urgently need someone in Cairo who can report on the military situation there. We have received some information from our Egyptian friends, but it seems rather dubious. If you are agreeable we will brief you in the next few days and then there will be nothing standing in the way of your departure for Cairo."

"What do you mean by 'brief?"

"Well, you must learn long lists of Egyptian resistance fighters and their addresses. You will have to be able to handle cyphers, memorize certain codes and so on and so on."

Afterwards there was not a sound, one could have heard the proverbial pin drop. Castor poured himself another cognac and the shipping agent flirted with the chambermaid as she cleared away the dishes. I could sense what Margret was thinking. She suspected what was in store for her and gave me a long, questioning look. The she reacted like a shot from a pistol.

"I have a few questions."

"And they are?" asked Castor, astonished.

"Let's assume that I go to work in Cairo. What will become of me if I should be discovered? What will become of me after the war; because I can probably write off my marriage to my English husband."

"Don't worry about it. In the event you are discovered you will be exchanged within several months for allied spies, several dozen of whom we already have under lock and key. You will be at the very top of the priority list. After the war you will automatically receive a Major's pension, enough to provide for you very well for as long as you live. Of course we expect good results. But you'll be able to get them, especially since you won't be alone there. Our informant in Cairo, a certain Gamal Abdel Nasser, will take you under his wing. As well he has Mr. Nagib and a certain Anwar al Sadat at his side. (The significance of these names would not dawn on me until much later!) You will pass on all information provided you by these and other freedom fighters to Lisbon. You will be given the precise address just before you leave Bucharest."

Believing he had won, Major Castor poured himself another drink and waited for Margret's reaction. But she suddenly changed the subject. Castor realized that he should put off his request until another day. Both men soon took their leave and I showed them to the door.

"Come to my office tomorrow morning, say at about 11 o'clock if that's alright with you," said the cockroach hypocritically. What could I say but "*Jawohl, Herr Major.*"

When I came back in the house Margret was waiting for me. "What do you have to say about it."

"You know," I replied, "I'm in a no-win situation. If I advise you to go and something happens to you in the course of your dangerous assignment in Cairo, I'd never forgive myself. But if you are determined to work for Germany, then tell me. As long as you're here I will stay at your side, you know that."

She looked at me reflectively for a long time. Then she said: "when you see Castor tomorrow morning tell him that I've decided to work for you."

I didn't know what to say. In this field I was a complete layman. On the other hand I also had to think of my country, in whose service I was there. It was, to put it politely, a miserable game in which I had become involved. The next morning found Margret in excellent spirits. She got ready and accompanied me into the city. Snow had fallen overnight, transforming Bucharest into an ice palace. Horse-drawn sleighs glided noiselessly through the streets, the quiet interrupted only by the jingling of bells.

Major Castor was in high spirits when he greeted us. "May I introduce Major Rossbach who has just arrived from Berlin. He has the latest news from Egypt, which may interest you, dear lady," he said candidly. "How about a glass of champagne to celebrate the occasion?"

Margret declined and so they got down to business. Castor was overjoyed at Margret's acceptance and observed, "If it's alright with you, dear lady, we'll begin the first lesson this evening at your house."

Margret nodded slowly and then we were dismissed. We had a little something to eat at the Athenei Palace and promptly ran into the English military attache, the "stinker" whom I disliked so much. Margret snubbed him. If only he knew! That evening the three of them arrived: Castor, Rossbach and Schenkermann, the agent. Margret was visibly nervous, but nevertheless got down to business. First Castor explained how they made a special secret ink and the correct way in which to place information on harmless picture postcards. Then he handed over a list with the names of the people with whom Margret was to make contact as well as an English novel in which was concealed the code necessary for decoding later messages. I had to admit it was clever.

Castor went on to explain: "You are to send all postcards to Lisbon. As I said earlier you will receive the address shortly before your departure. Oh, before I forget, I want you to learn what a company, a battalion, a regiment and a division are. Your house guest can surely explain this to you better than the three of us put together," he observed, gesturing to me. The idiot, I would dearly have loved to have punched him in the mouth. By now it had grown late. I informed the gentlemen that it was time for them to be going. The next day saw us studying hard. Margret learned very quickly and easily. In no time she had memorized the long list of Egyptian freedom fighters and knew how many soldiers there were in a battalion, regiment and division. It had been determined that she was to sail from Constanta to Cairo via Palestine. Once again all the participants met in Margret's house. Castor brought Margret's steamer ticket as well as money, quite a bit of money actually. In typical shopkeeper fashion he asked for a receipt, but Margret declined and observed that as the entire affair was based on trust such ceremonies were superfluous. The gentlemen gave in. Then it was time to leave. Margret shed no tears, although it couldn't have been easy for her. Her journey into uncertainty began.

She left me the huge house with car, chauffeur, servant, cook, and gardener for as long as I needed it. I wasn't to have it very long.

". . .but otherwise he was quite sympathetic!"

He was quite ordinary, our *Gefreiter* Gottschalk. He put in his time punctually in the telephone exchange and was liked by his comrades. He spent some time window shopping in the bordello quarter, but that was about it. In short Gottschalk was a typical German soldier. He had one vice, however, which he kept secret. He liked to gamble, be it poker, "seventeen and four," or the simple shell game which the gypsies there had down to a science. We were unaware that he was becoming more and more a part of the Bucharest gambling circle and getting himself in trouble. We had been in the country half a year by then, and almost everyone had made contacts among the population of Bucharest. Some had become engaged, some had even made wedding plans. Our people prepared for a long stay while the fighting and dying was going on on the western front. Then, completely unexpectedly, we received news that a certain Werner G. had run up considerable gambling debts in Bucharest and was in no position to make good on them. The CO summoned the *Gefreiter*, who denied everything, declaring that he had been slandered. As a result the CO dropped the whole affair, after all he had a fighter unit to run and God knows he had more important things to do than worry about his soldiers' gambling problems. Weeks passed until the Romanian secret service received a tip. There was a leak out at the German airfield. Secret information was being passed on to the Turks, who were then forwarding it to London. The news struck us like a bomb. We had thought that such activities were not a problem, at least in our area. There was speculation everywhere, especially since it was extremely difficult to find the "leak" among more than 300 soldiers, to say nothing of the foreign auxiliaries. But things have a strange way of working out. One fine day an attractive young lady, Romanian, appeared out of the blue to see the "old man." She was the girlfriend of Werner Gottschalk and had become pregnant by him. He had promised to marry her but had left, presumably for another. She came from a good family and was not prepared to stand for this. Furthermore she had loaned him money. She wanted advice from our CO; what should she do? He was on the horns of a dilemma, how should he advise the young lady? In the end nothing came of it. The two came to terms. The "old man" promised to give the young man a dressing down, but that was it. In any case the name Gottschalk soon ceased to be a topic of conversation and from then on the *Gefreiter* was shadowed by the Romanian secret service. Weeks passed, until one evening our paragon was caught passing information to an older Turk. Both were taken into custody. The Romanian interrogation methods appeared to be rather crude, in any case the two soon confessed: Gottschalk had been selling highly-sensitive information to the Turk for months. In this way Gottschalk had been able to pay off some of his gambling debts. Gottschalk came before a German court martial and was sentenced to death by firing squad; the Turk was found guilty by a Romanian court and hung the same day. Gottschalk's execution was to take place at Pipera airfield. Men were selected for an execution squad. The condemned man was placed behind bars on the upper storey of the barracks. A guard was placed at the door to prevent escape. It was only several hours before his execution. Shortly after midnight Gottschalk began banging on the cell door like mad and crying for help. Uffz. Demel, the guard, heard him groaning and moaning. In his naivete he probably thought Gottschalk was dying and cautiously opened the door, contrary to orders. He shouldn't have done it. The guard found Gottschalk lying on the floor, writhing in pain. Demel stood his rifle in the corner and tried to lift the "deathly ill" man onto the cot. Then it happened. A punch in the face, a blow on the neck, and Uffz. Demel fell to the floor unconscious. Gottschalk tied and gagged him, closed the cell door behind him and disappeared for good. Weeks later we received a picture postcard from Istanbul which was signed: ". . .with sincerest greetings, I remain your very loyal Werner Gottschalk." . . .but otherwise he was not unsympathetic!

"and never made it to Knossos!"

A few days after Margret's departure we, the entire "shop", were transferred head over heels to Greece. Crete was to be taken. I heard nothing more of Margret Wilson. That isn't quite true, I did hear one thing. A few weeks after arriving in Athens I chanced to meet *Major* Rossbach and learned that Margret was doing outstanding work through Lisbon. Consolation for me? I doubted it. What a rotten trick! Oh, before I forget: I was able to sell our "house of joy" to a reconnaissance unit for a good price.

We were late landing in Athens, having wasted too much time refuelling at Plovdiv, Bulgaria. Athens, the city of my dreams. How often as a schoolboy had I listened to Professor Sebrante describe ancient Greece and wished that I could stand at the Acropolis, to touch the stones in which were carved the millennia, history of our culture, influenced by the Greek spirit. The hotel they put us up in was lousy. The street beneath my window was filled with traffic; sleep was out of the question. I got dressed again, went outside and hailed a taxi. I had the driver take me to the Acropolis. There wasn't another person to be seen anywhere. All alone, I climbed the many worn-down steps to the sacred shrine. Gleaming in the moonlight, it lay before me like a manifestation, the Acropolis. Its huge columns almost overwhelmed me. Their long shadows seemed to lose themselves in infinity. Awe-struck, I stood there speechless. A light tremor penetrated my soul and body, nearly taking my breath away. Where are you Athens? For a moment it almost seemed as if the distant Kryatides had begun to move. Were they trying to shake off their heavy burden? It almost seemed so to me. No, I thought, you were deceiving yourself. It was only the shadows of clouds in the moonlight, spreading slowly over this magical shrine. How long I stood there I'm not sure. I felt the cold, time to return to the present. Slowly I turned away and walked down the many steps. The taxi driver was happy to take me back to dirty, loud, hectic Athens. In the morning I was uncertain; had it all been a dream? I was no longer able to fathom it.

Soon we were transferred to the South-Peleponnes, from where we were to fly missions over Crete. Not far to the south lay the islands of Kythera and Antikythera, well known from Greek mythology. Only a few days later they were to serve as markers when we returned, our aircraft shot up, from low-level attacks against British flak positions on that history-rich island. It was soon to become the mass grave of the German paratroops. Thousands were killed in one of the most senseless operations of the war.

"Traveller, go to Sparta!"

Late one evening, well past midnight, I met Ernst Rickmer on the "thunder beam." Like many of us, his intestines were having a hard time coping with the native Mediterranean bacteria. There wasn't much to talk about, so the discussion inevitably turned toward the coming missions over the historic island of Crete, whose snow-capped mountains we could see each day.

"Do you have the morning patrol?" asked Rickmer, who, like me, was suffering from intestinal pain.

"No," I answered, exhausted, "my mill has engine trouble and won't be ready until sometime tomorrow."

"You know," said Rickmer, "Hannes Zobel and I were originally supposed to patrol the south side of Crete today, but Hannes is in the first-aid tent with a fever, a recurrence of the malaria he caught in the Danube delta. You can go in his place, especially since his 'One' is a faster bird!"

"I'd love to come, especially since I'm not familiar with the south side, but I'll have to ask the 'old man' first. By the way, the area around there is supposed to be plastered with damned accurate Tommy flak batteries. We'll probably see each other at breakfast!"

Quickly we sprinkled the obligatory lime over our "leavings" and hobbled into our dust-covered tents on the lousy airfield south of that history-laden city, Sparta.

It was cool that morning. Low-hanging clouds swept ponderously over the South Peleponnes like huge, grey canvas buckets. The small Greek city which lay near our airfield had disappeared behind a portentous wall of fog. Men and machines slowly came to life. It was just five o'clock on my alarm clock when the tent flap was opened from the outside.

The "old man" peered inside and said, "glad to see you're awake, you're to fly the early patrol with Rickmer. Take Zobel's machine. Takeoff at 0530."

Even before I could jump to my feet and adopt the mandatory stance he had disappeared again. My morning toilet routine was out. I had a few quick bites of the awful military bread, tipped back a cup of malt coffee and then ran to my aircraft. Rickmer was already sitting in his aircraft. The two mechanics were waiting beside "my" 109. Wäschke was squatting on the left wing, Ebert was standing on the right holding the starter crank. I put on my parachute and climbed into my "steamboat." Once inside I put on my flying helmet and closed the canopy. The man began to turn the crank, faster and faster. The inertia starter gave out a high-pitched howl, I pulled the starter lever and my Daimler-Benz began shattering the morning silence with its sonorous drone. I carried out a radio check, then we taxied out for takeoff.

We lifted off in a tremendous cloud of dust and were soon over the Mediterranean. Its green depths looked as if they would liked to have told us of Odysseus and his adventures, but there was no time for such mysteries. I climbed steeply into the misty, but cloud-free sky over Crete. Rickmer was close by, just behind me and to my left, we had agreed upon radio silence. In less than ten minutes we were over Malemes, that fateful airfield on the northwest corner of the island. Visibility was unrestricted, I guessed more than 50 kilometres. The sky was a deep blue as the coming day dawned. The sun emerged from the flood, casting its brilliant rays into the sky. One could have forgotten that we were in the midst of a terrible event.

The Tommies were certain to become aware of us in such a hotly-contested area, and as if to confirm my premonition the first black flak bursts began flaming up in front of us. They were far to the right, so there was no danger at first. I sideslipped quickly, with Rickmer behind me, lost several hundred metres of altitude and then continued south over the snow-covered flank of the 2,450-metre-high Idhi Oros. The Mediterranean was also a deep blue on this side of the island.

The flak had ceased firing, apparently the Tommies' expectations of success hadn't been high. After a left turn we flew east along the coast. I began to yawn, the night had simply been too short. Rickmer was probably nodding off too, in any case there wasn't anything going on. There were several fishing boats off the eastern tip of the island. A little farther to the south was the island of Koufonisi; we ought to pay it a visit one day, I thought to myself. I lost height and suddenly tracer hissed towards us. Now then, were there Tommies down there? It had to be 20mm flak, the shellbursts were tiny. Very well then, in we go Uncle Otto! I broke radio silence and called to Rickmer: "Let's have a closer look."

Following a half-roll and dive we were right over the entire flotilla, which was apparently on its way to Egypt. Almost all the boats were firing now. There were a good dozen fishing boats and in their midst several English motor torpedo boats, all loaded with soldiers, munitions, and equipment.

"Low-level attack!" I called over to Rickmer.

I flipped up the safety catch and opened fire. The Tommies weren't old men and they put up a veritable wall of fire to meet us. I heard several thumps, it sounded like I had been hit aft in the fuselage. Rickmer had a tulip in his right wing, a shell had passed clean through. One of the torpedo boats began to glow bright red like a street light and seconds later blew apart. It was time to get away, fuel was running low, we had to get home and lick our wounds. I climbed toward the mountains. Soon Heraklion was below us. It was still in English hands and heavy anti-aircraft guns began firing. Then we were over Suda Bay, in which lay numerous English warships, sunk by our people. I turned north over Malemes and was already looking forward to lunch. Then, suddenly, tracer flashed past my cockpit and at the same time Rickmer screamed: "Hurricanes, four of them behind you!"

I was able to pull up to the right just in time and then I spotted the Tommies. How had they moved in so close without us seeing them? But there was no time for further consideration. Rickmer had dived away. Below us was Antikythera, in front of me the Tommies. They turned toward me. I was alone, where the devil was Rickmer? The battle drifted northward. I turned tighter than my opponents and in fractions of a second I had the first one square in my Revi. A press on the triggers and tracer poured into the Hurricane. It began to smoke and peeled away. I was still at 1,000 metres. Suddenly bullets struck my cockpit. The instrument panel caught the full force of the burst and was riddled like swiss cheese. What was worse, glycol vapour was streaming into my face, that meant that the radiators had been hit. I dove away steeply. The other Hurricanes had disappeared, thank God! I searched for a place to land. At 300 metres I spotted a machine lying on its belly on the beach, its British roundels stood out clearly. I lowered the flaps, left the landing gear up, and set my machine down on the sand next to the Tommy. The underwing radiators were ripped off, the ailerons flew away. I opened the canopy, jumped out, and ran away from my smoking Messerschmitt. Taking cover behind a large rock, I waited for the aircraft to explode. But nothing happened and the smoke slowly died out. I left cover and began thinking about the Tommy I had brought down, who must be hiding in the botany somewhere nearby. As a precaution I pulled my 7.65mm pistol from my fur-lined boot and looked all around me. But there was no sign of life, no one for me to take prisoner. Where could the fellow be hiding? Not ten minutes had passed since his forced landing. I looked inside his machine; the parachute was still in the cockpit. His instrument panel had been shot up just like mine, and there were several holes in the fuselage as well. But there was no sign of blood. It appeared that he had escaped unhurt, I didn't grudge him that.

In view of the difficult terrain there didn't seem to be much sense in searching further. So I took my parachute out of my Messerschmitt, which was riddled with bullet holes, threw it over my shoulder and began walking in the direction of the interior. After several hours of walking I came to a small fishing village, whose name I have forgotten. In an instant I was surrounded. They all spoke to me but my schoolboy Greek seemed not to be understood there. Then, finally, an old man came up to me and spoke to me in English. I explained that I needed a car to get back to my airfield, which lay not ten kilometres from there, and soon a donkey-drawn cart appeared. The old man drove me through the area at a leisurely pace and we began to talk. He told me quite openly that we Germans weren't welcome there, after all we had invaded his country. When I asked him if he knew the whereabouts of the shot-down Tommy he smiled to himself and asked me: "Would you turn in a friend?"

Right then I knew that Greek patriots had hidden "my" Englishman in a safe place. Finally, late in the afternoon, I arrived back at my airfield, dirty and disappointed, but otherwise none the worse for wear. I reported my return to the "old man."

"My dear fellow," he began, "where did you come from, we gave you up for lost a long time ago. Rickmer has been back for some time. He got away with a few bullet holes. Make your report after you've eaten."

I was unable to have my kill confirmed. No witness, no confirmation, that was it! That's how it was in that part of the world.

"Fly over and see if Malemes airfield is suitable for a transfer of the unit," said the "old man."

My mechanic fired up the engine and soon I was hanging over the blue Mediterranean. Antikythera soon disappeared from view, then the snow-covered flanks of the Ida Mountains came into sight. I turned onto an easterly heading and a few minutes later Khania, the small city which had been so bitterly fought over, was beneath me. Not far away was Suda Bay, full of sunken British warships. Malemes airfield, only a few kilometres to the west, appeared to have been completely destroyed. The runway was full of bomb craters and to the left and right of it there were hundreds of shattered German transport aircraft. It was a scene of devastation. I made a low pass and spotted an area between the bomb craters where I could put my Messerschmitt down in one piece. I lowered the undercarriage, set the flaps in the landing position, adjusted the propeller pitch, and began my approach to land. There were a few bumps after I touched down but I came to a safe stop at the end of the runway. I was greeted by German alpine troops who helped me from my aircraft. For the first time I saw the extent of the bloodbath which the German units had been caught up in. Numerous fresh graves were evidence of bitter fighting with elite British troops. To the left and right of the runway the destroyed Ju 52s, burnt and bunched together, formed a disturbing scene. The sweet smell of decay hung over the area. The destroyed Junkers still contained the charred bodies of German soldiers. I couldn't and didn't want to stay there any longer. A transfer of our unit to Malemes was automatically out of the question. A car drove me into shattered Khania. A British military camp at the entrance to the town made me curious. German soldiers were helping themselves, with sacks full of raisins, English bread, canned butter, and so on and so on. But a stack of records in a corner was being ignored, so I had a closer look. On one side was "Night and Day," and on the flip side, in very poor German, *"Bei mir bist du scheen."* What awful German, I thought to myself, and took the record along with me. (Actually I ought to return the booty to the British Empire, but I don't know exactly to whom I should send it. To "Queen Mum," to Queen Elizabeth, or perhaps even to the Prime Minister? Maybe they don't even want back such an old record? Can anyone help me? It really is embarrassing!)

The sun was setting. I had to get back to the *Geschwader.*

So I took off between the bomb craters, past the mass grave of the Ju 52s and the nearby hills of the Ida Mountains. By the time I landed it was already dark. I taxied past my comrades' tents with some difficulty and first applied the brakes as I approached the end of the runway with its genista bushes. My lateness had made the "old man" sour and my news did nothing to cheer him up. I heard him mutter under his breath that my description was probably exaggerated. So we stayed where we were, on that lousy airfield not far from Sparta. In the evening a Greek Orthodox priest arrived at the command post. The priest, who spoke perfect English, invited us to dinner at his house.

"Naturally I can't have the entire unit over, but my wife and I would be very happy if perhaps five or six pilots could come," explained the tall man with the long, white beard.

Amazed at such friendliness, we just stared at each other at first.

Then the CO said, "We're going to do the man this favour, therefore Zimmermann, Schade, Graf, Ehrenberg, and you Dickfeld will honour the holy man. You're not to anything to embarrass me, like fooling around with women, is that understood?"

We agreed willingly and soon we were sitting in the Kübel like tinned herrings. Away we went, to a nearby village. "His Holiness" had us pull up to the left near the entrance to the village. We climbed out and stood before a typical cube-shaped whitewashed Greek house. There were no windows on the side facing the street, only a tiny opening through a framework with a heavy wooden door. We crawled more than we walked through and came into a large inner courtyard, which could have been compared to paradise. An oasis among the palms. We were immediately surrounded by a swarm of children. The priest's wife greeted us warmly and led us up a narrow wooden stair onto the roof. A huge table covered with savory delicacies made our mouths water. We stared at one another in amazement. Our host brought us out of our astonishment and invited us to help ourselves. Red wine was poured and we soon hoed in as if we were threatened with starvation, completely forgetting our table manners. The conversation between the priest and ourselves was carried on in English, while madame, who spoke only Greek, took part through enthusiastic gestures. Unfortunately they couldn't seem to understand the ancient Greek I had learned at school. Or had I learned another language by mistake? I'll probably never get to the bottom of it. The conversation was limited to the house, courtyard, children, and the harvest. We consciously avoided any mention of the war, and quite rightly so because after all we were here as occupiers and not as liberators. This enjoyable evening passed quickly and as we went on our way before darkness fell we realized that we had found a friend in this unfriendly land. Before leaving we asked him and his lovely wife to be our guests two nights hence.

A brilliant morning was dawning as I stumbled out of my tent, still dead tired. Water was scarce in the arid South-Peleppones and there was just enough for a cat's lick and to brush my teeth. Shaving was accomplished with our oh so wonderful watery coffee and that was it. My comrades were already squatting in the mess tent.

"Now then, Alf," said Ernst Ehrenberg, "how was your night? I got bitten by fleas, stung all over, want to look?"

And in fact Ernst's face was covered with blotches. He looked like a freshly-peeled tomato. But it wasn't flea bites. A little later Dr. Sander examined him and found that he had caught chicken-pox. I heard the doctor say, "off to the nearest hospital," then the CO cornered me.

"Dickfeld, today I have something special for you," he said affably in the fine "English" manner he sometimes displayed. "Hundreds of English ships are supposed to be making off in the direction of Egypt off the southeast tip of Crete. Go and have a look, perhaps we can 'help' them a little. Take Uffz. Reuter with you."

We took off at about 0900 and headed toward Malemes. I planned to cross the Ida Mountains on the south side of Crete and then search east along the coast. Soon we were at 3,500 metres and climbed on to 4,000. Beneath us lay abandoned English positions which only a few days earlier had made life difficult for us with their anti-aircraft fire. But that was now past, thank God. I was able to cross the mountains unconcerned. Then the coast appeared before us. There was nothing going on below, not a ship as far as the eye could see. Surely a latrine rumour, so common at the front, I thought. Sunshine flooded my cockpit and I was forced to lower my sunglasses. Reuter hung beside me, likewise straining his eyes to see something. We had been in the air forty minutes already and were quickly nearing the southeast corner of that history-rich and now so ravaged, yet still magical island.

All at once Reuter called: "Beneath us on the water, anti-aircraft fire!"

In fact there was tracer snaking up towards us like strings of pearls, and at that moment I saw a group of about a dozen ships apparently headed in the direction of Egypt. I called over to Reuter: "Let's have a closer look at this bunch."

I rolled my Me onto its back and plunged toward the armada. The anti-aircraft fire grew heavier and was damned accurate. I broke left to avoid being hit. By now every ship was blazing away with everything it had. I was somewhat dizzy in the face of all this firepower but what choice did I have?

"Attack the last three boats," I called to Reuter.

I opened fire in the dive. The trailing ship filled my gunsight and I aimed at the deck. A stream of fire from my guns disappeared into the ship and I saw Tommies fall from their gun position into the sea. In fractions of a second everything was behind me. As I pulled up I saw Reuter attack. He, too, came through unscathed and soon he was hanging beside me again. I denied myself another attack, however, as I considered it too risky. Instead we set course for the Ida Mountains. Looking back I saw two of the ships explode in balls of fire. So it appeared our attack had had some effect after all. "Any damage?" I asked Reuter. He answered no but informed me that I had been hit in the fuselage and both wings. I had suspected as much as there had been several considerable bangs in my aircraft. I was hopeful that my mill would hold out. We landed at our airfield with only drops of fuel remaining.

Nights in the tents were comfortable. It was warm and a light sea breeze refreshed body and soul. I had just gone to sleep when a loud droning, like that of aircraft, awoke me. Then all hell broke loose. I heard shouts of "Alarm!" The first bombs were already falling. I raced from the tent and jumped into the nearest slit trench. I was bounced about in my foxhole by the shockwaves from the exploding bombs. Sand sprinkled down in my face. It seemed like an eternity before this surprise attack finally came to an end. I crawled out of my trench. The British bombers had put down their entire bombload to one side and the only casualty was the head cook's provisions tent. There'll probably only be potato pancakes tomorrow, I thought to myself, but that was better than the standard one pot meals anytime. Crete was firmly in German hands and our days in Greece were numbered. Nothing more came of our invitation to the priest's family. We heard nothing more from them, perhaps they were sick and tired of the nightly bombings by the Tommies. In any case it was a pity, they were such nice people.

Back we went to Rumania. I would gladly have bought back my "establishment" but the new owners, a bomber unit, weren't interested in selling no matter how much I upped the price. They were happy to allow our men to make use of the brothel, but at greatly increased prices. There was a warm welcome from the women though. Old friendships, even love affairs, bloomed anew, one could only shake one's head. But Bucharest was no longer what it had once been. A strange mood had prevailed there since our return from Greece, as if something undefinable was awaiting us. I couldn't explain it. We were reequipped. Missing aircraft were replaced and new pilots arrived daily from all over the Reich. They were totally inexperienced and knew nothing of the great bloodletting. The newcomers were amazed at the way we flew.

The days passed and spring came to the land. Rumania was like a sea of flowers. It was a land of milk and honey. The stores were filled with fruit and delicacies of every kind. We sent home large numbers of thick salami sausages. Those who had leave took it now, but it wasn't much: exactly two weeks including the long trip there and back. Too little time to recover. I was lucky. A courier aircraft had to be flown back to Germany. The thing was slow and had an open cockpit, but outfitted with flying helmet, sun glasses and long underwear I was able to endure it. Better a bad trip by air than a long train journey. The family was quite ecstatic when I landed in the old crow. My leave passed all too quickly. I hopped a ride back in a Ju 52 carrying munitions to Bucharest. For the entire trip I sat on wooden boxes, contents: 88mm anti-aircraft shells. With every bit of turbulence the boxes went up into the air before crashing back down onto the floor of the aircraft with a tremendous bang. A first-class trip to heaven! But I survived this too.

As had been our custom in the past, we had a mess dinner for the Rumanians once a month. On one such occasion I went to the door for a moment to get a breath of air. There was a strange droning noise. Soon an aircraft appeared in the pitch-black sky and tried to land at our blacked-out airfield with the aid of his landing light. He'll never make it, I thought, but the aircraft swept in and made an admirable night landing. The Ju 52 taxied toward me. Several German officers jumped out. The red stripes on their trousers identified them as general staff officers. It was Antonious, a Major according to his badges of rank. I had known him in Berlin. He spotted me at once and came toward me. We greeted each other warmly.

"What are you doing here?" was my first question.

"I have good news," he explained. "Can you supply a car for me and my officers quickly, we have to go to the German Mission."

I quickly scrounged up a Kübelwagen and driver and the group disappeared into the night. What might they have, I asked myself. Serious faces all round! Lost in thought, I returned to the mess dinner. The Rumanians sang their national anthem boisterously. The party went on until morning. I looked at my watch. It was just three o'clock.

The Sacrifices Begin

We were hauled out of our beds again at about 0500: highest state of readiness. Soon we were in the air above Rumania. Auspicious Bucharest disappeared behind us. We set course for the Black Sea, destination: Mamaia. We landed on the beach of what was later to become a famous seaside resort. No preparations had been made, so we simply waited around. Our ground personnel were still on their way. Soon we were splashing about in the warm sea. Not until evening did our men arrive. They pitched tents around the barren airfield, camouflaged and dispersed. Pots bubbled everywhere and we passed the day by swimming, writing letters, or simply dozing. Soon however everyone was enjoying a well-earned sleep. The only sound was the occasional whispering among the sentries. In the morning we learned that German forces had crossed the Russian border and were on the advance. We were stunned. This was the last thing we had expected. Soon we were placed at Alert Level I, cockpit readiness. Everyone climbed into his mill, the mechanics squatted on the ground. Not until evening, by which time our rear ends were sore, was the alert cancelled.

The night passed quietly except for the activities of the flies which emerged from the nearby swamp. At dawn we climbed back into our crates. A magical scene greeted us. On the horizon the huge disc of the sun emerged from the sea in a tremendous explosion of colour. We were still quite enthraled when the sirens started howling and through our headsets came the order to scramble. We swept out of dusty Mamaia airfield.

"Russian bombers approaching Constanta," reported the new CO.

He flew ahead, the *Staffeln* formed up behind him. We climbed to 4,000 meters and there they came. This was the first time we had made contact with the Red Air Force. An entire squadron of bombers, twin-engined, approached quickly from out of the morning sun. They were painted green with huge, red Soviet stars on their wings and tail fins. They flew in close formation, definitely heading for the port of Constanta.

"Prepare to attack!"

The *Staffeln* moved into firing position. I cocked my weapons, checked the reflector sight again, and was the first to reach the end of the bomber stream. A brief press on my firing buttons and a burst of fire bored into the closest machine. It caught fire immediately and sheared out of formation. Square parachutes opened up and floated toward the sea. I attacked again. The second one caught fire. There was chaos all around me. Messerschmitts swarmed round the Russian bombers. One after another they fell into the sea. The air was full of burning bombers and white parachutes. Only then did I notice that Russian warships were also attacking Constanta harbour. They ran into a Romanian minefield and exploded in an inferno. Enormous shock waves buffeted my aircraft. At the end of the battle almost all of the Soviet bombers had been shot down. We hadn't lost a single machine. One pilot had to make a belly landing. His undercarriage was stuck and refused to come despite all his efforts to dislodge it.

Then for a week there was a pause, not a Russian to be seen in the sky. Picket boats reported that Soviet flying boats were approaching the coast by night in an effort to mine the harbour. This had to be stopped, cost what it may. We therefore sent out flights of two aircraft each at dawn to search for these rare birds over the Black Sea. It was a case of the famous search for a needle in a haystack. The range of our Messerschmitts was not too great, and it was easy to calculate our chances of success. In my view running into one of these birds was purely a matter of chance. We had no idea what type of flying boat we were dealing with but we knew where they were coming from, from the Crimea or from the Danube delta, half of which was Russian. For days we roared up and down the sea like this, wasting time, to say nothing of valuable fuel. But the General Staff in Bucharest was insistent. Franz Schlosser from Linz finally caught up with one of the Russian seaplanes. He was flying high and far out over the sea with his school friend Sepp Fernsebner at his side when he spotted something low over the water.

"Franz," called Sepp, "I think there's a ship down below to the north of us, but it might be driftwood."

Stare as he might Schlosser couldn't see a thing. "Where is it?" he asked back.

"Man have you got tomatoes for eyes? I'll lead you to it." Fernsebner rolled his Messerschmitt onto its back and dove toward the unidentified object with Schlosser close behind. In no time they were diving at 600 kph. Then they saw it.

"It's a flying boat!" called Sepp over the radio. The pair levelled out low over the water and tracer immediately began flashing past the Messerschmitts. Schlosser was hit.

"I've been hit in the radiator," he screamed. His cockpit filled with white glycol mist. Unable to see, he jettisoned his canopy, pulled up and headed for home. However moments later his engine stopped. Wanting to avoid a belly landing in the water, he loosened his shoulder and belly straps and leaped from the plunging Messerschmitt. His parachute opened and moments later he landed in the warm sea, more than 100 kilometres from land. Fernsebner was horrified. He circled low over Schlosser and signalled that he was going to fly home and send help. Then Schlosser was alone. He was unable to see the Ivan from his small life raft, which he had inflated in the meantime. Fernsebner reported the drama by radio long before he reached our airfield. Four aircraft took off for the area where Schlosser had come down. At the same time a German flying boat took off from Constanta harbour. The unlucky pilot was fished out of the water, but there was not a trace of the Russian flying boat, pity. For days we strained our eyes searching for the amphibious Ivans, but no Ivan, no flying boat, no victory. Perhaps it was better that way for all concerned. Much later we learned that the Russians were operating a group from the Crimea equipped with American Catalina flying boats for mine laying and other mischief.

Soon we were faced with other problems. The first cases of malaria appeared. The swamp behind our airfield was infected. No one suspected, no one knew, least of all the Rumanians. Doctor Sander soon had his hands full. We were inoculated with Atebrin as a preventive measure. The stuff tasted awful and soon our faces were as yellow as a quince. A few slanted eyes and we would have made perfect Chinamen. Very soon more than 50% of our ground personnel were deathly ill. Several pilots caught the disease as well. We had to get out of there quickly or the entire *Gruppe* would be put out of action. So we transferred back to Bucharest. But our joy was to be short lived. By now the German armed forces had advanced deep into Russia. One fine day we spread our wings and landed in the Ukraine. The airfield was near a place called Poltava. The airfield consisted of nothing at all, absolutely nothing. Accommodations, as usual, were in tents. The nights were warm but there were other discomforts. As a precaution each of us had dug a hole in the ground and placed his tent over it. In this way we weren't completely exposed to the nightly hail of bombs from the Ivans. Even if the next morning the tent looked like a sieve, the main thing was that one still had all his extremities, including his head. Not far from us was a factory. Huge tanks projected against the sky. What they made there we had no idea. Because of the constant missions we had no chance to get organized. This meant another night under the bombs. I pressed myself into my hole in the ground, but the bombs fell nearby. How I kept my nerve I have no idea. It was still dark, morning was a long way off. It seemed to be getting wet beneath my air mattress. I reached under with my hand and felt paste, or something like it. It was coming down the walls of my hole from above. I didn't want to show a light, but I didn't want to leave the hole either. What to do? Slowly I splashed about in my foxhole. More and more of the liquid came in. Now I had to get out no matter what. Next to my hole was that of Hans Wiek. He too was just crawling out. Both of us were soaked from top to bottom. I sniffed at the stuff but couldn't tell what it was. "Perhaps it's a new Russian secret weapon?"

Then my mechanic Hilgers called out: "It's sunflower oil, the finest quality. Help yourself! Ivan hit his own tanks tonight and the oil's running out."

It was a terrible mess and more and more of the oil swelled out onto our airfield. We couldn't stay in our holes in the ground any longer. In an instant everyone was heading for the airfield like a swarm of bees. Everyone was on his feet and running toward the tanks with pots, buckets, mess tins and other containers. The precious golden liquid continued to run out of the tanks in a dense stream, enough to supply a medium-sized city for years. Our cook arrived with butter tins and "filled up," with enough, I believe, for the rest of the war. Prisoners of war were brought in to clean up and aviation fuel was used to try and overcome the oily mess. My things were completely soaked. We were still cleaning when low-flying Russian aircraft caught us by surprise. MiGs roared over the airfield at treetop height and opened fire. I threw myself flat onto the ground. A burst of machine-gun fire struck the dirt nearby, straddling me. As quickly as they had come they disappeared again. The Russians didn't turn around for another pass as we would have done. They left behind two sieves: one shot-up Bf 109 and a riddled supply tent with burst pickle barrels inside. This didn't bother the cook as the pickles were already partly spoiled. As the only one with a radio receiver, I was able to follow, at least in rough outlines, the events being played out around us. And every evening we tuned in Radio Belgrade to hear the song which was so popular on both sides during the war: Lili Marlene. Lale Andersen sang it with such feeling that many of our people were moved to tears and I must admit that I was not unaffected myself. What a shitty war!

Since the first aria we had occupied other quarters far from the airfield. In this way we were able to sleep more peacefully; it was no fun having to fly all day and then to be deprived of one's sleep at night by bombing. All of us, pilots and ground staff, looked like ghosts. Our bodies were thin and emaciated, with ash-grey faces and hollow cheeks, and we were plagued by stomach trouble and weakened by constant diarrhoea. At night when we weren't lying in the slit trenches we were sitting painfully man by man on the "thunder beam." Tablets brought no relief. We were long overdue for leave, but the war knew no pity. Winter arrived abruptly one night. The wind whistled about my tent and I crawled deeper into my sleeping bag. Soon the first snowflakes were swirling in my face. When morning came our airfield was a skating rink. The ground crews were taken completely by surprise. Our "mills" refused to start. The temperature was minus 15 degrees; the previous day it had been plus 18. No aircraft could endure that, to say nothing of the men. Chattering and freezing we squatted in the supply tent. There were shocked faces all around, not excluding the CO. Outside the first Messerschmitt finally started, followed by the other "crates." We were operational again, thank God. Transfer orders arrived at about noon. Our destination was Kharkov, a city of more than a million inhabitants. It had only recently been taken. We quickly tied up our bundles and soon we were hanging in the snow-filled sky above the Ukraine. The ground personnel followed us over muddy roads, the poor swine! The ceiling was barely 50 metres and the entire unit approached Kharkov at low level, following every contour of the terrain. Suddenly there was a Soviet bomber squadron, equally low, coming towards us. Both formations were taken completely by surprise. We flashed past each other in seconds, engaging them was out of the question. We were already low on fuel and only just managed to reach Kharkov. Landing in the deep snow wasn't a problem, but the accommodations, to put it mildly, were lousy.

Close to the airfield was a former sanatorium which the Soviets had blown up just before their departure. We were housed in the section which was still standing. Just about everyone built a tiny stove from the bricks which were lying about and soon the chimneys were smoking. The temperature had meanwhile fallen to minus 42 degrees. Flying was out of the question. Only now and there was there a mission over the front, usually without success. We thus had time to look around the metropolis. Freezing, Hermann Graf and I squatted in an open Kübelwagen. We slid over the icy roads more than we drove. The suburbs were virtually deserted, the only sign of habitation we saw was an occasional thickly-wrapped woman. We rolled slowly down the main street, which was called Sumskaya. Once upon a time it had probably been a magnificent boulevard, but there was no sign of magnificence now. From a distance we saw odd-looking bundles turning in the icy wind like large puppets. But then, as we got closer, we froze. I stopped the car. It was unbelievable. The puppets were hanged people, men and women! There were hundreds of them, all along the Sumskaya, always two to a balcony. We looked at each other in shock, unable to make any sense of it. I was speechless, and Hermann, who was sitting beside me, was the same. I quickly took a photograph with my Leica, turned the car around and somehow found my way back to our meagre accommodations at the edge of the metropolis. (This photograph later caused major problems for my family in the GDR. They seriously believed that I had personally hung all those people. What idiots!)

We reported what we had seen to the CO, who was able to shed some light on the horrible scene. A few days before our arrival Russian partisans had blown up a house occupied by the headquarters of a German division. The General commanding the division, as well as hundreds of his officers and men, had been inside at the time of the blast. The German response was immediate. Two-hundred captured partisans, who a military court had determined were not fighting troops, were hanged. This didn't happen by chance!

On their arrival the German troops had been received by the Ukrainian population with flowers, bread and salt, happy to be free of Stalin's terror at last. But what had they exchanged it for? Hitler's murderous eastern policy suffocated the political opportunities through the brutal exploitation of the population and the execution of thousands of Russians, especially minor communist functionaries, Jewish citizens, and the like. Within the space of a few weeks genuinely sympathetic Ukrainians became patriotic, vengeful partisans, men and women. However we fighter pilots, who had little contact with the other fighting units, knew nothing of this as yet. It was soon to dawn on me though, because I came into closer contact with the population than probably anyone else in our unit. The following day I had to go back into Kharkov.

"Drive into the city and organize some heating material," said the "old man," "you're the military welfare officer aren't you?"

He makes it sound so damned easy, I thought to myself naively. Where in the devil's name was I supposed to find wood or coal in this lousy city which itself lay frozen in the cold? But as we all know, orders are orders! I climbed into my Kübel and set off. The partisans were still hanging along the Sumskaya. Men, women and children walked past beneath their swinging feet, scarcely taking notice of them. But something was different about the bodies. During the night their shoes and socks had been removed. Who could say how scarce clothing was among the civilian population in this cold? Thousands were starving and we, with our limited resources, were unable to help them. Before leaving Kharkov Soviet troops blew up mills and food stocks. Fires blazed all round the metropolis. Thousands who had starved to death could not be buried as the ground was too hard. The bodies were stacked in the graveyards like piles of wood in the forest, twenty straight, twenty crosswise, 400 to a pile. An infantry Major gave me a tip. One could get coal, if it was to be had at all, from the city administration in the Losonov. There was a busy flow of traffic in front of the large office building. I spoke with a German interpreter.

"Coal? Second floor, Room 28, City Inspector Barsova," he told me.

I raced upstairs and found myself standing in a large room. "City Inspector Barsova?" I asked, and a pretty, young woman stood up from behind one of the desks.

"I am City Inspector Barsova," she said in a deep voice in fluent German, "but simply call me Olga."

I was flabbergasted at first and she seemed to notice this.

"You must want wood or coal," she asked.

"Precisely," I replied, "how did you know?"

"You're the twenty-second today, but we've been completely cleaned out."

Those were her exact words!

Then she said, "An SS unit got the last of the coal." I must have made a very sad face, because suddenly she began to laugh and said, "I still have a tiny supply in reserve, but you'll have to pick it up some distance from here."

"How far?"

"Eight kilometres south of Kharkov."

"Agreed, but first I'll have to organize a truck from the airfield. Shall we say tomorrow morning at the same time?"

The young woman nodded and the agreement was sealed. It snowed heavily on the return trip; I could scarcely see my hand in front of my face. Suddenly, in the ditch along the icy road, I saw an old man and beside him a young girl who lay shivering on the frozen ground. Apparently she was no longer able to walk. I stopped. Using sign language the old man explained that the girl had broken her left leg. Carefully we lifted the child, who was moaning in pain, into the car and set out for the airfield. The man and his granddaughter were very scared, fearful that they would be killed by the Germans. But Dr. Sander's gentle manner soon dispelled their fears. We treated the child's injury and gave both a hearty lunch. Then we gave them bread, butter, sugar, and a package of cigars for grandfather. The ice was broken. I drove them back into the city, taking notice of the street and house number where I dropped them off. I saw them often and always gave them a little something. Hunger drove the inhabitants of the city out to our airfield in hope of a piece of bread or a bowl of soup. We had the goulash cannon running full bore. At first it was a few dozen, mostly women and children. But then the numbers started to grow. Word spread quickly, but we couldn't feed a starving city of more than a million people no matter how good our intentions. So we handed out food vouchers which had to be picked up from us the day before, and that worked. To be sure many came without vouchers, but they always got a little something.

One day I was summoned by the CO.

"Tell me about the brothel in Bucharest. Didn't you and Dr. Sander set one up?"

"That's correct, *Herr Major*, but you don't intend to establish something like that here, do you?" I asked astonished and unwilling.

"I have an idea," he continued. "We could ask some of the starving women to make themselves available in return for good pay and generous provisions. I have a feeling that our soldiers are badly in need of them. They aren't having any luck in the city, the women there are more than unapproachable."

No wonder, I thought to myself, we're unwelcome occupiers here, but I kept my mouth shut. Let him find out for himself. In any case I didn't want anything to do with this silly idea at any price. He sensed that he was wasting his time with me and summoned Hans Sander.

The doctor said, "I'll be glad to try it, but I doubt that we'll get a sufficient number of women."

The old man was disappointed. "Try it anyway, Sander!"

"*Jawohl, Herr Major*, I can ask them at noon."

That day an especially large number of women and children pressed toward our field kitchen. I saw Hans Sander and an interpreter, already "on the job." They were obviously discussing how best to approach the subject. Then Vassili called out to the throng:

"Listen to me. We require about 30 women to make themselves available to our soldiers in return for good pay. Who is interested?"

First there was stunned silence, then we saw something that we wouldn't have considered possible in view of the hunger and distress. All the women turned away, took their children by the hand, and left us standing there.

One of them called to us, "We would rather die with our children here in the street! What do you know of the value of a Russian woman?"

Sander, as well as Vassili the interpreter, were stunned, I saw it in their faces. Surely the latter, a Russian himself, should have known what to expect. But he was a prisoner of war and was simply following orders, nothing else. At that moment I felt nothing but shame, but this was soon replaced by admiration! Admiration for these women. Hats off to their attitude. All this altered my opinion of the Russian people and it has not changed to this day. Even though Soviet politicians with their Leninism, Stalinism, Marxism, and other "isms" have long kept this people, no this multi-racial state, in a great concentration camp behind barbed wire and minefields, they haven't lost their souls. From that point on I purposely sought contact with the suffering population. My additional duties as military welfare officer gave me the opportunity to do so, interrupted only by missions against the Ivans. The "brothel aria" was finished for me, thank God, but not for Doctor Sander!

Visit from Bucharest!

On this particular day there was nothing going on at the front. Fog everywhere, visibility less than 50 metres, and heavy rain to boot: all flying was cancelled.

Right after breakfast Hans Sander came over to me and said secretively: "Want to hear the latest? We're bringing the brothel from Bucharest. The 'old man' has just authorized it. Tomorrow morning the IVa and his 'war chest' are flying out in a Ju 52. I've heard that the bomber unit at Pipera is urgently seeking a buyer, not too expensive, at least no more than we were asking before we went to Crete."

I breathed a sigh of relief at this good news, I was no longer concerned with the party and this disreputable business.

"Anyway," continued Sander, "it's supposed to be the same crew, only the house mother was changed, supposedly because she wasn't exactly young any more."

The news spread among the men like wildfire. All were full of expectation. They already knew each other and many of the men were describing the coming joy in the brightest colours. Then the moment arrived. A Ju 52 swept in, landed and turned toward the "Seventh"'s dispersal. The doors flew open and out stepped what everyone had been waiting for. The women, who were impressively made up, were soon surrounded by an eager throng. Several fell into the arms of the waiting soldiers; we hadn't had such a happy day for a long time. The women soon occupied their quarters, twenty-one in all. But there should have been more. Had the bomber boys in Bucharest pulled one over on Sander? In any case the doctor was kept busy in the next few days with medical examinations. The men wore satisfied expressions and this happy situation continued for quite some time until we were transferred with very little notice. Hamann had quite a job pawning the "operation" off onto the SS. It must have been a miserable business. However the fate of these women was to be a terrible one. When, a year later, the fortunes of war turned in favour of the Soviets and they seized Kharkov, the SS were forced to hastily evacuate the city. The "establishment," which had been set up so hopefully, fell into the hands of the Soviets, who immediately put it to use for their own people. The SS chased the Ivans out of the city again only a few weeks later and got their women back. What finally became of the Romanian women after the Soviets recaptured the city for good this chronicler does not know. All trace of them was lost in the endlessness of the taiga. What a fate!

Bitter Routine in Kharkov

Once again the CO approached me: "Can't you do something for the unit in the way of theatre or something?" he asked.

"What do you mean by 'or something' *Herr Major?*" I asked, suddenly suspicious.

"I've heard that a theatre is setting up again. It's called Chevchenko, or something like that."

"I'll be glad to check into it, especially since I have to go into the city tomorrow anyway," I replied. The next morning, following a sleepless night (the Ivans made life difficult for us with their bombs), I climbed into the truck beside *Obergefreiter* Labske and off we went into the city. Olga, the inspector, had been waiting for me for days, but enemy action had repeatedly upset my schedule.

Olga greeted me with a reproachful look: "I'd begun to think you weren't coming at all," she said.

"Is the coal still available?" I asked apologetically.

"You're in luck, I was just about to give it to another unit. Do you have your truck with you? Then we can go. I think the weather will hold. We couldn't get through yesterday. Too much snow outside the city."

Barsova slipped into her thin coat and took her place between us without ceremony. The drive out of Kharkov was difficult. Constant checks by military police delayed us unnecessarily, but we finally reached our destination. It was a low, rickety shed, in which the coal was supposed to be hidden. Soon the three of us were busy shovelling. Olga appeared to be used to hard work. She kept right up with Harnisch and me. Where did the woman find the strength? Soon we were covered in coal dust like chimney sweeps, but I had my truck full of this badly needed, precious commodity. Olga gladly accepted my invitation to come along, especially since I promised her a shower in the first-aid barracks with hot water and precious soap. A warm welcome awaited the three coal miners when we finally pulled up in front of the mess. The CO did Olga the honour of personally welcoming her, and that was to have consequences. The evening passed harmoniously. We were amazed at Olga's outstanding German.

60

"I studied German at the university for eight semesters before you Germans ended my studies," she observed cheerfully.

It was late when I finally took her home. I quickly pressed several bars of chocolate from my flight rations into her hand. The streets were deserted and ice-covered. She guided me into the city centre, to the Red Square, where she lived with her parents in one of the tall apartment buildings. Olga was about 25 years old, a dark beauty with a slightly slavic face and pearl white teeth. She knew very well how to keep a certain distance. This impressed me. I offered to escort her to her apartment, but she declined the offer politely but firmly.

"Perhaps the next time, *Herr Leutnant*, and thank you for everything."

Then she disappeared up the long stairway. On my way back I met an armoured column. The poor swine, I thought, in this cold, it must be 35 below. Dead tired, I fell into bed. However the cold soon woke me up. Harnisch had forgotten to bank the stove, so I got up again and shovelled what was in the coal bin into the stove. We were very poorly equipped. They had forgotten to supply us with winter clothing in time. Our families helped out by mail. Even three undershirts, three pairs of underwear (the long type naturally) and two pairs of socks wasn't enough to keep us even relatively warm on operations. At altitudes of 7,000 metres we had to endure temperatures of minus 70 degrees in our unheated cockpits. Fear for one's life in aerial combat was enough to warm us up however. I shared my only pair of fur-lined gloves with my mechanic, who wore them while working with oil and grease. When the next takeoff came he handed them back to me. They were completely saturated, but at least they were warm. Many times I asked myself: wouldn't you be better off as a member of the ground crew, rather than hanging with your rear end in the sky each day, never knowing whether you'll return from the next mission? Hard to say!

It was odd. The more we endured the terrible cold the more our bodies grew accustomed to it. It was already February and hopes of a Russian spring grew daily. One day I received a visitor. Hanisch came in with an older, distinguished looking gentleman. He spoke broken but understandable German and introduced himself as director of the Kharkov Zoological Gardens, which were known all over the Soviet Union.

"Excuse me for calling on you here, but my niece, Olga Barsova, told me that you might be able to help."

I was surprised at first. "How might I help you and your zoo?" I asked politely. I had no idea what the man wanted.

"Hundreds of our valuable animals are dying daily. We've already had to slaughter many and give the meat to the starving population. But we can't save the lions, tigers, apes and many others. Olga said that you are on good terms with the German agricultural director who is responsible for the entire supply of the army and air force."

"That must be a mistake," I replied. "Olga seems to think that I'm a wizard."

The man apologized. "I will gladly come with some of my comrades and select several animals which we can keep alive here as long as we aren't transferred."

Disappointed, the zoo director left. The next day the thermometer rose to the zero mark for the first time. There was widespread fog, no weather for flying. What we found at the zoo would chill the heart of any animal lover. The cages were filled with the bodies of dead animals. Even the lions and tigers had died. Only in the monkey house was there still life; several long-tailed monkeys raised their heads when we arrived. The zoo director asked us to at least take these with us. An attendant opened the doors of the cages. Near death, the animals crawled slowly toward us on all fours. A pitiful picture! The poor creatures apathetically let us pick them up.

"We still have several grey parrots and macaws in the aviary, perhaps you could take them too."

I interrupted: "Of course we'll take them. How many are there?"

"Come I'll show them to you." In the aviary the same picture. Dead birds, hundreds of them, lay in the huge bird cage, starved, frozen. Huddled on the floor, scarcely moving, were five macaws and three grey parrots. The attendant gave us several cages in which to transport the animals. It took some time to carefully load them all. The zoo director had expected more of us, especially, I believe, feed, but where were we supposed to get it? The drive back to the airfield went without a hitch. There was a warm welcome from the *Staffeln* when we arrived and in no time the animals had been handed out among the units. We were to drag this monkey and parrot circus around with us for months, even as far as the Caucasus.

There were rear-echelon stallions and parasites in the city. They preyed upon the starving population, trading food for their last possessions, like jewellery, antiques, paintings, valuable rugs, even wedding rings. Quite by chance I learned from the family of Professor Tomaschek that one such crook, a "golden pheasant" who passed himself off as an agricultural director, had already taken the family jewels in exchange for flour, corn, rice, and potatoes. I obtained the man's name and unit from the professor and notified the military police. But no one there would take responsibility for this parasite. So I informed our "old man," and he passed it on. I never learned what came of it all. Even today my stomach still turns when I think of it. I'm convinced that these figures are still among us today, holding high offices, with their service medals, as honourable members of our community.

At the Gates of Hell!

We desperately needed labour forces to build bunkers and blast pens, because enemy bombing and strafing attacks had increased noticeably in recent days. It was easy to figure out that we would soon suffer major losses in men and materiel if we didn't go underground with our men, equipment, and munitions. One day the "old man" summoned me.

"You should go and have a look in a POW camp and bring us back a few strong Ivans."

"Is there such a camp in the area, *Herr Major*?" I replied.

"Yes, yes, there's supposed to be a very large camp west of Kharkov near Liubotin, or something like that, with more than a thousand POWs. Take the Kübelwagen and see what can be done. I think we could best use about 10 to 15 men. I'll give you a requisition for the commandant."

The next morning saw me in an open car on the ice-covered road, crawling from pot-hole to pot-hole. The weather was clear, not a cloud in the sky, but damned cold, I would estimate 35 degrees below zero. Good weather for the Ivans to attack. Along the way I met army units, panzers and combat engineer outfits with bridging equipment, all heading towards Kharkov. The devil take this damned Liubotin I thought to myself. Just then I heard bombs exploding behind me and the next instant they were overhead, Il-2 *Stormaviks*, the notorious Soviet close-support aircraft which had earned the grim respect of our ground forces. I jumped from the car and threw myself into the ditch. Bursts of machine-gun fire whizzed past to the left and right, sawing the snow banks into small chunks. Rockets smashed into the midst of the tank formation, which had come to a halt. The Soviet aircraft disappeared behind the nearest chain of hills as quickly as they had come. Damage appeared to be minor. Nothing had happened to the tanks, they had simply "closed up shop." The only casualty appeared to be one wounded engineer. My car had taken a good twenty hits but none of them were serious, so I climbed back in and rumbled on from hole to hole. Finally I came to that God-forsaken place Liubotin. Military police confirmed that there was in fact a POW camp at the western exit from the village. The houses and cottages had been burned down to the foundations. I quickly neared the entrance to the camp. It was a huge barracks complex surrounded by barbed wire. Infantry guards asked me what I wanted and soon I was standing before an older *Hauptmann* who had just been enjoying a siesta. My arrival had obviously taken him by surprise and he hadn't had time to take off his slippers. His uniform shirt was open, revealing a rather soiled undershirt. I saw how embarrassed he was and before he could find his voice I said: *Herr Hauptmann*, please remain calm. I'm sorry if I've disturbed your nap. I've just come to borrow a few POWs from you, nothing else."

By now he had regained his composure. He buttoned up his shirt and stepped out of his slippers and into his boots.

"That can be arranged," he said, "how many do you need?"

"My CO is thinking of 15 to 20 strong men."

Embarrassed, he said, "Strong men? Come with me and have a look at the skeletons. Dozens of Ivans starve to death on me daily, spotted fever and typhus take more. We have and receive almost no provisions. More than anything I would like to release them all!"

Then we went outside. There was an infernal stench among the barracks, it was almost impossible to endure. Russian soldiers, who in fact resembled skeletons, staggered about between the barracks, searching for food. Several prisoners were rooting around in a pile of garbage by a latrine looking for anything edible. Peering through the open windows, I saw emaciated figures lying on three-tier bunk beds. Their hollow eyes stared at me apathetically. I could have been sick. I had never seen anything so awful and asked the *Hauptmann*: "How can you stand this, how can you be responsible for something like this?"

For a while he was silent. Then, in a quiet voice, he said, "For weeks I've been requesting a transfer to the front just to get out of here. I would rather die at the front than have to continue to endure this hell. I can't take it any more, I can't accept responsibility for it any longer. What will I tell my children?"

We returned to his office in silence. He suggested that I select several prisoners myself, but I simply didn't want to and couldn't bring myself do it. We agreed that I would send a truck the next day and that he would select fifteen men. I didn't look back as I left that hell-hole, I just wanted to get away. The following could well have hung above the entrance:

"Whoever enters this place is doomed! He is blown away, there is nothing, not a trace left of him!

He cannot go back, cannot go forward!

He is an outcast in this place, shunned by God, even by hell!

He is not day, he is not night, he is nothing, has never existed!

He is too large for infinity and too tiny for the grain of sand.

He has never existed and has never been conceived!

May his ashes at least find peace!

It was obvious that we would first have to build up the strength of the prisoners and get rid of the vermin they carried. It would thus be some weeks before we could expect much work from them. The trip back was quick. A truck from a transport unit towed me. The springs of my Kübelwagen crashed frightfully and I thought we might be torn apart at any minute, but nevertheless I arrived home safe and sound after midnight. *Major* Huberts wasn't exactly enthusiastic as he listened to my report, but in the end he decided in favour of my solution. The next morning we sent a truck to Liubotin and a day later the emaciated figures from the dreadful

POW camp arrived. We never regretted saving these poor creatures from that hellish place. They stayed with us almost to the end, dependable, willing, loyal helpers. Right after the war they were repatriated to Russia, where thousands of them were denounced as collaborators, executed by the NKVD, Stalin's murder organization, and buried in mass graves. Previously I could not understand why we had moved against communism, but now I know!

What a Senseless Sacrifice!

It had been clear to us for some time that our "old man" needed a rest. His clothes hung from his frame, in short he was a bundle of misery. Nevertheless he flew every mission. Each night he shared the "thunder beam" with the rest us. It was obvious that he couldn't go on like this. When I returned from Liubotin I there was finally good news: he had been ordered on rest leave. There was a brief farewell and then he and his Messerschmitt disappeared into a fat cumulus, direction Germany. He was to be gone six weeks, much too short a time for him. We waited for the new commander to arrive. Things could have carried on quite well without one, but service regulations demanded it, even at the front. Who would the new CO be? Rumours swirled about in the *Staffel*. Would he be an old hand, an experienced pilot, perhaps an ace? The days passed and we continued to fly our missions. There was nothing to be seen or heard of our new old man. One morning a Kübel came around the corner of the Seventh's dispersal and out climbed a man who was obviously getting on in years. His hair was already streaked with grey (I've nothing against grey hair, by the way). Then the man introduced himself as our new CO. We had been expecting a daring display of aerobatics over our base by the newcomer before he revealed himself as our new boss. Everyone was dumbstruck. That evening in the mess the man slowly thawed out a little. We learned that he had been in Göring's Staffel in the First World War. Now, during our real CO's absence, he was to look after things and experience life at the front once more. He couldn't fly the 109 and therefore his place was with the ground personnel. That didn't bother us and given the frequent low-level attacks by the Ivans it was enough to earn him the Iron Cross, Second Class. Actually I felt sorry for the man, who was a Major by the way. The days passed. Then orders arrived for yet another move. We soon collected our things, climbed hurriedly into our machines, and disappeared into the snow-laced sky of the Ukraine. I can still see him, our ersatz-CO, squatting in the foxhole he had had dug next to the command post. He never reached our new base and no trace of him or his car was ever found. He may have lost his way in the expanses of Russia and fallen prey to the partisans, who were growing stronger by the day. The only thing we knew for certain was that he lay somewhere, covered by the cool, brown earth of mother Russia, which had never refused a stranger. It was a pity about the man. He had his merits, at least in the First War, so why was he sacrificed in this way? Yes, it was strange how things happened in this God-damned conflict into which we had been blown like a swarm of bothersome flies. How were we ever to escape from this inferno?

A Curious Guest

The He 111 touched down and taxied over to our command post. The aircraft came to a stop and a fur-trimmed figure climbed down hand over hand from the tall machine and came towards us. He was tall with blond hair, blue eyes, and a narrow nordic face, a perfect Widukind from the heroic saga.

"Is this the *Jagdgeschwader?*" he asked.

"Yes it is," answered Franz König warily.

"I would very much like to speak to Herr Huberts."

He can't be one of our lot, I thought to myself, he's acting too strange. Then our CO arrived, went up to the stranger and greeted him:

"Welcome *Herr Gruppenführer*, we've been expecting you. The telex arrived just an hour ago."

The two of them disappeared into the command post barracks. That evening in the mess Huberts introduced the newcomer.

"*Gruppenführer* Heydrich will be our guest for a few days. He wants to see a little of the front and has already flown the Bf 109."

Taken aback, we looked at one other. What did a *Gruppenführer*, one in civilian clothes no less, want here with us? What kind of party ace was he? SA or SS, perhaps *Fliegerkorps*? Surely he didn't intend to fly combat missions with us.

"That's Wotan over there," said Fw. Rassmann pensively.

The next morning there was perfect "bomber weather" and Huberts flew a brief sortie with Heydrich. The two returned after about fifteen minutes. There was a worried look on Huberts' face; what now, we asked ourselves? Afterwards the two had a long talk alone in the command post barracks. Finally *Hauptmann* König was summoned. That afternoon the "old man" called me in.

"Could you fly a brief sortie with *Herr Gruppenführer* Heydrich? There must be no aerial combat, just let him see that we're not firing blanks up here."

I wasn't exactly enthusiastic about the idea, but I couldn't refuse my CO.

"If I must," I answered rather coolly, "but I can't be held responsible for his life."

I gave Heydrich a graphic description of what might happen to him in the event of an encounter with enemy aircraft and strongly urged him to stay at my side. I tried to impress upon him that if it came to do or die he was better off to run for it rather than to let himself get involved in any sort of adventure with the Ivans, because they were better than a *Gruppenführer* any time, even a well-motivated one. He took it all in and we climbed into our machines. Radio check: all in order. We taxied out for takeoff. Within minutes we were over the front. As a precautionary measure I climbed to 3,500 metres, one never knew. But all seemed quiet, in the air as well as on the ground. Then I spotted flak bursts far to the north in the direction of Kursk. Must be a Soviet reconnaissance aircraft, I thought to myself. Although I could have been on him in a matter of a few minutes I let the poor swine alone. That's simply how it was sometimes, perhaps I just didn't have the nerve at that particular moment. "My *Gruppenführer*" hung in the sky to my left, keenly holding position. But then I saw something I could scarcely believe: beneath us were about a dozen Soviet close-support aircraft, Stormaviks. They were low over our lines, blazing away with all they had and making life difficult for the infantry. I peeled off to the left. Heydrich followed and in no time we had caught up with the trailing Ivan. He hadn't spotted us yet.

"White Four stay close but don't fire," I called to Heydrich.

This Soviet aircraft was so heavily armoured that there was no point in making a standard attack from behind and above. Only an attack from behind and below, concentrating on the oil cooler, could lead to success. I moved into position just beneath the Ivan. He was damned low, just above the weeds. I hoped he wouldn't go any lower, otherwise I'd be in a fine mess. I couldn't worry about Heydrich any more. The Ivan's engine began to smoke after my first burst. The other Soviets had meanwhile disappeared over the horizon, so I had this bird all to myself. The fellow in the enemy aircraft didn't react. I fired another burst. Various pieces flew off, some of them banging against my wings and fuselage. By now we were so low that we were brushing the grass. The Soviet pilot lowered his flaps and set down his blazing wreck next to our troops. I climbed back up and called Heydrich, but there was no answer. Down below the German soldiers waved to me and hauled the Ivan out of his crate. Now I began to get worried. I raced towards Kharkov. As I approached to land I saw Heydrich's aircraft, parked nicely in front of *Gruppe* headquarters.

"Where did you get to?" I asked.

A slightly annoyed *Gruppenführer* said, "Everything was happening too fast for me. I didn't want to bother you, so I flew back."

In the subsequent "debriefing" by the CO I was informed that it had been my sworn duty to protect such an important man as Heydrich, not to go chasing around after a kill. Had anything happened to him as a result of my leaving him to look after himself I would have been held responsible. That was my reprimand. The next morning the He 111 disappeared in the direction of Germany with one *Gruppenführer* on board.

I never saw him again, but I was to hear about him. None of us knew it at the time, but he was head of the Gestapo in Berlin. A short time later, while acting Reich Protector of Bohemia and Moravia, Heydrich was killed in a bombing attack by Czech resistance fighters. The assassination took the life of Hitler's favourite.

On May 27, 1942, in an operation code-named "Anthropoid," two Czech agents, who had parachuted into Czechoslovakia, succeeded in liquidating Heydrich as he was driving to Prague airport. Two Czech Sergeants, Jan Kubis and Josef Gabcik, had been trained for the assassination attempt in Scotland by the British Secret Service. Together with other resistance fighters, the two remained hidden in the tombs of Prague's Karel-Boromejska Church for three weeks after the assassination. But then they were betrayed. Surrounded by the Gestapo, on June 18 they all committed suicide. Heydrich's death unleashed the frightful bloodbath, carried out by special detachments of the SS, which came to be known as Lidice and Lezaky. All the inhabitants, including the children, were murdered by the SS. The two villages were razed to the ground and the occupied nation terrorized. It would have been better if Heydrich had met a hero's death with us, better for him and better for all those involved in what later took place. Needless to say, I would have been drawn into the affair myself had Heydrich fallen into Russian hands alive while flying with me. It doesn't bear thinking about!

"Paule"

In normal life he was called Edmund Roßmann. He must have been from somewhere in the country, as he occasionally mentioned that his parents owned a farm. What would I have been without him, my faithful "Kaczmarek". I hade been flying with him for months and it was he who kept the Ivans away from me whenever they got it into their minds to get on my tail. His eye was that of the falcon and I wish that I had had his far-sightedness, int the truest sense of the word. Nothing could shake him. His coolness and dependability were the best life insurance for those of us permitted to fly with him, he was a true comrade. It wasn't until he was taken from us in March to serve as a flight instructor somewhere in the rear that we realized what we had lost in him.

But in June he was back. The "Gruppenkommandeur" assigned us both "freie Jagd". It was already almost noon nad I had no desire to have my rear end hanging in the air so soon before lunch, after all we were having potato salad with small sausgaes, my favourite dish. But, as we all know, orders are orders. Even the Ivans preferred to hang around their "goulash cannon" at this time of day rather than go on tangling with us "Germanskis".

In any case we climbed into our mills and set off in the direction of the front. Radio communication with Paule were in order and I had just called to him tht nothing was going on when he suddenly shouted "beneath us!" and rolled his Messerschmitt onto its back and dove away.

I must have had tomatoes over my eyes, for all I could see were German soldiers, with trucks and horse-drawn wagons, moving along the road. But then Paule opened fire with everything he had and I saw him. An Ivan!

The fellow was flying along the road in his Stormavik and firing into the midst of our people. But in a matter of seconds the Red was on fire and moments later he set down his blazing machine in a ploughed field. I saw Ivan run into the nearest hay barn, but he wasn't allowed to remain there long, for German infantry had already circled the building. I believe it was Paule's 48th kill, perhaps his 50th, it has been so many years.

Unfortunately I didn't have Paule by my side much longer. Rommel was already casting his shadow over me. Fate was cruel to Paule. In July he led a "Schwarm" into the Oboyan area on a reconnaissance and "freie Jagd" mission. The weather was poor, the mission was a sheer waste of fuel, but then everything changed.

In an instant the "Schwarm" was involved in a "hairy" air battle. Paule lost sight of his charges except for one, and he had to make a forced landing. After Paule saw his pilot land safely and climb out of his crate, he decided to land beside him and pick him up. But then Russian infantry appeared. They opened fire and hit Lt. Seyler, as he was climbing into Roßmann's machine killing him. Roßmann was taken prisoner and was not released, by then a sick and malnourished man, until 1949.

The Knight's Cross, which he received for 93 kills and almost 700 combat missions, was small consolation for what he had to endure in those long years under the Soviet yoke. I don't know if anyone else has told his story. In any case I would like to dedicate this brief chapter to him. I never had the chance to ask him where he got that nickname. Perhaps he will read this book and write to me, Paule let me hear from you.

"Days of Rest"

Easter, deep inside Russia, brought forth no spring-like feelings, neither in me nor in my comrades. The weather was awful, so we kept our "hornets" on the ground. Since it was Huberts' birthday we began passing round the bottle early that morning. What else was there to do in this lousy war but have a drink in the hope that it might let us forget all that was going on around us? We could hear the Ivan's radio traffic from the command post, but who knew what they were babbling about. My knowledge of Russian was absolutely zero. Our Hiwi, a captured Russian who served as interpreter, was still drunk from the night before and lay in his foxhole snoring loudly to himself. There was no point in waking him up and asking him about the babbling from the other side. I was just thinking that I wouldn't mind a few days of such quiet when the alarm siren at the airfield perimeter began to howl loudly. Russian aircraft swept across the airfield at treetop height: MiGs, LaGGs and other Ivans, firing everything they had. My faithful Me was the first to go up in flames and others soon followed. Ammunition exploded in a sea of flames. Bullets hissed randomly over the field, slashing people, tents, trucks, and anything else in their way. In short all hell had broken loose. Hess and I jumped from our hole in the ground and ran towards the nearest still-intact machine. Hess turned the starter crank like a man possessed and the engine roared to life. I raced through the chaos, straight across the airfield, and set off after the Ivans. A fifty foot ceiling, drizzle, visibility virtually nil, and I, poor madman that I was, really thought I had a chance of catching the enemy. But what was that in front of me? The outline of a MiG appeared from out of the mist. I turned the gunsight illumination to maximum and closed to less than 50 metres. I was about to press the cannon button when a burst of fire entered the cockpit from the left side past my shoulder and struck the instrument panel. A LaGG was sitting behind me, firing for all it was worth. I applied full rudder and climbed into the clouds. All my instruments were smashed and I had to fly by feel. A few seconds later I dropped back down out of the clouds. There was no sign of the Ivans. I was obviously deep inside Russian territory as I was being fired on by Russian infantry. Completely disorientated, I felt rotten. Where was I, where was west, how was I going to get home? Rifle bullets smacked into my fuselage and wings again. How long before they hit me? It was clear that I was finished if I landed in Russian territory. But then I regained my senses and said to myself, "Whatever you decide, your chances of finding your way back are about zero. Simply follow your nose and stick to it. Either you land in enemy territory and are captured or you make it." Before me lay broad, yellow wheat fields, extending as far as the horizon. I steered towards them, my whole body shaking. I was so agitated I became nauseous and vomited. Suddenly I spotted Russian Il-2s in front of me. Now I knew where west was, because the Russian aircraft were on their way to attack our infantry. I followed at a distance, then they descended and opened fire. German flak gave them a hot reception, however I had absolutely no desire to attack them. The fright I had received was still too deep in my bones. A thousand angels must have been helping, because I saw my airfield below me. Wobbly-kneed and with soiled trousers, I staggered to the command post and made my report.

The CO snarled at me: "Who gave you permission to take off anyway? You're grounded for three days."

A great weight was lifted from my shoulders. That's exactly what I needed, because going back into the air that day, or even the next, would have been too much for me.

"Günther"

Actually his name is Günther Rall, a Schwabian by birth and temperament, always ready for a joke and dependable, whether in battle or anywhere else. I have fond memories of his amusing songs. I still remember his verses by heart. He liked me a lot, but secretly he considered me an especially ardent Nazi. It was for this reason that he suspected that

I had been to the Reich Speakers School, for I could speak on almost any subject at length without any difficulty. I didn't think any worse of Günther, for humour was badly needed at the front where death was a daily occurrence.

Early one morning the old man said to Rall and me, "You have 'freie Jagd'. There's not much going on up front, but perhaps you can find out where Ivan is."

Günther looked at me and nodded and we walked out to our mills. I hadn't been well for days. I had terrible diarrhoea (green tomatoes), but I clenched my teeth and climbed into the 109.

Rall was "Rottenführer" and so I taxied out behind him. We took off and, staying low, headed toward the front.

Before us were our people's trenches and opposite them those of the Russians, who today waved up at us. Perhaps they had mistaken us for MIGs or LaGGs, in any case they didn't shoot at us. It was a good thing, for we could have easily have taken a hit in the radiator or been shot in the backside, in which case it would have been all over.

The weather was mixed, a little fog and here and there the sun broke through. Beneath us the terrain varied between low hills and flat grassland. In short there was nothing going on. We maintained radio silence. Now and then there was a crackle in my headset, otherwise, nothing.

Suddenly Günther called over to me: "Alf, isn't that two MiGs?"

I stared straight ahead. "No, nothing seen, it's probably dirt on your windscreen."

Just then Günther opened fire. A tremendous stream of fire left his guns and in fact, right below us, almost close enough to touch, were two Ivans. Immediately flames spurted from the cockpit of the first. Günther pulled up over him and was soon on the tail of the second. I was in no position to attack, so quickly he had dispatched both Russians. Hats off to Günther Rall, an outstanding fighter pilot. Somewhat ashamed I followed him home, where I confirmed both of his kills. Yes, one must be able to fly, my inner Schweinhund reminded me. Even if I hadn't shot anything down I at least had my pants full (damned diarrhoea), which provided Rall with the inspiration for another sdong.

After the war Rall went on to become General Inspector of the Bundesluftwaffe. However, he didn't keep the post long as he came into conflict with the Minister of Defence. It was clear from the beginning that Rall wouldn't last, a pity. Today Günther lives in a lodge in Bavaria. Perhaps I'll hear from him again.

"Let Him Live"

Day after day we inflicted tremendous losses on the Ivans, losses which they couldn't cope with in the long run. Over and over again we asked ourselves where they got the aircraft. Over time we learned that the Americans were sending Boston bombers, Airacobra fighters, and Catalina flying boats through Alaska and across the Bering Strait, to say nothing of other weapons and ammunition, but until these deliveries reached their stride we pretty much ran the Russians into the ground. At least that's what we believed in our naivete. One night there was a terrific snowstorm. The thermometer outside the window showed minus forty degrees. When it became somewhat lighter at about 0800 I made a brave, manly decision:

"Stay in bed today, remember the old saying: 'Worry about your troubles tomorrow.' The Ivans won't come in these idiotic temperatures and weather so lousy that even the birds would walk if they could."

I rolled over onto my other side. Unnoticed by me Zierenberg had hopped out of bed and tossed a few pieces of wood into the stove. It was thus quite pleasant in bed and I could very easily have slept through until New Year. I was just trying to remember what I had been dreaming about when a frightful explosion threw me from my bed. Pieces of glass flew past. A bomb! The stovepipe fell lengthwise towards me and in no time ice-cold wind was whistling about my ears. I managed to jump into my things and dashed out into the corridor. Fred Burck had also felt the effects of the blast; he looked like a miner at the end of a shift.

"That was a bomb," he said, "it must have hit the hangar."

In view of the snow piling up outside, there seemed little sense in running to the hangar, especially since all the ground crew were indoors. Even if some aircraft had been hit there was little we could do about it. But then I began to think and it occurred to me: how on earth could an Ivan find the hangar from the air in this snowstorm and hit it?

Hauptmann Huberts observed pensively: "That was an explosive charge, gentlemen, and not a bomb! Partisans I would think, sabotage."

Perhaps he was right. By ten o'clock the snow had let up and it had become somewhat brighter, enabling us to see the mess. The hangar was finished. The roof was gone as was one wall. The two Messerschmitts inside had been destroyed and it was obvious that an explosive charge of considerable size had been responsible, probably placed there during the night and detonated later. Insinuations, speculations, and rumours swirled about like blow-flies. I had my suspicions too, but I dismissed them. Could Maria or Nina, or even Olga have had something to do with it? No, never!

The weather improved from minute to minute and soon the first aircraft were ready for action. At about twelve the alarm siren began to wail: we clambered into our machines. The mechanics were already hanging on to the starters began cranking for all they were worth. I counted the aircraft as I lifted off: there were ten of us. The command post called:

"*Achtung, Achtung!* I-153s attacking infantry south of Belgorod."

Staying low, the formation turned north. We raced along in the assigned direction, just above the treetops, and then we spotted the maneuverable biplanes as they dove and fired on our men in the trenches. In unison we rammed our throttles forward to the stops, picked up speed and in no time we were in the midst of the swarm. Koppen was the first one there and right away he got on to the tail of an Ivan. However the Russian shot past him, only to be caught by *Hauptmann* König. The enemy biplane caught fire and crashed in a bright red ball of fire not far from the German trenches. I was unable to take part in the action as my guns had jammed. Damned mess! The air was filled with tracer. A bullet whistled through the cockpit behind me, in the left side and out the right. Plexiglass splinters struck my neck and blood trickled down my collar. Close call! After what couldn't have been more than ten minutes there were about a dozen of our comrades from the other side burning on the ground. Only one Ivan was left. Obviously an outstanding pilot, he simply refused to go down. Six Messerschmitts swirled round him but he escaped every attack by elegantly half-rolling and diving away. I had to admire the fellow. Not quite sure of what drove me to do it, I pressed the transmit button and called to the others, "Don't shoot him down, don't shoot him down. Let him live, we'll escort him home."

Seconds later the air battle ended. The Ivan immediately dropped down to just above the ground and turned east. Remaining above and behind him, six of us followed the Russian. Repeatedly he turned his head to look at us, not believing in his "freedom." However his machine was just too slow. Even with landing gear and flaps down we were still too fast to stay with him. So we waved farewell and left him to return in peace, home to his airfield, the only one of twenty-one I-153 biplanes to do so. What must he have told them about us, the damned Nazi, capitalist swine?

Action On the Ground As Well

Almost daily we were reminded that our opposite numbers were past masters of camouflage and improvisation. One day I caught Ivan at a new trick. It seemed odd, but whenever I went roaming about behind the Russian front (we called it *freie Jagd*, or free hunting), there were always sleighs laden with manure moving about. But never did I see a field to be fertilized. On this day steam rose from the manure and the driver didn't stop even when I roared overhead at treetop height. On the contrary, he waved to me from his seat. It was already late. The sun would be setting soon and I had to get on my way if I was to find the airfield, which wasn't so easy in a snow-covered landscape. Suddenly I came under rifle fire from below. Four Ivans were standing not far from the manure sleigh aiming their rifles at me. Bullets smacked into the fuselage but the aircraft continued to respond normally. I turned back and found to my amazement that the four men had disappeared; it was as if the ground had swallowed them up. They could only be underneath the sleigh, which had meanwhile come to a stop. The manure continued to steam. The driver raced away from the sleigh and threw himself down behind a large tree. I cocked my weapons, dropped down and fired a burst of tracer through the manure. A tremendous explosion blew the sleigh into a thousand pieces, almost taking me with it. All that was left was a black smudge in the snow. The sleigh had been transporting artillery shells. The sun had long since set and I was still roaming about over Russian territory like a stupid man. It was almost dark when I landed. *Freie Jagd* was ordered for the coming morning. The target? Manure sleighs! It wasn't long before many black patches in the white snow marked the scene of yet another tragedy in the depths of Russia.

Strictly speaking, knocking out enemy tanks wasn't our role, but when they made trouble for our infantry we were often pressed into service. The Ivans had scored a major hit with their T 34 tank. The Soviets threw tens of thousands of these things against our ground forces and air support was vital. Knocking out one of these heavily-armoured tanks wasn't an easy thing to do. But like Siegfried and the linden leaf, the T 34 also had its vulnerable spot. In this case it lay between the turret and the engine compartment. The Ivans knew this and unless we hit them with a surprise attack there was little to show for our efforts other than a huge cloud of smoke. They almost always turned to face us and blasted us with their special machine-gun. Then we were left holding a bad hand. Our 20mm shells bounced off the thick frontal armour like drops of water off a hot griddle. But when we were carrying solid jacket, incendiary-explosive and armour-piercing ammunition they were done for. We had to wean them of an entirely new trick. Of late when their outposts reported our approach the T 34s would drive unscrupulously into the nearest farm house and stay there. In this way entire armoured units would disappear from view. We would roar about the area, straining our eyes and wasting valuable fuel. As soon as we had to depart to refuel, the "comrades" emerged from the houses and went back to making life miserable for our infantry. But that was soon to change. From then on we took turns, so that there were always several Me's hanging around above the Ivans from sunrise until dark. Not much went on at the front during the night. One day Koppen came back from a sortie over the front.

"Have you heard the latest? Those farmhouses the T 34s have been disappearing into aren't farmhouses at all. They're fakes, built by special units where armoured operations are planned. The things are made out of wood, wire and cardboard, I just shot one up."

The Ivans were able to conjure up airfields in nothing flat; how they did it was a mystery to us. It was not until later that we learned the answer. Whenever a new landing strip was needed the Soviets called out the inhabitants of entire villages, bag and baggage, hundreds of them. They simply tramped an airfield out of the metre-deep snow. This took barely half a day and then the Soviet fighter and bomber units were able to begin operations from the new strip. After we put a stop to the manure sleighs the Soviets resorted to using civilians to transport fuel and munitions. We often saw them, rolling fuel drums from one village to another and hauling crates of ammunition on small sleighs. Actually, given the nature of their activities, we ought to have simply shot them down. It would have been simple to do so, but to simply kill hundreds of women, old men and children in this way! My stomach turns when I think of it. What a miserable business that would have been.

In Terror's Courtyard

It had become colder again. The winter simply didn't want to end. Then one day Hermann Graf and I received an invitation. There it was in black and white, a certain *Standartenführer* Dr. Weinmann had the honour of inviting us to a *Sakuska*. Neither of us knew exactly why such an honour had befallen us, but since food was involved and our rations were miserable, we were more than happy to go, especially since a real Russian *Sakuska* consisted of a whole series of courses (it was supposed to be twenty-one but many had twice that number). The feast began with famous Russian borscht and ended with caviar. One drank a vodka after every course, bottoms up you understand.

"They're said to have their mess in the school building," observed Hermann.

"*Standartenführer*," sounds very much like SS or something," I mused out loud.

"Oh rubbish," said Graf, "It could be SA or *Fliegerkorps*, perhaps even motor corps, they have such designations. The main thing is that they have something good cooking."

We searched for a long time in the darkness until we finally found the dimly-lit school. In a guard house stood two heavily-wrapped SS men with submachine-guns. They checked our pay books, then the two snapped to attention and saluted smartly. What sort of reputation must fighter pilots have here, I asked myself, people had stopped saluting us that way long ago.

"Second floor please," said one of the guards and we went up the wide, dimly-lit stairs.

We could hear voices from a long way off and then we were standing before the brightly-lit cloakroom. An SS officer wearing the white braid of an adjutant saluted and relieved us of our pitiful things. We looked threadbare next to this spruced-up young man. Then the *Standartenführer* came and introduced himself.

"Welcome to our modest hovel," he said cheerfully, "Good that you could come. I've heard a great deal about you fighter pilots out there, it was high time I got to know you."

I thought the man made a good impression. The *Standartenführer* led us into a large reception room. It was packed. Officers from the infantry and the armoured forces, signals people, army flak, doctors, administrators and others were already engaged in lively conversation. There was plenty of alcohol, served by buxom, well-dressed waitresses.

"Man," I said to Hermann, "Those are Russians, no doubt about it. Where did they get the pretty girls?"

Then an infantry General came over to us and saluted.

"Fighter pilots, if I'm correct?" he asked. "Out there we see you only in the air. If one of you ever came down among us you would seem like an apparition."

The man was right. Contact with the ground forces was extremely limited, we didn't even have radio communications with them.

"Come, you must try this Crimean champagne, it's delicious," the General said jovially. Then someone tapped on a glass. Everyone sat down and the *Standartenführer* began his welcoming speech. He spoke of the Reich, the Führer, the enemy and of home, the honour of being allowed to fight, including the SS forces in their role of protecting the troops in this insecure area. What surprised me straight away was that he spoke not a word about the desperate, starving, dying people in the city. Then there was a toast to the Führer and the *Sakuska* began. It was about time, my stomach was already growling. Hermann Graf smiled at me, he was obviously thinking the same thing. The feast began. As the guests of honour we sat at the head table. There was Dr. Weinmann, his adjutant, the infantry General, Hermann, and I.

"How do you like our orderlies?" our host asked the table expectantly.

"Elegant, *Standartenführer*, elegant," I said. "The girls are pretty and obviously Russian, where did you get them? We could use some like that out at the airfield."

"Yes that's a fact. They were partisans and actually they were supposed to have been shot. But we gave them a choice and now they're here. Better for them and for us. They're still alive and we have them under control."

The General's lower jaw dropped. He hasn't had that much to drink, I thought to myself.

"Slick, very slick," he said with a light Bavarian accent, "But we're not that lucky at the front. However we've heard that the Russians are now employing female battalions, perhaps we'll catch a few too."

The General almost split his sides laughing at his own joke. Hermann glanced at me with a questioning look. The first course, the borscht, was excellent. Everyone stood up, the first vodka was tossed back, then the whole assembly sat back down. There now followed course after course and vodka after vodka, and soon the entire party was quite drunk. I lost count of the courses and vodkas. The *Standartenführer* and the General had left our table, Hermann and I were alone. I was just saying that I thought it was time for us to quietly slip away, when a very drunk *Sturmbannführer* came up to our table and nonchalantly began to speak.

"You may be very good fighter pilots, but we do something here that you can't."

I had no idea what he was talking about.

"You can kill perhaps one or two a day, but here we do things much, much more efficiently."

As he spoke drool ran from the corner of his mouth.

"If you like I can show you something, but you'll have to come down into the courtyard."

That suited Graf and me very well, as it was the quickest way out.

"Gladly," I said. The distasteful man was already making his way unsteadily down the stairs. Without bothering to say goodnight we grabbed our things and followed him. He would surely have fallen head over heels had it not been for the hand-rail. In the school yard fat, fluffy flakes of snow were falling on a row of furniture vans. The cold, sharp wind blowing straight in our faces sobered us up quickly. The *Sturmbannführer* staggered over to one of the huge vans and opened up one side of the compact double doors.

"As you see, you can't see anything," he began, speaking thickly. "I'll show you why you can't see anything."

Then he opened the other half of the door. The beam of his flashlight illuminated the entire van, but inside it was empty and dark. I was thinking that this was all a trick of some sort when he began to speak:

"As you know, we catch partisans, all kinds of partisans. And an order from the Führer is an order from the Führer. The political commissars belong to us too, and what does the dear SS do with all its enemies? Well boys we make them small, very, very small."

Graf and I looked at one another in shock. Hermann and I were probably both thinking the same thing: he's crazy.

"Yes, one first has to get to the bottom of the matter. You fighter pilots have it in the bottom, but we have it in the head, understand?"

The SS man belched loudly.

"Hermann, let's go," I said.

But the fellow grabbed us by the arm and said, "Abracadabra, here's the secret. Imagine the van full of partisans, nothing but partisans. The door shuts, away it goes, and when it reaches the outskirts of the city they're all dear little angels, with tiny wings and hallelujah and so on. Now do you know what I mean? Listen both of you, we simply lead the exhaust gas into the van, ha, ha, ha! Oh you're both stupid!"

The SS man finished speaking and vomited into the snow. Graf and I were speechless; we simply couldn't believe what we had just heard. We both thought that the fellow was raving, trying to make himself sound important. Graf and I left the man and his vans without saluting. Neither of us spoke a word on the way home, we were both too deeply engrossed in what we had just seen. The next morning I reported to the CO and told him of our unusual evening. He, too, wrote it off as a wild notion of someone who had had too much to drink and let it go at that. Heavy action in the following days and weeks soon pushed aside this unusual occurrence.

Lousy Business!

All of us, ground crew, mechanics, pilots, supply personnel, were infested with vermin! There was every kind, from body and head lice to crabs! Fleas were the least of our problems. Strangely enough they held themselves back somewhat, at least at first. It was probably too cold for them. Like the rest of us they were waiting for spring, then they'd show us. Dr. Sander's concern for the tiny creatures was touching and he always had gifts for them like Cuprex (which burned like hell), or a yellow powder which he tossed onto our clothes, or a creosote soap with which to wash ourselves and our clothes. It was strange, but the crab lice would climb as far as the eyebrows and not one step farther, for above the head lice guarded their territory jealously. Only the lice in our clothing could eat where they liked; they could be found in every region of the body. Dr. Sander had one other surprise for the greedy creatures. We had pre-heaters which we used to warm up our engines in the biting cold. They were easily capable of producing air as hot as 150 degrees. We tried using them to heat our clothing in empty gasoline canisters. The results were striking. Not a single louse or louse egg survived the procedure. But enough said about that, I start itching again whenever I think about it.

"Kharkov? Excellent Culture!"

Olga Barsova visited us more often now. She had organized a horse and sleigh and came out to see us whenever she could. Usually she was our guest in the mess for lunch. Everyone liked her. Our "old man" had apparently fallen for her. Previously he had spent his time in the mess playing skat, but now he got dressed up every evening and stayed out late. We were all happy for him, especially since Olga wasn't a bad catch. Coal and wood were no longer a problem. The "old man" finally broke through and obtained several of the women who were constantly begging for cooking and cleaning duties. My room was now cleaned by one Maria Chekovka, a modern languages student at Kharkov University. (I had no idea then that she would one day save my life! But many bitter years were to pass first.) Her German was passable and she was a cheerful soul. She lived with her parents in a barracks camp not far away. I liked her and we soon became friends. I gave her part of the special rations we pilots received, such as coffee and chocolate, as well as cigarettes for her father. These were treasures more valuable than gold in that plundered land. My wife sent clothes and warm underthings by post, especially for Maria's elderly mother. In the meantime Maria had taught my grey parrot a few words of German. Whenever I returned from a sortie it cried loudly, "Hey grandpa!" When I shouted back "shut up!" he replied: "Stupid dog!" Naturally everything else he said was in Russian. He always wanted to know what time it was. He would ask for the time until someone told him it was two seventy-five or five ninety-six, then he shut up. I don't think Maria quite understood what she was teaching him, but it may have been that my batman Zierenberg had put her up to it. I think if he had carried on I'd have choked him! But Zierenberg took good care of "Kreck," my cocker spaniel. I had little time for him myself. He was a gift from Bucharest. Ilse Schiller gave him to me and he was my companion for a long, long time.

One day Hannes Timm and Herbert Mittag failed to return from a mission. They were both shot down in flames during a strafing attack on Russian flak positions and crashed not far from the guns. That evening their stools were empty. They were gone, that's all there was to it. Just prior to takeoff Hannes had clapped me on the shoulder and said, "Will you fly in my place, I just don't feel up to it."

The CO instructed me to collect their things for shipment to their parents. He himself wrote the sympathy letters. They always had the same text:

"It is with deep regret that we must inform you that your son, in true fulfilment of duty for Führer, Volk, and Fatherland, failed to return from a combat mission. We will honour his memory. Enclosed find his personal belongings. With the German salute, your. . . . ."

Deeply depressed, we sat a while at the table, but then the pitiless life at the front went on. Everyone was thinking the same thing: perhaps tomorrow it will be your turn and then they'll sit around your empty chair. Soon the worn cards were brought out again and the skat game got under way. It was all an effort to get back to normal as quickly as possible. Now and then someone might mention the "poor swine," but that was it. One simply couldn't take it.

The war was now in its third year. Spring had finally arrived. Life in Kharkov reawakened. The great dying-off had slackened and the authorities had finally got a handle on the supplying of the civilian population. A steady flow of supply trains now rolled from Poland loaded with basic foodstuffs such as potatoes, flour, corn, and cooking oil. There was also a cautious reawakening of the city's cultural life. Finally, it happened that I became involved with the Chevchenko Theatre. It was to open soon and was to begin with an operetta. When I walked into the large theatre vestibule I was approached by a young woman, who asked me what I wanted. She spoke good German, so I explained to her that we, my unit, were interested in seeing a performance.

"Well you've come at the right time. We're just rehearsing an operetta by Johann Strauss, 'Gypsy Baron.' Do you know it? Not in German, naturally, but the music is what matters most. We've had to fill some gaps in our orchestra, as the men are gone. But we've been able to engage some women who are quite outstanding artists. Come back tomorrow at about nine for rehearsal. I'm a pianist by the way, my name is Nina Bobrinova."

When I arrived at the Chevchenko the next morning the rehearsal was already under way. Nina was sitting in the orchestra pit, apparently directing the orchestra, which apart from two older musicians, consisted entirely of women. I counted a total of twelve members. On stage a dance group was practising to the music of a Strauss waltz, "Vienna Blood." They weren't bad. Nina accompanied on the piano. The leader of the dance group, an elderly ballerina, had the ladies well in hand. Then there was a break. Nina, who had spotted me as I entered, came up to me.

"Well, what do you think of our rehearsal?"

"Not bad," I replied. "I liked the dance group best of all. Tell me, could we invite the ladies to come out for an evening of dancing?"

"Come with me," said Nina. She took me straight to the ballerina and introduced me.

"Yes, that could be done. We would gladly dance for food, if that were possible," she declared engagingly.

I agreed. "We'll pick you and the piano up here at the theatre at six in the afternoon the day after tomorrow." Out at the airfield there was great enthusiasm when I informed the CO of my "conquest."

Interlude!

The Soviets had broken through near Kursk and had overrun the German lines with masses of tanks. The next morning we were scrambled and sent north to help the hard-pressed infantry. The scene of the fighting was scarcely an hour's flying time away. What was supposed to be our destination airfield lay beneath us under a deep blanket of snow. All that was visible was a single long strip which the soldiers had shovelled clear. There were high snowbanks to the left and right of the narrow runway. A strong crosswind was blowing snow back onto the cleared strip. Even from a considerable altitude it was obvious that our chances of landing safely were negligible. But there was no going back. We had barely 10 minutes of fuel left, not enough to return to our base. The old man's voice came through my headset:

"Line up, I'll land first. Watch the crosswind."

He began his landing approach. I saw him touch down briefly. He skidded left, right, left, right, then crashed into one of the piles of snow. The aircraft flipped over onto its back. The adjutant followed. He hit the ground the same way, except he ended up on the other side. One crash landing followed another. I was one of the last. I was scared to death as disaster approached. I raced across the landing strip and ended up with my aircraft flipping onto its back. After much effort I was able to squirm out from under my Me. The other pilots had been helped from their crates by the infantry. Seldom have I seen so many silly faces, the CO included, as after this drama. Luckily no one had been hurt. The entire unit out of commission; enemy action: nil! A Ju 52 flew us back to Kharkov the same day.

The old Chevchenko could never even have dreamed of such a thing! We arrived back in time for the ballet dance evening. I showed up punctually with the bus and a truck. There were more women than we had bargained on, five more than we had "booked." But it was all the same to us. We drove them all, Nina Bobrova included, out to the airfield. Everything had been spruced up. The mess shone in the candlelight, the CO made a brief speech and then the evening got under way. Nina pounded the keys with a vengeance. The elderly ballerina chased the ladies about to the melodies of Johann Strauss. There was enthusiastic applause. Then supper was served by candlelight. Actually they weren't candles but a type of trench lamp, which I believe were called Hindenburg lamps. It wasn't much but we enjoyed it. After supper there was dancing. Addresses were exchanged. When the evening ended everyone was in high spirits and satisfied. Each of the women received a large food parcel to take home with them containing sausage, butter, cooking oil, chocolate, cookies, and cigarettes. The union of Germany and the Ukraine seemed perfect. What we could not know was that we would never see each other again. After the war Nina Bobrinova and many other women were publicly hanged in Kharkov's Red square for collaborating with the enemy. I mourn for her!

The knock on my door came earlier than normal. Maria brought my laundry, clean and pressed.
"My parents would like to invite you over this evening. Can you come?"
"I can't say. I don't know yet if I'm on duty tonight."
With the significantly improved weather the number of combat sorties had increased considerably. We had quite a lot to do up front. None of us liked strafing attacks on the Russian anti-aircraft guns which had been making our lives difficult for weeks, but they had to be flown. Today it was my turn. It wasn't that I was an out and out coward, but I always had a great fear of this type of mission. Four of us took off, the CO, his wingman, *Leutnant* Freytag, and I. Flying time to the enemy flak positions was only ten minutes, so close were we to the Ivans, or so close were they to us,

depending on how one looked at it. We made our approach at very low altitude, taking advantage of every fold in the terrain, every wood, so as to approach the anti-aircraft positions unseen and hopefully take them by surprise. Radio silence was a necessity as the enemy monitored our communications. I cocked my weapons and then we were there. A hailstorm of fire met us. We fired for all we were worth and in a matter of seconds we had roared over the positions and disappeared behind the nearest wood. I felt a minor jolt and a huge hole appeared in my left wing. I had been hit by flak! My bird still handled normally so it wasn't so bad. *Hauptmann* Huberts appeared to have been hit as well, his engine was smoking quite heavily. Adjutant Derflinger had been hit a number of times in the tail and ailerons. Someone must have informed the Ivans as soon as we took off, otherwise how could they have been ready for us? *Leutnant* Freytag was missing. The CO called him, but no answer. The old man landed safely, his aircraft still smoking heavily. Derflinger made it as well. I was unable to get my undercarriage to come down however. I pressed the button but nothing happened. There was no other choice but to land on my belly at the edge of the field. There was a crash as I touched down. Pieces of the landing flaps, ailerons, and radiators flew about, the propeller blades bent back. Then there was silence. A huge cloud of snow shrouded me for a while. I had made it safely once again. We discussed the mission at length. *Leutnant* Freytag had apparently bought it.

That evening I drove with Maria to her parents' place. I packed the car with bread, butter, potatoes, and candles, as well as some good cognac for her father and chocolate for the mother. Some coal, which had been delivered the day before by Olga Barsova, already lay in the back of the Kübelwagen. I was curious to see how they lived as I'd never visited a Russian family. Maria guided me skilfully through the darkness, avoiding deep holes and puddles. Before long we were in the midst of a horrible barracks camp. We stopped in front of a weather-beaten door. Two elderly, care-worn people greeted me warmly and led me into a large, cold room. A candle on the only table illuminated the poverty of these people. The parents spoke only Russian, so Maria interpreted for the rest of the evening. There were tears in the eyes of the old couple when I unpacked the delicacies. Maria brought the coal in from the Kübelwagen and built a roaring fire in their small stove. The two elderly people were deeply moved and couldn't thank me enough. I felt ashamed. The room warmed up quickly. The old woman began making potato pancakes on a griddle, while father and I sampled the cognac. From him I learned that when the Russian troops withdrew before the advancing Germans, they had forced every male inhabitant from the ages of 12 to 60 to go with them. Since he was 64 he had been allowed to stay at home. Then it was time for supper. The potato pancakes were excellent. The candles I had brought with me made the room somewhat brighter and I realized that this one room was their entire apartment. Outside, in the open, was the sole toilet for the hundreds of people living in the barracks. The brand name on the facility was "Plumpsklo." Like hundreds of thousands in the Kharkov area, they had been living in these pitiful quarters for about fifteen years, blessings from the workers' and farmers' paradise. Father and I were soon mildly drunk. He produced a balalaika from beneath his bed and together we sang "On the Volga" and "Black Eyes," he in Russian, I in German. We soon got into our stride, singing loudly even when we didn't know all the words. In any case there was soon banging on the walls left and right. The neighbours were complaining. When the cognac was gone mother brought out a home brew. Then Maria's father told me something that quickly sobered me up:

"There are mass graves behind our small birch wood! I've seen them. Many hundreds of Polish officers and soldiers lie buried there."

As he spoke he pulled a cardboard box out from under his bed. In it were badges of rank bearing the Polish eagle.

"They were shot twenty at a time in front of a trench they had been forced to dig themselves!"

Then he placed his right index finger to his lips in a gesture for me to keep this to myself. Maria interpreted everything, but then she said to me, "Father talks too much when he's drinking. Don't believe everything he tells you."

I thought he was talking rubbish too, after all why should Polish officers come to Kharkov to have themselves shot? I therefore decided to keep this information to myself. (Much later I learned of the crimes committed there by Stalin. Not until 1990 were the remains of more than 4,000 Polish officers and soldiers exhumed.) An article in the *Frankfurter Allgemeinen Zeitung* stated:

Moscow, August 12 (dpa/Tass):
"President Gorbachev has ordered an investigation into the circumstances surrounding the mass shootings of several thousand Polish officers and soldiers carried out by the KGB on the outskirts of Kharkov in 1940. It was on this day that the mass graves of the murdered men were discovered."

Maria's father hadn't been so drunk after all!

It was getting late and I tried to take my leave, but Maria and her parents wouldn't hear of it. I'm not sure how I got into the child's crib, one with a white wire screen no less, but when Maria woke me every joint was sore. Mother had made breakfast. Father was still in bed snoring away, in Russian of course. It wasn't until about ten that I arrived back at the airfield. The "old man" gave me a blast which made itself felt. A formation was just returning from a mission in which I was supposed to have taken part.

I could only half hear the CO because of my headache. If I understood him correctly I was grounded for ten days. It was unlikely the Russians would notice. I therefore had time to worry about other things, for example the miserable living conditions of our ground personnel, their inadequate winter clothing and their poor rations. By comparison we pilots were pampered and I felt that we were obliged to share our special rations with our ground crews.

We were sitting in the mess when the alert *Rotte* took off. A high-flying reconnaissance aircraft was supposed to be over our base. The two aircraft soon disappeared into the blue sky. Just as we were about to go outside we heard a distant drone, then a whistling and howling. We threw ourselves to the ground and seconds later bombs struck an empty hangar not far away. Oh well, it was no great loss, there were no aircraft inside. But our astonishment was even greater when moments later the bombs were followed by thousands of white leaflets. Printed in awful German, they bore the following message:

"The intelligent act of *Leutnant* Freitag! Comrades! It is time to end Hitler's bloody terror. End the madness and throw down your weapons. For you the war is over! Follow the courageous example of your *Leutnant* Freitag. The Committee for Friendship Among Peoples. Signed Walter Ulbricht, Erich Mielke."

(The mention of this name still makes the bile rise in my throat. Had it not been Mielke who murdered the two police officers in Berlin in 1931 and then fled to safety in Moscow? One of the policemen's names was Captain Anlauff. Why have the authorities not charged him with this capital crime? Yes, and to mention Ulbricht, that dark figure, would bring shame to every word!)

Freitag's case remained a topic of discussion for some time, because we weren't sure whether he had been forced to land and branded a deserter or if he had really gone over to the other side. The ten days flew by, and I used them to have a look around the city. Olga Barsova was our "old man"'s constant guest; it seemed as if a romance was blooming. Since we no longer needed heating material I scarcely ever saw her. My contacts with the pianist Nina Bobrinova were all the more pleasant. I gladly accepted an invitation to visit her parents, and one fine day I drove to an apartment building not far from the Sumskaya, armed with bread, tinned meat, coffee, and chocolate. It was still light. The four-storey building looked rather run down. The Bobrinovs lived on the second floor. Nina, who was expecting me, watched from a window. Her parents were nice people. The father repaired typewriters, an occupation which in more normal times had allowed him to earn a reasonable living. But in this household, too, hunger was the order of the day. Thus my visit was all the more welcome. The evening passed pleasantly with much piano playing. Maria played splendidly, mostly show pieces. Her repertoire included Liszt and Beethoven, naturally, but Tchaikovsky and Rachaninov as well. Then it was late and time for me to go. I wanted to avoid a repeat of the drama resulting from my visit to Maria's parents, so I started my "sixty horsepower" in plenty of time. On the way I met five furniture vans which were being led by an open SS Kübel. All were heading down the Sumskaya at high speed. In a flash it came to me: the vehicles from the *Standartenführer*'s schoolyard! Although it made no sense to me at the time, I felt it important to report my encounter to the CO. He decided to file a report.

Hermann Graf said to me reflectively: "Perhaps there was something to that drunken SS man's fantasy after all."

Just a Grave in the Taiga

The alert *Schwarm* took off one icy morning. One of the four aircraft failed to return. *Leutnant* Walter's first combat mission appeared to have been his last. The formation leader, *Feldwebel* Rasmann, last saw him at his side as they entered a snowstorm at low altitude. We waited for an hour until his fuel must have run out, but in vain. Missing in action. It was a fate that already had snatched many from our midst. The weather cleared at about midday. Mounting a search for Walter in the vastness of the taiga seemed hopeless. That evening the "old man" summoned me and informed me that he had just received a report from "up front." Some infantry unit had found Walter and his aircraft and had buried him with honours at the western exit from the village of Volstoya. He had crashed into a depression while flying at very low altitude, his aircraft exploding on impact.

"I want you to go over there tomorrow morning and try and recover his personal effects as well as his identity disc. Take a camera with you and take a photograph of the grave for the parents."

After a long search I finally found the place on the map, about 90 kilometres north of us. Given the poor road conditions that meant two days or more. I packed my things in the open Mercedes Kübelwagen and set out the next morning while it was still dark. The thermometer showed minus 21 degrees. Even though I had bundled up well I was still cold. Just outside Kharkov I reached the "highway," the only line of communication from the front to the rear and vice versa. Armoured units were trying to move up through bottomless holes in the mud and filth; the tracked vehicles towed trucks and smaller vehicles which would never have been able to get anywhere on their own. I was in a hopeless state in view of this situation. If decided that if I couldn't find a tank or tracked vehicle to tow me I was turning back. Not far away sat a Tiger tank. The crew had climbed out and were working on the left track. Snow blew across the road. I passed cigarettes around.

"Where are you going?" I asked harmlessly.

"To Kursk."

A young *Leutnant*, frozen blue and obviously the tank commander, sensed what I wanted and asked: "You're trying to get up front? We can take you with us. Do you have a tow cable?"

"Yes, thank you, it's in the luggage compartment."

Then the young officer asked: "exactly where are you going?"

I told him my destination, which lay right on this road. Soon I was hanging behind the Tiger, which dragged me through the filth, mud, and potholes at a rapid rate. I feared that my car wouldn't last long in spite of its Mercedes star. It had become daylight in the meantime. Everyone kept an eye out for Russian aircraft, which had a habit of cruising the roads shooting up anything that moved, and there was plenty moving here! I shouldn't have mentioned it. In the next second a good dozen Russian close-support aircraft came racing towards us, guns blazing. The Tiger stopped, its commander shut the hatch and disappeared inside. Left out in the open, I dove from my car and threw myself into the ditch. Tracer sprayed about my ears. It appeared that I hadn't been hit, so I got up, dirty from top to bottom, and banged on the side of the Tiger with a stone. The hatch opened and the *Leutnant* appeared:

"How many were there?" he asked innocently. He didn't seem to be interested in how I had fared.

"Alright, let's get going then," he said nonchalantly, and the caravan set itself in motion again. Near evening we arrived at Volstoya, which was no more than a collection of straw-roofed shacks. The *Leutnant* tossed me my tow rope and disappeared into the darkness without saying goodbye. I steered toward the most prosperous looking cottage, which sat at the entrance to the village. I knocked on the door and an old woman appeared and asked me what I wanted. Then she motioned me inside with a friendly gesture. I immediately found myself in a large, poorly lit room, crowned by a huge, square, tiled stove in the centre. Around this was a bench. From around the stove many curious eyes looked me over from top to bottom, however in the semi-darkness I was unable to distinguish male from female. A pleasant warmth surrounded me. I unpacked my sleeping back and air mattress, as well as bread, butter, one of the notorious tubes of cheese, chocolate, cigarettes, coffee, and a bottle of vodka. The eyes up above grew larger and finally everyone came down from on top of the stove: the master of the house—Boris was his name—, a kindly grandfather, and his two grandchildren, Boris and Nina. Seldom have I seen anyone tuck in so blissfully as did these lovely people. Dog tired, I climbed up onto the stove and quickly fell into a deep sleep from which I didn't awaken until morning. When I awoke I found myself surrounded by the entire snoring family, which, unnoticed by me, had taken me into its midst. Grunting especially loudly was the grandfather, who had taken several large drinks from the vodka bottle. I carefully crawled over the sleepers so as not to wake them, but the grandmother nevertheless got up immediately. It was still dark outside with no sign of daylight. The window panes vibrated slightly from the thunder of gunfire at the front. I scratched away some of the thick frost. Outside it was clear and cold. My car was completely covered with snow and barely visible. Using the coffee I had brought with me, the mother made a lovely brew which the rest of the family, who had got up in the meantime, enjoyed noisily. As I suspected, the beast at the door refused to start. Not until a charitable truck gave me a tow did the engine spring to life. It took no time to find *Leutnant* Walter's grave. It lay close to the road buried under the snow; all that was visible was a wooden cross with his name. The infantry unit which had buried him had long since moved on. I scraped away the snow with my bare hands, removed his identity disk and took a picture.

"Lonely comrade, who will visit your grave here in distant Russia?"

I offered a silent prayer for him and then I went on my way, for here on the main road the fighting and dying went on. Perhaps it would be my turn next. It took me all of thirteen hours to get back to Kharkov, thirteen hours to drive a lousy ninety kilometres.

Does Anyone Know Anything About the Tartar Trench?

At about midday it leaked out that we were to be transferred. As the ground personnel were preparing for a long trip, it seemed that we were leaving Kharkov for good. The next morning the "old man" let the cat out of the bag. We were moving far to the south, to the entrance to the Crimean Peninsula. Maria must have suspected something. That evening she appeared at my room and hung around looking sad and sorrowful:

"Is it true that you're about to leave us for good?"

I was surprised at her question, because secrecy concerning our unit was absolute: Secret Command Matter!

"Where did you hear that?" I asked Maria.

"I heard in the kitchen that you're leaving in the next few days. Please take me with you, I'm a part of the fighter unit too!"

It became clear to me at that moment that secrecy was impossible with all the civilians crawling around our operation. Some time later I was to learn just how true this was. We were ready to leave and Maria had brought my things out to my aircraft.

"Where are you going," she asked, "please tell me. I'll follow you if it's not too far, please tell me!"

We took off and as I climbed away I could still see Maria waving.

Kharkov was far behind us when the CO's voice came through my headset:

"White 13"—that was me—"close up with the first *Schwarm*!"

Finally I took up my position in the formation.

"Base course 180 degrees," called the "old man."

Actually he was a young and sympathetic fellow whom I had quite grown to like.

"How had he parted with Olga Barsova?" I asked myself. Surely he knew of our transfer much sooner than we and was in a position to take his leave of her calmly. *Hauptmann* Huberts' voice rang out through my headset:

"We'll be landing in about 25 minutes."

Where were we? With all the talking to myself and my musings I hadn't been paying attention. I laboriously worked the map out of its pocket behind me. The Bf 109's luggage compartment was very tiny. I had stuffed my sleeping gear, which included my toilet bag, and my few clothes inside. I diagnosed this as a design flaw. Beneath us lay broad, endless Russia. The Dniepr, that ancient, fabled river, accompanied us. Winding restlessly, it formed huge chains of lakes before returning to its course. In the sunshine the river looked up at us with its deep green water as if to say: "What do you strangers want here in our land?"

Lost in thought I asked myself: "Do we intend to snap up, occupy, or simply exploit all this forever as breadbasket for Führer, Volk, and Fatherland?"

But my philosophizing was interrupted. The CO called:

"We're going to land, the *Stabsschwarm* first followed by the First, the Third, and then the Second. No delay refuelling!"

Getting everyone down on the ground was a wearisome process. The place was called Dniepropetrovsk. It was the site of a huge dam whose giant turbines had once supplied power for the surrounding industrial centres. The Ivans had blown up the dam shortly before they left. Now it lay useless below us. The water poured through numerous huge holes in the quay wall, flowing uselessly toward the Black Sea. Refuelling proceeded quickly, aided by many capable hands, including Russian prisoners of war. Then we took off. We were not yet at cruising altitude when the "old man" checked in:

"Our destination today is an airfield not far from Perekop, the entrance to the Crimea. It's supposedly called Chaplinka and is little more than a huge field. Our dispersal is at the south end of the field."

Then he resumed radio silence. The terrain climbed gradually. The first peaks of the Jaila Mountains appeared in the distance.

"Prepare to land, usual sequence."

We touched down and taxied in. To the left and right were other, diverse units: bomber, tactical and strategic reconnaissance, fighter and close-support. Sevastopol, the gigantic fortress in the southwestern corner of the Crimea, was to be taken. A tough nut!

Hadn't Sevastopol been conquered once before? When was that? Oh yes, in the famous Crimean War of 1853 to 1856, when the Turks allied themselves with England and France against Russia. But the main battle had been over Sevastopol. It was a good thing I had paid attention in school. Professor Sebrandtke would surely have given me an A.

The tents were pitched quickly. It was to be a restless night with frequent alerts. Soviet bombers searched for us and they had to get rid of their loads somewhere. Soon bombs were falling. There was an eerie howling and screaming, a moment of silence, and then an inferno of explosions: dozens, hundreds. My ears hurt. Blast waves raced through my tent. Outside there were screams. Machines burned and exploded, and with them their ammunition, which hissed across the field. The tactical reconnaissance unit had been hit.

The next morning it rained hard. We squatted in the mess tent of a neighbouring unit. Only the birds knew when our ground personnel were going to arrive. Dr. Hans Sander stumbled into my tent.

"What do you say, should we use this bad weather to organize things a little? I've just heard that we're not far from a collective farm. They have all kinds of hens and so on. My colleague from the close-support unit next door has loaned me his car."

Actually I wasn't interested. After the short night and the rain I craved a nap much more than scrounging for food. But then Huberts, the CO, also looked in on me and said, "You know Sander is right. Bring me back a chicken."

What choice did I have but to say "*Jawohl!*" I struggled to my feet and took money, cigarettes, and plenty of chocolate. The latter was canned and was called "Schokakola." Hans Sander and I were soon on the road to the Isthmus of Perekop. The collective farm was supposedly close to the so-called "Tartar Trench." But there was nothing to be seen in the rain apart from a few poncho-shrouded German soldiers trudging south along the road. After a short time we saw Russian prisoners of war coming toward us. All alone, they were trotting north, soaked to the skin. There was no one at all watching them. I stopped and, using sign language, asked them where they were going. Laughing, they said Zaporozhye and pointed to a sort of meat inspector's stamp which had been placed on their left breast: "Released by the 481st Infantry Regiment."

It was odd that they wore no badges of rank. There was no way to tell a General from a simple soldier. Then a giant of a man stepped out of the group and spoke to me in French. They had been released from captivity and were going home as they all came from the coal basin around Zaporozhye. Hans passed out a few cigarettes, which disappeared like hot rolls. Then an idea came to me.

"Would you be interested in helping me as interpreter," I asked the giant, "we want to buy food from a collective farm, you won't regret it."

The man jumped into our vehicle and introduced himself as Boris Berenkov.

"What was your position in your unit?" I asked.

"Colonel," he answered, looking rather embarrassed. The weather cleared and soon we were standing before a tremendous wall of earth. I estimate it was 20-25 meters high.

"This must be the Tartar Trench," I said to Dr. Sander. Then our new interpreter jumped in and explained that it had once been much higher but had been badly eroded by the weather. "But where is the trench," I asked. Boris the Colonel told us that in order to build the wall they naturally had to excavate a huge trench. Over the course of the years all that had entered the local vernacular concerning the wall of earth was the trench. Catherine the Great had had this structure built in response to frequent invasions of her empire by swarms of Tartars coming from the Caucasus via the Crimea.

"You know the man is not uneducated," I observed to Sander. The road was one great pothole. The Opel rocked as if on the high sea. Muck sprayed into the car and soiled us from head to toe.

"Over there," said the giant, "is that the collective farm you are seeking?"

In fact he was right. We turned onto a country road and moments later found ourselves in front of a line of buildings. An old man with a white beard stepped out of one of the buildings. He noticed us immediately and came over. Our Colonel made the introductions.

"This man is the collective farm's bookkeeper. He wishes to know what we want," he translated.

"We would very much like several hens, in return for payment of course," I explained. There then followed a long palaver between our interpreter and the old man. It turned out that all but a few of the farm's hens (there had once been 25,000 there) had been confiscated and taken away by various German units.

"And what about the rest?" I asked indignantly. The old man told us that he could let us have 24, the rest he needed for his own people. "Tell him we'll take them and that he's to kill and prepare them straight away."

The old man called two female workers who immediately set to work. Meanwhile the bookkeeper invited us into his office, took a bottle of vodka from the cupboard and began to pour.

"We are very angry with the Germans," began the old man, repeatedly stroking his long, white beard with his right hand. "The first soldiers who arrived here were very kind and took nothing from us. On the contrary, this vodka came from them. But the rearguard ravaged everything here. Even our sheep and goats were confiscated. So now we're without any kind of livelihood, no one thinks of payment."

I was dismayed and astonished at the same time at how bravely the old man expressed his opinion. Turning to Boris, I said: "Tell him we will of course pay what he asks." The old man poured another round and began figuring out a price on an ancient abacus. It was just like the ones I had played with as a child, only much larger. Nevertheless he worked away on it, like Einstein with his theory of relativity. Then, like a shot from a pistol, he said, "Twelve Rubles per chicken."

I pulled out my "war chest." He refused to take German money as he wasn't familiar with it. I therefore paid him with the few rubles I had brought with me from Kharkov. The "broilers" were soon stowed away in the car. We took one more in exchange for all the chocolate and cigarettes we had with us. Soon we were on the main road heading home. Russian prisoners continued to stream north. On taking a closer look I realized to my astonishment that they were women, female soldiers, covered with dirt from top to bottom and completely exhausted from walking. I stopped by one such group. They had two litters in their midst, each one carried by four women. On the litters were two badly wounded young women. Dr. Sander had Boris translate and learned that one had a belly wound while the other had lost her left leg below the knee.

"We're taking them with us, otherwise they don't stand a chance of surviving."

Carefully we lifted the two litters into our Opel "Captain." Boris Berenkov we left to walk with the women. I explained where our airfield was and drove away while Hans Sander tended to the women. I was unable to avoid all the holes and the two severely injured women frequently groaned in pain. Finally we were home. Dr. Sander called in his colleague from the bomber unit and the two doctors set to work in the hospital tent. In all the excitement I had forgotten the chickens which everyone was so eagerly awaiting. That evening however they were in the pot. Seldom has a supper tasted so good. The next morning Hans came into my tent.

"The 'belly wound' died during the night. The gangrene couldn't be stopped. The 'lower leg' has regained consciousness and is quite chipper. You know the infantry battalion also put its 'meat packing stamp' on the women, but on the right side of the chest."

We buried the "belly wound" at the edge of the airfield at noon. We had no idea who she was or what she was called. I had a miserable feeling in the pit of my stomach as I placed a few flowers on her unmarked grave. Who would weep for her?

A *General* Richthofen landed at our field to tell us that our loafing about was at an end.

"From tomorrow on expect heavy action. The Crimea is not yet in our hands. The Russians are bringing in units from the Caucasus across the Kerch narrows. It's your job to prevent this."

Hauptmann Huberts came to attention and saluted. The *General* immediately climbed back into his Fieseler *Storch*, which soon disappeared in a cloud of dust. There were stunned faces all round. As if we had been twiddling our thumbs the past month! Why our *Geschwader* was the most successful on the entire Eastern Front. What an idiot, I thought to myself. Expressing this opinion verbally would surely have got me into a lot of trouble. That evening Boris Berenkov, the Russian

Colonel, strolled into camp. With him were three women who could barely walk.

"Ameobic dysentery," confirmed Dr. Sander. "There's not much I can do. I've given them a shot. They can rest here a while and them move on. If this keeps up we'll soon have half the Soviet Army in our hospital."

I informed the CO of Boris' arrival and left the decision to him. Keep him or send him on his way was the question. We had need of an interpreter, but he knew only French and what's more he was a Colonel! The CO decided to send him on his way. I had to tell Berenkov. I can still see his disappointed face, but war is war and who knows what trouble we might have got into?"

It rained heavily again that night. My tent leaked badly. Soon my air mattress and I were lying in a warm, brown brew waiting for morning. The latter came slow as a snail. It continued to pour. Slowly I pulled up the tent flap and looked outside. It couldn't be true! The entire airfield was white, as if it had snowed. I reached out my hand and discovered that they were mushrooms. On closer inspection I realized that they were Champignons, real Champignons, hundreds, thousands, what am I saying, millions of them, as far as the eye could see! Our units were in the middle of a giant mushroom farm. I can scarcely describe what followed. Our men came out with pots, sacks, canisters, cans and anything else available and filled them all with mushrooms. However, when the first alert *Rotte* scrambled, the mushroom aria came to an abrupt end.

Things happened quickly from then on. One *Staffel* after another took off and headed south. Soon I, too, was hanging in the cloudless sky over the Crimean Peninsula. Target: Sevastopol. In front of us was a unit of He 111s which we were to guard against Russian fighters. Soon their bomb bay doors opened and hundreds of special heavy, concrete-piercing bombs rained down on the huge fortress. The bombers' aim was good and the bombs fell precisely within the fortress zone. Each explosion sent up a shock wave and we were catapulted into the air as if by a giant fist. There was no sign of enemy fighters. On the way back we were ordered to carry out strafing attacks. We caught a fully loaded freight train. First we knocked out the locomotive. Realizing what was up, the engineer jumped from the moving train. Seconds later the locomotive spit out its steaming life and came to a stop. Franz Dreher attacked the last car. Tracer flashed toward the car. Then there was a brilliant flash and the car went up in a tremendous explosion. One car after another blew up in a chain reaction. Seconds later there was just a huge, black crater where seconds before there had been a long train. The explosion of the munitions train was so great that even the locomotive had disappeared. Bathed in sweat we landed back at our mushroom farm. I can't say that I was exactly happy.

That evening there was a *Geschwader* briefing. "Daddy" Mölders, the CO of all COs, had come to say farewell. It was to be goodbye forever. I can still see him disappearing into the night in the He 111. He was killed when his aircraft crashed near Breslau, halfway to Berlin, on his way to the state funeral for the great First World War pilot Ernst Udet. Things now moved quickly. Sevastopol simply refused to fall. The next morning I received orders to fly cover over the largest railway gun of the war. The huge gun, which was called "Dora," was being moved in for action against this monster of a fortress. Not far from Perekop we found the giant, moving slowly toward us. For the first time I realized that what we were dealing with wasn't just a single gun, but an endlessly long train with a tremendous, shrouded something in the middle. As far as I could tell from the air the thing had to have seventy wheels. It must have been terrifically heavy. There were four of us and we were much too fast for this sluggish operation. There was nothing to do but circle high above, watchful as falcons. The approaching night took this rolling apocalypse under its protecting wing. We later learned that the monster weighed 1,350 tonnes and had 80 wheels, no wonder with that weight. The entire train consisted of 100 cars. "Dora"'s effectiveness was indisputable: in only five days, firing a total of 48 shells from a range of 30 kilometres, it reduced the fortress of Sevastopol to a pile of rubble. It had supposedly been impregnable. What is impregnable today, I asked myself.

At breakfast one morning the CO said to me: "You can get on your feet and organize a few things. We're short of everything. We've no flour, no butter, nothing to spread on our bread at all. Some fruit and vegetables wouldn't be bad either. It might be days before our ground personnel arrive. Take the *Storch* and go cross-country."

God in heaven! What was I now, the supply officer? It was easier said than done. Organizing something there in the desolate steppe was something like searching for the famous haystack, to say nothing of the famous needle. Following orders, I set out in the *Storch* with several empty butter tins stowed in the fuselage behind me. One never knew. I felt a certain amount of anxiety, for in such a slow machine I would be easy prey for enemy fighters. There couldn't have been a better serving dish, with me as the roast beef. I tooled along at low altitude, looking more behind me than ahead, for Ivan usually attacked from the rear. I flew toward the east without knowing the exact path of the front. The onrushing panzer units left a great deal of territory behind them each day which could only be characterized as no-man's-land. The panzers rolled past fully operational Russian units without paying them any heed. Our infantry followed too slowly and no one knew what was played out between the two groups. Nevertheless I was of good cheer. A village appeared in the steppe in front of me. On its left side was a huge wall of earth on which trees were growing and beside it the tall mast and huge propeller of a wind-driven generator. Ah, I thought, this is a good place to come down. I pushed the *Storch* under the spreading acacias to protect it from the sun. It was a small village with all its houses along the road. A few crooked cottages to the left and a few to the right. The houses were empty, there wasn't a soul to be seen. The situation didn't strike me as risky, nevertheless I went from house to house. I had gone through almost all of them when I stopped short. In one of the huts lay an old woman, apparently sick and abandoned. When she saw me she crossed herself out of fear. I couldn't blame her for being afraid. Using sign language I learned that she had nothing more to eat. Just then I heard singing in the distance, which struck me as very odd. It sounded as if soldiers were coming along the village street. I was standing beside the bed of the old woman. Who could describe my horror when, through the small window, I saw that a Russian unit, in full battle order, was marching along the street singing. I dropped down under the window and waited until this apparition had passed. My main concern now was, what about my *Storch*? Cautiously I stole out the back door and ascertained that the coast was clear. They hadn't discovered my aircraft as it was too well hidden beneath the spreading trees at the water reservoir. What was I to do with *Matka*, the old one? I have scruples, but as bad as I felt I had to leave her there. I pushed my *Storch* out from under the trees and with several flaps of my wings I took off for home. Somewhat to the left of my course I spotted a huge, green, rectangular field. Around it were hundreds of small boxes. At one of the corners there was a small house. A man looked up at me and waved. I turned left, lowered the flaps and touched down beside him. After shaking hands I took a closer look at the small boxes. Beehives, beehives and more beehives. The fellow caught on in spite of the limitations of my sign language. In his small house there were dozens of wooden containers full of golden honey. He saw my greedy eyes and invited me to help myself. The empty butter tins flew out and soon my *Storch* was loaded to the collar with the rare delicacy. I gave the friendly old man a receipt voucher for the requisition, but not without leaving him with a bonus in the form of bread, coffee, chocolate, sugar and cigarettes. It took quite some time just to get my overloaded steamer airborne. I wobbled along like a lame crow, my wheels grazing the blades of grass. Meanwhile an air battle seemed to have developed above me. Russian fighters and bombers crashed to my left and right with tremendous explosions. Russian parachutes, recognizable by their trapezoidal shape, floated to earth; one landed right beside the old beekeeper. I had left enough honey behind for the man in the parachute, which ought to have at least sweetened his disaster somewhat! Pushing the throttle all the way forward, I tried to escape this inferno. After what seemed like an eternity I touched down, bathed in sweat, between landing and departing Messerschmitts which were either returning from or leaving on a sortie. I almost got knocked over in the hustle and bustle. I received a big welcome from my unit when I finally unloaded my booty. Distribution was seen to by our administration mandarin, better known by the title "Four A" (IVa).

"A shame you weren't there today," observed Franz Winter. "We knocked down a whole series of Ivans."

"They must have been the ones that nearly fell on my head, thanks very much," I replied.

"Honey or victories," said *Leutnant* Schmude, joining in the conversation, "That is the question."

The CO was quite thrilled by my "capture" and said, "Tomorrow morning you can go looking for something meatier. Our ground unit has just arrived from Kharkov, completely burnt out and without rations. You'd better take the IVa with you, he knows best what we need."

I decided to say nothing about my encounter with the Russian infantry unit and the sick old woman lest he send me scrounging in a Bf 109!

The next morning I grabbed our inspector and away we went, back over the familiar fields. Flying into the rear would have been pointless as our ground forces had long since taken control and sifted the area. Therefore we flew farther forward, toward the east. Hamann made himself comfortable in the *Storch*, I shoved the throttle forward and we lifted off into the unknown, into frightening no-man's-land. The air above us was damned plumbiferous and already full of activity. Air battles were in full swing, which meant: eyes open! More than anything I would liked to have flown below the blades of grass.

"You'd better sit with your back to me and keep a sharp eye out behind," I called to Hamann, "I have the situation in hand to the front. Call out as loud as you can as soon as you see an aircraft approaching from behind that looks suspicious to you, it's a matter of life or death."

"Yes, I'll do that," came the timid reply. My passenger seemed to be somewhat frightened. Honestly speaking I was scared too, but I didn't let on that I was. Outturning an enemy fighter in the *Storch* was no easy task, especially since one was completely naked, meaning unarmed, and the bird was simply too lame. Keeping all this in mind, I crept through the countryside. I made out a collective farm ahead of us and prepared to land. The people were surprised but friendly. The famous bookkeeper was summoned and as Hamann spoke some Russian we quickly got down to business. They were able to offer us an ox and 125 geese in exchange for gasoline and diesel fuel: 100 litres of gasoline for the ox and 100 litres of diesel for the geese. We quickly came to terms and sealed the deal with a handshake. I explained to the old man that our trucks would come for the animals that afternoon. Soon we were back in the air above the steppe. Then, suddenly, Hamann cried out: "Fighter from behind! Fighter from behind!"

I hauled the *Storch* around in steep turn; tracer was already flashing past the cockpit. A Russian MiG, the most modern fighter the Ivans had at that time, zoomed past overhead. Its propwash almost drove us into the ground. I hauled my aircraft around again in order to keep the MiG in sight, a necessity if I was to evade the next attack in time. I hoped he wouldn't come out of the sun, or we'd be done for. I spotted a small wood in front of us, perhaps I might be able to reach it! I was right, the MiG pulled up in a steep turn in preparation for another pass. I saw it diving towards us at tremendous speed. Full throttle, left rudder and my *Storch* slipped sideways so quickly that the tracer missed us and struck the ground. I raced toward the wood. "Get out, get out," I shouted to Hamann. We leapt out of the machine, left it standing with its engine running and raced through the thicket. Our only thought was to get away. By the time the MiG returned for its next pass we had disappeared into a gully beneath some trees, scratching into the earth with our hands out of fright. There was the sound of gunfire, then an explosion, and our bird burst into flames. We saw the MiG disappear in the distance behind a thick cumulus cloud. And our faithful *Storch*? It was a write-off; black smoke poured from the wreckage. We set out on foot and headed west. After a long walk we ran into some pioneers who generously took us back to our "shop" in their car. The "old man" didn't look too amused as we told him about our drama, but his expression brightened somewhat when we informed him of the plus side: 1 ox and 125 geese. Soon afterward Hamann and our cook set out for the collective farm with the fuel we had promised the bookkeeper. They returned towards evening. Even from a distance we could see the royal buffalo and the geese fluttering about him beneath the camouflage net. And then began the night of the long knives. The ox was shot on the loading ramp, the geese beheaded on a chopping block. By morning it was all over and in the afternoon there was roast goose.

Geschwader briefing: "Sevastopol has fallen. The unit is transferring in an hour."

Once again I had to pack my bundle, only this time "Kreck," my cocker spaniel, had to go into the baggage compartment too. The dog loved to fly, especially in the large transport aircraft. Often he was en route for weeks before he was returned to me thanks to a badge around his neck on which was marked his name and the name of our unit. He had been to Norway, Berlin naturally, to Sicily and had once even dropped in on Rommel in North Africa.

We flew in three *Staffeln* and arrived at our destination in scarcely twenty minutes. It could scarcely be called an airfield. Far and wide there was only steppe, nevertheless we landed at our imaginary airfield. We had just climbed out of our machines when Hermann Graf shouted clearly and loudly: "Strafing attack, everyone get down!"

I had "Kreck" under my arm at the time and both of us stuck our noses into the yellow sand, making ourselves as small and thin as possible. The inferno was upon us in seconds. Ivans, fighters and bombers, pounded the field with machine-gun and cannon fire as well as bombs. At that moment all I wanted to know was what idiot had selected this place for us. There was no cover anywhere, only naked steppe. Fragments whizzed over our heads with a frightful noise. Machine-gun bullets sawed through the dry steppe grass. All was quiet for a second, then there was a terrific explosion directly behind me. "Kreck" broke free. Exactly how long I lay in the dirt I cannot say, but when everything seemed to be over I slowly turned around and found myself staring into the fuselage of a Russian fighter. To my horror I saw the pilot, covered in blood, hanging in his straps. He had crashed right behind me. It wasn't until I stood up on my wobbly legs and looked around that I realized what the attack had cost us. Wounded cried out, an atmosphere of general chaos ruled. Then a wet nose nuzzled my hand.

"Ah Kreck, I'd forgotten all about you. Where have you been?"

The dog was bleeding heavily from a wound in his belly and I rolled him onto his back with some concern. No doubt, he had been hit. He held quite still even though he must have been in pain. I immediately applied a bandage to stop the bleeding. That evening Dr. Sander took a look at him. His diagnosis: a simple grazing wound.

"He'll be alright," he said confidently, "We'll pull him through. Is 'Kreck' now due for the Wound Badge in Gold," asked the doctor.

"I don't know," I replied. "It's best if we don't say anything to him about it," I replied, "Otherwise he might demand what he's entitled to."

The phrase "entitled to" always reminds me of a former instructor, the intellectually somewhat limited *Feldwebel* Krupinski. In class he would often ask: "What does a soldier have on his bread?" My answer: "Margarine, *Herr Feldwebel*." Each time he would shout, "He's entitled to bread, remember that you stupid man, that's all he's entitled to. Next time I'll give you what for."

"Wretched Creature"

Actually I quite liked our *Oberleutnant* from the technical personnel. He was a fine fellow, a good sport, and the kind of man one could trust his sister with. That was how I felt, at least until that fateful day. I don't know how we began talking, but in any case he took me aside after breakfast and said:

"Picture this: at dawn this morning, I see three partisans at the edge of the airfield. I can't believe my eyes. I crawl up to them with my submachine-gun and take them completely by surprise. I make them lie on their bellies and frisk them for weapons one after the other. Then I place my gun on single fire, there are three bangs, and that's it. Do you want to see?"

At first I didn't know what to say. I felt sick, but then I collected myself and asked, "Were they armed?"

"No," he said, "But they were partisans, that was reason enough to let them have it."

"Couldn't they have been released Ivans who were on their way home like the many we've met lately?" I asked.

"Oh what difference do three Ivans more or less make anyway?"

Wordlessly I turned away and went into my tent, I had to digest all I'd heard. A thousand thoughts swirled in my head: it was war after all, perhaps I shouldn't be so prudish. According to the rules of war partisans weren't considered combatants. Luckily there was a scramble minutes later which interrupted my deliberations. On my return I reported to the CO. He was as appalled as I, and simply couldn't believe it. The adjutant was sent to where the bodies were and a few minutes later we knew the truth: they were released prisoners of war who had passed by our base purely by chance. The release stamp of a German infantry unit was clearly visible on their chests. I had the unpleasant duty of filing a report against a previously esteemed comrade. I shivered, even though it was warm outside. We buried the three Russians the same day. I don't know what came of this distasteful affair, but I could easily place myself in the psyche of this man who had served so admirably until then. From that morning on I went out of my way to avoid him. Fortunately he was transferred far, far away soon afterward, but I will never be able to forget him.

Behind Ivan's Lines

It was clear to all of us that it was only a matter of time until we were brought down by Ivan, either in aerial combat, by flak during a low-level attack, or simply by the rapid-firing rifles of the Russian infantry. The statistics proved it. However no one wanted to think about what awaited him in such an event. The more missions one flew the closer the day came when he might not come back. Russian leaflets, which poured down from the heavens, promised us that the workers and farmers paradise awaited us in captivity, but we had our doubts which were later confirmed. On this particular day I led the morning *Rotte* with Fw. Reiter as my wingman. It was exactly five o'clock. We quickly disappeared into the morning mist. Our mission was *freie Jagd*, which meant that we could engage anything we found. Enemy aircraft were most often encountered at low altitude, only rarely high in the Soviet sky. We crossed the front lines in a matter of minutes. A duel was under way between German and Soviet heavy artillery. I could clearly see shells bursting in the Soviet positions. Their infantry had to be concealed somewhere down there. I could recognize ours by their trenches, etched neatly across the terrain, precise, just like the Prussians of old. Beneath us endless fields of corn stretched to the horizon. We flew along a road over which Russian truck columns, protected by anti-aircraft guns, were moving up toward the front. A huge yellow dust cloud followed the columns. They were obviously transporting munitions. I decided to make one strafing pass and turned toward the road. Tracer flashed toward us, so close that I decided to break off the attack. I had no wish to be shot down before breakfast. Reiter was holding position on my left. Suddenly he shouted: "MiGs!"

In the next instant a shower of bullets riddled my fuselage and wings. A second MiG roared past. I couldn't risk a half-roll and dive as I was much too low. Instead I sideslipped sharply, as a result of which the next bust of tracer went wide. I called to Reiter: "Where are they?"

There was no answer. The MiGs climbed up into the sun, obviously in preparation for another attack. I called Reiter again but there was no reply. My engine seemed to have escaped damage, because when I applied full throttle it responded as before. There was nothing to do but head home. I was wondering where Reiter was when he pulled up alongside. There was a huge hole in the fuselage; his radio had obviously been knocked out. He waved and gave me the thumbs up signal. As a precaution I made a steep turn to the right to search for the Ivans but the sky appeared empty. It had been foolish of me to cruise about so stupidly in such dangerous territory. I had behaved like a raw beginner! It was a good thing that Reiter's damage wasn't too serious. We were still a good 15 kilometres inside enemy territory. The two of us chirped along in the direction of home. The oil temperature was causing me concern, the indicator was almost in the red already. Hang on, hang on, I implored, don't give me anything to worry about now! Reiter was still with me. Suddenly there was a bang. Black smoke poured into my cockpit and the propeller stopped. I was barely 100 metres above the ground, beneath me was a large cornfield. I lowered my flaps, saw the Russian truck column off to my right and then dropped into the green field. The belly landing was smooth as butter. Corn stalks flew away to the left and right, then there was silence. Smoke poured from my engine and hot steam hissed from the radiators. Reiter circled overhead. After jumping out I indicated to him that I was alright and pointed in the direction of home. Then he disappeared from my view. The important thing now was to get away from the nearby road. I was certain that the Russians had seen me come down. The road was barely 100 metres away. First of all I had to get away from my aircraft, as far away as possible. I raced between the tall corn stalks then turned east, back into Ivanland. I reasoned that they wouldn't be looking for me there, assuming that I would take the shortest route home. I looked at my wristwatch; it was just after six. I had the whole day ahead of me. What would it bring, I asked myself? Then I remembered that I had a compass in my jacket. I held it tightly in my hand like a precious gem. With the compass I could follow a precise course, hide by day and attempt to reach the front lines by night. Any other course of action would have been doomed to failure. I heard rifle fire. Bullets whizzed through the corn. They were looking for me! My heart leapt into my throat and I became bathed in sweat. My fur-lined boots hindered my running so I took them off and hung them over my shoulder. My 7.65 pistol rattled reassuringly in my pocket. I could at least fire off a clip and if worse came to worst use the last bullet on myself. There were still Russian voices nearby, I had to keep moving. But then I felt my strength leaving me. I was simply all in and let myself drop to the ground. I allowed myself a short breather. I'm not sure how long I lay there, but soon I was on my feet again and running east, always east, away from the Russians, whose voices I could no longer hear. Then I came to a brook in the middle of the cornfield. I swallowed the cool water hungrily, scarcely able to stop. Completely exhausted, I fell asleep where I lay. When I awoke the sun was already low on the horizon. A look at my watch showed that it was five in the afternoon. I was completely soaked through and cold. I had to get out of the cornfield, had to get to the edge as quickly as possible, for I had to use the night, had to get to the front lines which I believed I could cross only at night. Following my compass, I marched south through the corn and soon reached the edge of the field. The sight that met me caused the blood to freeze in my veins. Right in front of me, not five metres away, a Soviet infantry unit was digging in! They were so engrossed in what they were doing that they didn't notice me. My heart raced with excitement. I immediately ducked back into the corn. It was obvious that from then on I was going to have to head west. It was soon dark. I left cover, pulled on my fur-lined boots and set off, following my compass. There was heavy artillery fire to my left, then silence. Unusual. I walked up a slope and down the other side and found myself facing a rather wide stream which was flowing south sluggishly in the starlight. I had to cross, there was no doubt. I hung my jacket and boots around my neck and waded in. The current was strong, but I was able to swim unhindered to the other side. Once there I collapsed from exhaustion; my legs simply couldn't go any farther. What's more I was shivering from the cold and my teeth chattered. The illuminated numbers on my watch showed 9 o'clock. How much farther was it to the front lines? I crawled into a depression in the ground and fell fast asleep. The cold of the night woke me. It was three in the morning. I got up and staggered onward. Before me was another cornfield, which I crossed bent low, my compass pointing west. I threw away my jacket and boots which had become water-logged and heavy. Suddenly I received a blow on the back of the head and lost consciousness. When I came to I heard German voices. A young infantry *Leutnant* was bending over me, my soggy paybook in his hand. "Man, you were lucky. We almost shot you, thought you were an Ivan. Where in God's name did you come from?"

"Help me up first," I replied groggily, "I was shot down over there by the Ivans. Please phone my unit at once."

Then I fell back into a deep sleep. It was late in the afternoon when the *Storch* came to pick me up. I had a headache for some time, a remembrance of my odyssey. Fw. Reiter had also been forced to put his aircraft down before reaching our base, but fortunately on our side of the lines.

"Between Mars and Diana"

It had rained the whole night. The inner walls of my tent were soaking wet. Kreck lay cuddled close beside me so that we could warm each other. It was four o'clock in the morning, but still dark and gloomy on account of the low-hanging clouds. Actually I had the morning *Rotte* with Paule but he was apparently still snoozing too. So I rolled onto my other side, almost squashing the dog, but he had become skilled at turning with me.

Then there was the sound of footsteps beside us, the tent flap was opened cautiously and the beam from a pocket lamp struck me in the face. I heard a familiar voice say "Get up!" It was Fw. Brunner, who was on watch.

"Herr Leutnant the morning *Rotte*. Fw. Roßmann is already at his machine."

Kreck yawned. Now wide awake I clambered out of the tent. My morning wash and other ceremonies were out of the question, so I put them off until later and strolled over to my 109. Paule looked angry. He turned toward his bird and climbed in without saying a word. Today I was flying the old man's machine. The rudder had to be changed on my bird. Yesterday I had taken three hits, Russian infantry with their dangerous automatic rifles, I believe they were able to fire twelve rounds at a time. Helmet on, canopy closed and locked. Grosser began turning the starter crank. Paule's engine was already running. I rolled to the end of the airfield with Roßmann behind me, opened the throttle and then we both lifted off. I still felt rather taciturn, but following procedure I called over to Paule:

"We'll climb to 1,000 first and see what's going on."

"Victor," came the reply and then all was silent. Below us was the broad steppe. Visibility was 5 kilometres, it was still raining. Nothing going on again today, I thought.

"Two MiGs below us," shouted Paule, "Flying in an easterly direction."

It must be the morning patrol from the other side, I thought. I rammed the throttle forward, cocked my weapons and was soon behind the pair of enemy fighters.

"They must be blind to fly around here like this," I thought to myself. A burst of fire left my weapons and the Ivan blew apart into small pieces. Amazingly the leader failed to notice the fate of his companion, and so I cautiously moved toward the second Ivan. I was within 50 metres of him, his propwash shook my aircraft. But what did the fellow do? He rolled his machine onto its back and dove away. I stayed right on his tail, not wanting to let him get away. He twisted and turned like an eel. Steep turn to the left, I followed. The MiG pulled up to the right; he shouldn't have done that. I moved into position behind him and pressed the firing buttons. A burst of fire left my guns and in a fraction of a second there was a red flash of an explosion in his cockpit. I saw him jettison his canopy and jump, but his parachute became hung up on the fin. The MiG spun to earth with its unfortunate pilot in an endless spiral. Seconds later a fireball in the Tiga marked the end of a brave opponent, but one who had had no chance.

Whewre was Roßmann? Iturned around to look. There he was, maintaining position off my left wing, holding up one thumb.

"Your left wheel is hanging" called Paule, and in fact there was a green light on the instrument panel. This was the signal that it was high time to head for home, for there was no sense in prowling about any further. The old man was going to curse me for "bending" his lovely ship.

Soon we were home. The other wheel came down obediantly and the landing was uneventful. The "Kommandeur" was obviously sour, but it was more important that the Ivans had been forced to write off two more of their hornets. The command post noted the date: 14 May 1942.

Finally I had a chance to visit the mess tent, my stomach growled loudly, vying with that of Kreck, the poor dog. Neither of us had eaten since yestewrday afternoon. We'll make up for it I thought, provided the supply chief has received some rations. Hermann Graf knocked aside the wet tent flap and asked "Now then, Alf, how was the morning *Rotte?*"

"Well," I replied, "Not much going on apart from two MiGs who had apparently had enough of living."

"No, no," observed Hermann, "Don't hide your light under a bushel. If I've counted correctly that was number 82 and 83, was it not?"

The old man walked in and Graf and I both came to attention. Then he turned to me and said, "I have news for you. After breakfast you can go out again with Uffz. Noe and have a look around up front. Four of Ivan's Il-2's have supposedly been making life difficult for the infantry since dawn; I'm surprised you didn't run into them. By the way '13' is serviceable again. Takeoff in 30 minutes."

"I'll be glad to look around, but Uffz. Noe has little frontline experience," I replied.

"You'll look after him," replied the chief, and then busied himself with his setter.

The miserable dog had peed in my flying boots early the previous morning while I lay in my tent. I would have loved to have given him a good kick in the rear end.

Noe and I forced down our army bread. Once again the coffee was awful. Either the cook was putting something in it (one rumor said that it was soda, to keep us from becoming too lusty) or else he must have been using some other type of bean. At least that's the way it tasted. I had been suspicious of the fellow for some time.

Outside it had stopped raining and Noe and I soon made our way to our machines. I had a brief chat with Noe, telling him how I expected him to behave. Radio communications were in order and we soon lifted off from the wet grass-covered surface of "Mother Russia."

We stayed low and in five minutes were over the front line. Something seemed to be happening, and I saw a large number of artillery shells bursting round about the trenches of our infantry.

We spotted flak bursts to our right and went over to have a look. And there they were, four Il-2s attacking our forward positions . They were flying at treetop height and firing rockets into the trenches.

"Stay with me!" I called to Noe.

Soon the first was in my reflector sight. He seemed to be still asleep and took no notice of me. I had to attack from behind and below to have a chance of shooting him down. I cocked my weapons, flipped up the safety catch and opened fire. A cloud of black smoke exploded from the enemy aircraft's fuselage. Seconds later the Il-2, its cockpit on fire, landed on its belly in front of our trenches. The other Ivans seemed not to have noticed and calmly flew on into our rear.

"White 3 are you still there?"

"Victor,, I'm to the left of you. That was great!"

I had already closed in on the second Ivan. I followed the same procedure but this time the enemy aircraft reversed course and tried to escape me. Now we were heqded back toward Russian territory. He flew so low that his propeller almost touched the ground. I had to stay above him and fired from the side, aiming at his exhausts. This tactic seemed to be working, because slowly but surely the aircraft began to burn. Moments later the Russian put his machine down onto the Taiga.

"An I-153 behind us and to the right!" screamed Noe.

I looked behind and sure enough a biplane was trying to get on my tail. I was now at 100 metres, but I pulled around sharply and had the fellow right in front of my guns. A burst of fire and he exploded. Noe clung bravely to my left wing and held up his thumb.

"Let's go home," I called to him.

We climbed to 1,000 metres. I had had enough and wanted simply to head back to base. Below us the land battle was in full swing. Tanks, T-34s, were attacking our lines. However, I couldn't take part, the chances of getting hit were too great. The field came into sight before us, but what was that, it can't be true! A good 1,000 metres above us was an SB 2 bomber, heading east. I simply couldn't let him get away.

"White 3 do you see the SB 2 above us?"

"No," came the reply, "I'll follow you."

A few minutes later I was sitting behind the enemy bomber. The rear gunner saw me and began to fire. Tracers flew about my ears. Bullets smacked agains the armour glass of my windscreen. I dropped down to escape the Ivan's defensive fire and then attacked from below. I pressed the firing buttons and poured explosive-incendinary rounds into his belly. His cockpit began to glow like a light bulb. The rear gunner climbed out and a four-cornered parachute swung toward the earth. The Ivan pulled up, but his aircraft stalled, fell off to the right and went into a spin. Minutes later it crashed and exploded.

"White 3 what is your fuel situation?"

"My red lamp is already on," he replied.

I dove away steeply. My "reserve" light began to blink as well. We landed moments later.

"Congratulations," offered the old man, "That's six for you today already. I think that's enough, you can take the afternoon off."

I went into the command tent and mae my report, Noe assisted. For lunch there was noodles with meat sauce. My dog enjoyed it more than I. Roßmann, too, made a wry face.

"I've still got a Mettwurst from home, care to join me?"

We made our way to Paule's tent. Together with some homemade bread it was the most delicious thing I had eaten recently. Then I crawled into my sleeping bag, intending to stay there all afternoon. One never knew, that night the Russians might decide to bless us with fragmentation bombs.

I was in the middle of a silly dream when there was a frightful crash. There was another crash and my tent flew awy, leaving me lying in the open. Overhead was a flock of aircraft, Tupolev SB 2 bombers, I-16 Rata fighters and then, at low level, a gaggle of Il-2s. The air was filled with howling and screaming aircraft which raced over the airfield. I lay on the ground, making myself quite flat. More than anything I would like to have disappeared into the earth. Only now did our alarm sirens begin to howl. The idiots had been asleep, even our quadruple flak remained silent. Ofw. Steinbatz' machine blazed fiercely; the ground crew were already busy putting out the fire as the worst was already over. Apart from a few bomb craters the Ivans had little to show for their attack, if one overlooked my riddled tent and a few burst pickle barrels belonging to the supply chief. I looked at my watch. It was time to head for the mess tent for a cup of coffee and recover from this midday surprise. There I found Sepp Fernsebner, Hannes Zimmermann and Franz Schlosser.

"Well, another one with bomb damage," joked Hannes. "You look quite depressed. I understand your tent was damaged and is still missing."

Suddenly I felt a damp dog's nose on my left hand. It was Kreck, the poor dog, the bombing attack had frightened him badly.

Suddenly the *Kommandeur* appeared. "Dickfeld, you're to fly the last *Rotte* with Graf. Shall we say at Five o'clock, and have a look at the Rata fighters, their base is said to be about 20 kilometres east of us."

"*Jawohl*, Herr Hauptmann, I know the place already, easy to find, it lies right on the Nayarska River where it makes a bend to the south."

I took my leave to seek out Hermann Graf. He was sitting in his tent writing in his diary.

"Now then Hermann, have you heard. We're flying the evening *Rotte*. Direction the Ratta airfield. We take off at five o'clock."

"The old man was already here, I know all about it. We've still got a good hour to go," he said, visibly angered.

"So what's with you?" I replied.

"Nothing, but I've already flown five missions today and I'm gradually becoming fed up. I'll see you at five."

Then it struck me that I should bring my own diary up to date, but in the foul mood I was now in, I decided to put it off until the next day. Hermann was just more diligent.

I walked out to my aircraft at about 04.30 hours. Hölzl was busy with the weapons, installing ammunitiojn belts.

"Have you put in enough HE-incendiary?" I asked. He nodded his head. Wagner was just driving the fuel truck away. I climbed into the machine and checked out the instruments, which appeared to be in order. The parachute could well be repacked, I had squashed the thing flat by sitting on it. Then Graf came with his setter. He, too, climbed into his machine. We made a quick communications check and then all was ready. We soon lifted of from the wet grass

I led the *Rotte*, with Graff off my left wing. We climbed to 1,500 metres, all seemed to be quiet. No artillary fire to be seen. Visibility was about 10 kilometres with scattered clouds. Before us, in the direction of the Rata airfield, a village was burning.

"Ratas beneath us!" called Hermann, and in fact, an entire squadron was approaching our lines. They hadn't spotted us yet. I rolled my machine onto its back and dove toward the enemy. Graf followed and soon I was on the tail of the trailing Ivan. A short burst and he exploded. Beside me Hermann had a second Ivan in trouble. The Rata caught fire and plunged earthward. How could the Ratas in front fail to notice anything, I asked myself. They continued flying in a westerly direction, in close formation. Then, suddenly they woke up. The Russian fighters pulled up and turned toward us. I had lost sight of Hermann. One Russian, apparently the squadron leader, came toward me with all guns blazing. I evaded the Russian and pulled up into a loop so as to dive back into the fray with increased airspeed. The enemy squadron leader was now in front of my guns. He tried to evade but my burst tore off his right wing. The pilot jumped out but his parachute failed to open. Far below I saw Graf engaged with three Ratas, but I was unable to help. A large number of Ivans attacked me like enraged hornets, quite bravely I must say. I was bathed in sweat. If I didn't get out of there I was likely to be hit.

"Hermann, where are you?" I called.

"Beneath you. We had better get out of here."

"Viktor," I replied, and we headed for home. It was slowly growing dark. Soon the airfield was beneath us. Hermann landed straight away and I had just lowered my undercarriage when a tracer flashed past the left side of my cockpit.

"Alf!" screamed Graf, "A LaGG behind you!"

I turned sharply to the right and then I saw him. I rammed the throttle forward, retracted the undercarriage and with a climbing turn got behind the Ivan. The latter tried to escape by flying low. Seconds later I was right on his tail. I fired all weapons and in seconds he had begun to smoke. His left wing broke away and struck my fuselage. There was a mighty crash, my cockpit hood flew away and I found myself sitting in the open. There was no point in bailing out as I was much too low.

Meanwhile it had become very dark. I found the airfield with some difficulty and, leaving the undercarriage up, made a belly landing. There was a great racket as the radiators and flaps were ripped off and flew away. The propeller turned itself into a corkscrew and then all was quiet. Ground crew hurried to the scene and I climbed out of the pile of wreackage. Blood was running down my back, I must have been hit at some point. The medical officer pulled a splinter out of my left shoulder blade, the devil knows where it came from, probably a stray fragment.

It is a day I still think of. Sometimes I relive it in dreams, wake up with a start, knowing that its over, but that the hunt was as successful as it was senseless. What good did it do to have shot down nine Ivans that day? The parable of dismay on the enemy side, the satisfaction of having served the Fatherland? Oh, Dianna, how simple it was for you millenia ago. How honourable to hunt in your fashion, for which even the God Mars himself would have braided the golden laurels in your black hair.

"Across the Rubicon"

Heavy fighting raged at the Strait of Kerch. Our forces were trying to break into the Caucasus. We had plenty to do and flew from morning until night, one sortie after another, often as many as seven per day. We were soon exhausted and barely able to stay on our feet. To make matters worse our acting commander, an *Oberleutnant*, Herbst was the dog's name, drove us mercilessly and even reproached us as cowards if we weren't successful. He kept his own fat behind in the command post, well protected behind sandbags, and issued orders. Our anger and hatred were so great that we considered shooting him down on his next mission—by mistake of course—if he ever decided to fly with us again. However reason won out over our pent-up hatred. I wouldn't have liked to have become involved in such business. Not long afterward a bomb brought his command to an abrupt end. May his ashes rest in peace. We had become modern-day gypsies. Scarcely had Kerch been taken and Armavir on the Kuban fallen into German hands, when they threw us into the next hot spot like a fire-brigade. "Kreck" didn't accompany me this time; having been wounded, he travelled with the ground personnel. Our new base was called Taganrog. From there we were to fly against the Russians based at Rostov on the Don. Except for one snag the flight was almost problem-free. Something wasn't right with my engine, it lacked "pull." Soon I was lagging far behind the *Gruppe*. The old man saw what was going on and called to me

: "Take your time, there's nothing going on today. White 3 stay with White 13."

Fred Burck turned toward me and took up position off my left wing. I couldn't explain it, but something didn't feel right. The others had soon disappeared on the horizon. Fred and I flew along. Beneath us were broad fields, not yet harvested, wheat I assumed. Now and then there was a collective farm. To our right was the Sea of Azov. I was just thinking to myself that it was quite big when Fred Burck shouted to me over the radio, "Alf, MiGs from behind!"

As he spoke one of the Russians opened fire. Tracer flashed past my cockpit. As I pulled up I saw a second MiG behind me and to one side. His guns were aimed directly at my left flank. The next second bullets pierced the canopy behind my head. Where was Fred?

"Alf," he shouted, "Abschuß," the first one's burning, dive away, I'm right behind the second one!"

I dove away vertically and made a tight right turn. It was an old trick of mine to escape a second attack. Burck called out another kill.

"There were two of them, where are you?"

"I'm at low level, right over the mouth of the river, heading for Taganrog," I answered.

"Right, I see you, I'm coming down from your left."

"My motor's just about finished, it's on its last legs!"

I didn't have much altitude in hand, barely 300 metres, so I prepared for a belly landing. Burck hung beside me.

"Are you going to land?"

"Yes, I have to," I answered curtly. Seconds later I touched down on the steppe. There was a bang and a crash, dust swirled into the air, the flaps flew away, the propeller blades bent back and I found myself on the ground still in one piece.

"Everything alright?" called Fred over the radio.

"Everything's OK, fly to Taganrog and send a car. I'll stay with the aircraft."

"*Viktor*, we'll come pick you up." Fred climbed away and soon disappeared on the horizon. I opened the canopy and climbed out. It was then that I first realized how damned lucky I'd been. I must have had an entire regiment of guardian angels with me! The small luggage compartment behind the cockpit had been completely riddled and with it my "luggage." My clothes were now little more than strips of cloth, while the contents of my toilet kit, apart from my toothbrush, were no longer usable. Even my shaving mirror had bought it. Horrified, I thought of "Kreck." If he'd been with me this time he'd have had it for sure. All around me there was absolute quiet. There was no sign of life anywhere, just two columns of black smoke in the sky behind me and to my left, Burck's two kills. I walked down to the water; pushed by the wind, light, green swells lapped the beach. It was now 1300. I calculated that if Fred landed at Taganrog in twenty minutes and got a car immediately he should be able to make it here before dark if road conditions were good. When I returned to my aircraft I found an old man standing there looking inside curiously. I quickly felt for my pistol, but the man seemed to pose no threat. I couldn't understand what he was saying, but he kept on pointing toward the north. Presumably that's where he lived, however I let him know by sign language that I was staying with my aircraft. We shook hands and he left. I had nothing with me to eat and I was thirsty too. I scooped up some of the sea water and cooled my face and hands. The water had a brackish taste in my mouth. It had now been three hours since Burck left. I climbed inside the aircraft and dozed a little. I had just fallen asleep when someone shook me. It was the old man again, but this time he was surrounded by a crowd of Russians civilians, men, women and several children. They had brought me bread, cooked potatoes, eggs and a large bottle of vodka. Bewildered, I didn't know what to say at first. They were all speaking to me but I had no idea what it meant, probably something like: "Eat and drink brother German."

I climbed out quickly and a massive, buxom woman came over and planted a hearty kiss full on my mouth. Everyone was laughing and they obviously wanted to take me to their homes, which were visible in the distance on the horizon. But I had to refuse and so everyone sat down and the fraternizing began. They soon began to sing as well. When I joined in in "On the Volga" in German their joy knew no bounds. But where was Fred Burck with the car? The afternoon was rapidly drawing to a close. I began to fear that I might not get out of there. In spite of the charming people, all their kind gestures and tasty vodka, I wanted to go home to my unit. But then I heard a distant drone and soon a *Storch* appeared on the horizon. The aircraft made an elegant left turn and set down right beside the public festival. The old man himself was piloting the *Storch* and he could scarcely believe his eyes. Even before climbing out he shouted to me, "What kind of circus is this?"

I explained the situation to him, but he was in a hurry as night was fast approaching. My farewell was brief but heartfelt. I gave *matka* a fat kiss on the cheek, quickly pulled the clock out of the aircraft and threw my parachute over my shoulder. There was much waving by both sides. Huberts lifted the *Storch* off the ground and we soon disappeared into the steppe, direction Taganrog. We stayed low, flying just above the blades of grass. There had been plenty of activity in the air that day and the CO didn't want to be chewed up by the Russians before supper. It was already dark when we landed. Fred Burck, who was waiting for us, informed me that he hadn't got away unscathed either. He had come home with 19 bullet holes in his aircraft, two of them just below the fuel tank.

We were elegantly quartered in a still-operating sanatorium, but as it turned out we didn't think much of it. It was just a better place to sleep, that's all. We still followed the same procedure: up at two-thirty in the morning, drive out to the airfield in an open Kübelwagen, climb into our freezing machines and take off with shaking knees into the morning twilight. The Sea of Azov as far as Rostov was now our playground. The soldiers at the front were plagued by Soviet night harassment raids carried out by ancient biplanes which they called "sewing machines." The Russian bombers dropped small bombs on the trenches and roads and generally made life miserable. They flew exclusively at night, at low altitude and often in bad weather, and were almost impossible to shoot down. As soon as we appeared on the scene they disappeared. I always hoped to catch one of these fellows, but the sea god who ruled the Sea of Azov apparently had other things in mind. On this particular morning they had roused us from our beds even earlier than usual. When we arrived at the airfield it was still dark. It was cold outside, so we slipped into the command tent. Sullen faces all round, taciturn too. Each was lost in his own thoughts.

"I don't think we'll see any action today," offered Hans Huber in his Old-Bavarian dialect, "You can scarcely see your hand in front of your face."

"Anyone for skat?" I asked. But no one was interested so I closed my eyes and began to doze. In the back of my head I could hear a droning noise; could it be an aircraft? Oh rubbish, who'd be flying in such weather? But then the others heard it too. Curious, I cautiously lifted the tent flap and looked outside. I thought I must be dreaming: a "sewing machine" was approaching our airfield at low level. I was about to sound the alarm when the biplane swooped down, landed and taxied right toward our tent. In an instant everyone was on his feet and wide awake. We all pulled our pistols. I carefully closed the tent flap again. The aircraft rolled to a stop beside our tent and the engine was switched off. Two Soviet officers, one with red stripes on his trousers, jumped out and, suspecting nothing, came towards us. Huber and Walch had meanwhile slipped out the back of the tent and just as the two Soviets were fumbling with the tent flap Huber shouted, "hands up!" The two officers raised their hands and allowed themselves to be disarmed. They were stunned and speechless. Huber then directed them into the command post where we were. The shocked looks on their faces lasted a long time. In the meantime it had become light. Our men now streamed in from all the tents around the field. Everyone wanted to see the "sewing machine Ivans." When the two Soviets finally regained the power of speech, we learned that they had mistaken our airfield for theirs. It was quite a catch for us! One of them was a Major, a general staff officer and in charge of the entire "sewing machine" operation. He had gone along on a mission to see how his firm did business. The other was a Captain and an experienced pilot. Neither could grasp what had happened to them. In their "sewing box" we found interesting papers concerning missions, airfields, names of pilots, codes and so on. What stupidity to fly around with such documents! Our CO had both men sent to *Fliegerkorps* straight away for interrogation. We never heard any more about them.

The capture of the biplane resulted in a variation in our flying routine. Sight-seeing trips were announced. As strange as it might sound, most of our people had never sat in an aircraft. Now each got his turn whenever weather and fuel availability allowed. Dr. Sander had his hands full. Not only did he have many wounded to care for as a result of the constant bombing and strafing attacks, but the unit was lice-infested as well. Every known variant from head and body lice to crabs appeared. It was no wonder, for hygiene had long since ceased to be a major concern with us. There was no soap and water and what was more the emaciated men were reluctant to pull themselves together in the morning, evening or whenever, what with the mud and filth, the night bombings and the cold. This style of camping in such "plumbiferous" surroundings left deep scars on all of us, physically and psychologically. By the grace of God we'd so far been spared serious illnesses like cholera, typhus and others. However amoebic dysentery, with all its unpleasant side affects, had begun to set in. Our sick rate was almost 50%. The ground crews' clothing hung in tatters and still there was no end in sight to this terrible war. The next winter was at hand. Morning temperatures were already at the zero mark. The fighting on the Mius Front had intensified. Low-level attacks to assist the hard-pressed infantry became more common. Russian T 34 tanks made their lives difficult. We had armour-piercing ammunition for our cannon and were thus able to stabilize the situation on the Mius. There was little activity in the air. It appeared as if the Russians had lost the last of their reserves in our air battle over Rostov. Fw. Rother was able to force a MiG to land at our airfield. The aircraft's pilot was an attractive woman, a Major. She was dismayed at having fallen into our hands, but she had no other choice. Rother had sat behind her and directed her with bursts of fire past her cockpit, now left, now right, now higher, now lower. She had to "listen" if she didn't want to be shot down. She was interrogated and it turned out that she was from Leningrad, the wife of an infantry Colonel and the mother of three children. A letter she was carrying described the situation in besieged Leningrad. It described the terrible famine in the city, with inhabitants dying by the thousands. Even mice and rats were being eaten. The letter was not two weeks old. But we knew all about such things from our time in Kharkov. At first we put madame to work in the kitchen, but later we had to hand her over to higher authorities even though we had captured her. We never learned what became of her. Hopefully she survived and today is able to tell her grandchildren what awful people the capitalists are.

The thermometer fell to minus thirty overnight. Our aircraft refused to start. *Feldwebel* Reinhardt organised some ether and soon had the engines running. There were repeated calls for help from the front. Our infantry, the *Leibstandarte Adolf Hitler* under Sepp Dietrich, was being hard pressed. Russian T 34s attacked relentlessly. My *Staffel* was scrambled. We stayed low as it was only a few minutes to the front. If we didn't stop them now the Russians would be at our door by lunchtime. Then we spotted huge pillars of smoke from burning T 34s. We could see the fiery paths of artillery rounds as they whistled over the snow-covered landscape. We attacked in tight line abreast formation. I flipped up the safety catch over the firing buttons. It was a good thing we had loaded armour-piercing and incendiary ammunition. I poured shells into the first T 34. It stopped but the damned thing wouldn't burn. I turned for another pass and just as I was approaching the tank it blew up with a tremendous explosion, almost taking me with it. Only a steep turn saved me from the worst. To my left and right my comrades were also busy.

"White 13 from Yellow 1, I've been hit in the radiator, heading back."

One of our number had caught it. But our work was finished and we could go home. There were burning tanks as far as the eye could see. Beneath us men waved enthusiastically from the trenches.

"To everyone, we're heading home."

Some distance in front of us was a Messerschmitt, trailing smoke. We closed up around him. Would he make it to Taganrog? A hit in the radiator meant three minutes before the engine seized and the propeller stopped.

"Yellow 1 from White 13, favourable terrain for a forced-landing below us."

"*Viktor*" came the reply.

Seconds later the aircraft set down in a tremendous cloud of snow. We circled the downed machine.

"Everything's OK, send the *Storch*."

"*Viktor, Viktor*, the *Storch* will be there without delay."

That evening we welcomed the "forced lander" back with a huge piss-up.

The next morning there was another call for help from the front. Berger and I took off immediately. The sun, which was just rising before us, was blinding, so I lowered my sunglasses. There was a fat "clunk" as I cocked my weapons. Berger was in position on my right. Suddenly he shouted: "White 13, cavalry on the horizon!"

I couldn't see anything but I kept looking. Then I saw them. I could scarcely believe my eyes. Approaching from out of the sun was a wave of Russian cavalry, I estimated a good 500 riders with their horses. Lances fixed, they charged toward the German lines. I pinched my arm to make sure I wasn't dreaming. The infantry were already firing everything they had. A bloody slaughter began on the broad, snow-covered field.

"Don't shoot," I called over to Berger.

"*Viktor*" came the reply.

We flew over the scene of the battle. I couldn't decide whether or not to intervene in this operation in which the Russians had absolutely no chance. As I pulled up I could see the full extent of the carnage. Hundreds of horses lay dead, torn and bleeding on the ground, among them their dead and wounded riders. What madness! The German infantry was still firing. Only a few riderless horses escaped.

"We're heading back," I called to Berger.

I didn't look back. On the way home I realized what stupidity the human mind was still capable of. "And you're one too," I thought to myself. But there was nothing I could do about that.

Ancient Culture in Taganrog

Near our quarters stood a museum. Curious, I went and had a look inside. An attendant greeted me and then I began to comprehend the museum's. purpose. It was amazing to see all those who had been here before us. Relics thousands of years old gazed at me. Babylonians, Persians, Greeks, Romans, Huns, and who knows before them had left their calling cards. So as conquerors or passing visitors we Germans were nothing new to this corner of the world. They had all left meagre relics, mere traces of their cultures. What were we likely to leave behind, apart from shattered machines, bombed-out houses and the bodies of our fallen comrades? I would liked to have visited the place more often, but unfortunately the god of war would not permit it.

In the meantime the Sea of Azov had frozen over, which posed a direct threat to us. The Ivans could easily cross the ice at night and attack our dispersal. The old man ordered the posting of additional sentries after dark. A quadruple flak was installed up at the beach and it was assumed that that would be sufficient. One night *Feldwebel* Hütter was on sentry duty. It was just after midnight. Scarcely able to believe his eyes, Hütter spotted a Russian company moving slowly across the ice toward our airfield. The Ivans, who were usually kept well informed by the local population, must have suspected nothing. The commander of the watch gave the order to open fire. The quadruple flak and 18 submachine-guns sprayed bullets across the ice. It was a tragic scene; not a single person escaped the bloodbath. The next morning our sentries counted 84 dead and 23 wounded. The rest surrendered, including a Major. The booty in captured weapons and sleighs was considerable.

Outside the snow was blowing. With visibility virtually zero it was pointless to leave the sanatorium. I finally had time to take care of some long-overdue mail, see to my uniforms and look after "Kreck," who had arrived the day before with the ground personnel. His belly wound was healing rapidly and he had regained his taste for chocolate, a good sign. However he still didn't like smoking. Preparations for Christmas were by now under way as several of us would be away on leave on Christmas Eve. I too was preoccupied with thoughts of the long trip, even if it was only for two weeks. But there was a hitch when it came to finding transportation. I would have hitched a ride on a returning transport aircraft, but scarcely any were getting through. Even the old man suggested that I should take my long overdue leave. Allowing for the trip there and back I would have a week with my wife and children if all went well. On the other hand if something went wrong I'd have to turn around in Breslau in order to reach the front again in time. I wasn't prepared to take that risk.

"What would you say if I offered you a courier aircraft which has to go to Berlin-Staaken for an overhaul?" the CO asked me rather casually.

"What, you mean the old, open cockpit Klemm?" I asked back.

"Exactly, it would be just the thing for you and when it's overhauled you can simply bring the thing back."

I made a quick mental calculation: three days to Breslau if the weather cooperated. I made my decision. "Thanks very much, *Herr Hauptmann*, I accept." It was still one week until Christmas Eve. As usual, the premature Christmas celebration ended up in a tremendous drunk. Worst off was a *Leutnant*. When I staggered to my room he was already in bed and had thrown up on himself. However his faithful Setter was taking pains to clean up whatever his master threw up on the covers. Then I got sick too. Oh well! It wasn't so bad, you understand.

In my subconsciousness I heard a shout of "alarm!" At first I didn't know where I was. But then when I heard running in the hall I quickly realized that this wasn't part of the Christmas celebration. I jumped up and banged my head on the corner of the bed. Weil tore the door open and shouted: "The Ivans have caught us with our pants down. Everything's burning out at the airfield."

I jumped into my clothes and moments later raced to the airfield. Even from a distance I could see burning aircraft and exploding ammunition dumps. Soldiers were running about the field, gathering wounded, dragging away the dead, there was chaos everywhere. When we reached the field we saw what the Soviet fighters and bombers had done in their dawn raid. We looked at each other. Without saying a word we walked to our machines. The command post ordered *freie Jagd*, absolute radio silence, low-level attack by *Schwarm*. There were eight of us and we took off into the rising sun. Our target was the Russian bomber base north of Rostov. We were sure that they must have come from there; we knew of no other Soviet airfields in the area. The place was plastered with a good dozen of the feared quadruple anti-aircraft guns, but at that moment we didn't care. We stayed very low, taking advantage of every fold in the terrain. Huberts led the two formations. Rostov soon appeared and we let it pass to our right. Then we flew over the still Don. We cocked our weapons as we approached the target. A nod of the head and both formations spread out into two rows. I stayed to the right. The Soviet airfield suddenly appeared in front of us. Approaching at treetop height, we caught the Soviets completely by surprise. On the airfield bombers were being refuelled and fighters rearmed. I began to fire. Long bursts of tracer spat from my Me, which shook from the recoil of the weapons. Down below the Ivans ran for cover. An explosion tossed me upward and in a flash I was past the inferno. As I climbed away I had a chance to see what was taking place below. Bombers burned fiercely, munitions dumps blew up with huge explosions. We had all completed our firing passes when the Soviet anti-aircraft guns began hacking the young morning to pieces. Too late! We dropped down to just above the ground and soon arrived back at our base. As I turned final I saw my Klemm 35 sitting undamaged at the airfield perimeter. I breathed a sigh of relief, my leave appeared to be assured.

When I made my mission report the CO asked me, "Where did you leave *Leutnant* Habel?" No one had seen him after the attack. "You write up the missing report."

Much later we learned from a downed Soviet pilot that *Leutnant* Habel's aircraft had flown into a tree and exploded immediately following the attack. That evening we sat in the sanatorium feeling somewhat hung over. *Leutnant* Habel's place at the long mess table was empty. We couldn't mourn too long, it might be someone else's turn tomorrow. The beer tasted good again and I lost one game of skat after another. *Hauptmann* Huberts was an ace at skat. Then an orderly came up to me and said, "there's a Russian woman outside who wants to speak with you."

"What sort of Russian woman?" I asked, "I don't know any. The devil with her!"

He went out, came back a short time later and handed me a note. On it I read: "Dear Sir, my name is Maria, from Kharkov. I'm the Maria whose parents you visited, don't you remember me."

I was speechless. Could it possibly be the Maria who had taken such good care of us in Kharkov? How had she made her way here, 500 kilometres from Kharkov? I hurried out and there she stood, a bundle of misery, her clothes in tatters. I took her in my arms and hugged her for a long time. My companions were shocked.

"Maria, how did you find us in this icy winter? Come in first and sit down."

Our CO called to Dr. Sander: "Take Maria to the first-aid tent at once. Give the girl a bath and then find her some suitable clothes. I'll donate a khaki shirt, who else will give something?"

In no time we had assembled a complete outfit. The size was a little big, after all Maria was only 1.65 metres tall and she had lost quite a bit of weight as well. But what did we have a *Staffel* tailor for? The discussion then turned to the girl. The most adventurous theories were put forward and then crossed off. The military things hung from her body, but she looked happy. After she had had something to eat Maria unravelled the mystery. After we flew away she learned from the ground personnel that we had been transferred and where to. A detachment from our unit stayed in Kharkov to await important parts and she learned from them of our subsequent move to Taganrog. Then she began her journey. Travelling with refugee columns, sometimes in panje wagons, sometimes on foot, and occasionally with German units, in bitter cold and snowstorms, it took her no more than three weeks. When the old man asked about Olga Barsova she fell silent. After much gentle persuasion she informed us that Olga was no more. Exposed as the leader of a Russian espionage ring in Kharkov, she had been shot by a firing squad. *Hauptmann* Huberts stood up without saying a word and went into his room. We all suspected what he was feeling, we all knew Olga as a frequent and popular guest in our mess. The evening passed quickly. By next morning Maria was firmly integrated into our kitchen again. She was to play an unbelievable role in my life and indeed that of my whole family, but more about that much, much later.

What a Leave!

We flew around eagerly seeking kills, but there wasn't a Russian to be seen. I was so close to the Knight's Cross that I was getting a lovely sore throat. Hermann Graf described it thus in his diary:

"Dickfeld and I sat in our mills daily. But the kills didn't come. Some time ago we had worked out a new tactic. We flew over the Russian airfields with four aircraft. If MiGs appeared two of us made as if to flee. Every time the Soviets made off after them. The higher pair, of which the Russians were unaware, could then calmly fall on them from behind and shoot them down. But then this tactic too failed to produce results. One day we tried something which was rather common. We made up a packet with chocolates and cigarettes, tied it to a small parachute, added an invitation in Russian, and dropped it over the Russian fighter airfield south of Rostov. It read:

'Comrades from the other side, we invite you to a dogfight over the Don delta south of Rostov tomorrow, Wednesday, at 1200, altitude 4,000 metres. We guarantee that we will come with only eight machines, you can bring as many Soviet machines as you want! Horridoh! In sincere friendship, your enemy.'

However we waited in vain."

"*Oh, Du Fröliche*" (Title of a German Christmas Carol)

It was high time for me to snap up the Klemm and go. Mechanic Hess checked the bird once again and reported: "In order, ready to fly. Are you really going to fly this lame duck to Berlin and Breslau?"

"What choice do I have," I replied, "My wife and children are waiting at home. I'm leaving at first light tomorrow no matter what the weather!"

"But it's forty degrees below zero outside," observed my capable technician, "I can't guarantee that the beast will start."

Where would I have been without Hess. "Bring out the ether; it'll start coughing as soon as it sees the bottle! Sister Erna over at the hospital has been keeping a bottle for me since yesterday."

There was no activity at the front all that day, no sign of any Russians ready to be shot down. Had Ivan lost his courage or was his delivery system for replacement aircraft not working, for his losses had been enormous. Since there was nothing going on, I reported myself off duty to the CO that evening and began preparing my things for this more than questionable adventure. Christmas presents? What was I supposed to take with me? There in vast, icy Russia there was nothing to warm the hearts of my wife and children. The cold en route gave me the most concern. To be sure I had warm things, but I wasn't sure if they'd be adequate for a flight in an open sporting aircraft. Dr. Sander gave me pair of thick fur-lined gloves. They were dirty, but he assured me that they were warm. Hannes Wiese loaned me a flying helmet. I had to smear my face with a thick layer of grease to prevent freezing. The maps for this 2,000-kilometre flight were a joke. I slept poorly, plagued by wild dreams. (In one case I erred by 180 degrees and landed at Novo Sibirsk instead of Breslau!) Finally the duty officer knocked on my door.

"*Herr Leutnant*, it's time."

I shot from my bed, jumped into my clothes, and hastily drank a cup of coffee. Hess was waiting at the door and together we went out to the airfield. The command post was reporting minus 41 degrees. It was still dark. The unfortunate Hess fiddled around with the aircraft in the cold. He splashed ether about, however the beast simply would not start. It slowly became light and I grew more and more uneasy, for all I needed now was for an attack to come and I could forget my dreams of home leave. It was going to be a clear, cold winter day. The trees around the airfield, bedecked with ice crystals, gave the impression of a fairy-tale landscape, but it was one filled with death and destruction. Hopefully the Soviets wouldn't come until I was away from the field! Finally the engine sputtered to life, spitting and snorting like a walrus. Hess had performed a miracle. I let the good old Klemm warm up and then it was time.

I quickly tossed my pitiful bundle into the open cockpit in front of me. A brief handshake and then I taxied out for takeoff. I applied full throttle and the nimble little aircraft lifted off after a few metres. It was a lousy feeling to be crawling along, totally helpless and defenceless. The aircraft's maximum speed was no more than 110 kilometres per hour. Only by staying at treetop height could I hope to avoid being discovered and shot down by enemy fighters. After two hours I climbed somewhat higher, relatively certain that I had escaped the danger zone. In spite of the layer of grease and the nose protector my face was ice-cold. The slipstream whistled about my helmet. I ducked down in the cockpit to get a little more protection from the icy blast. One cannot believe how long two hours can feel when one thinks he is about to be shot down at any minute and sent on to eternity. There is a little cowardice in all heroism. I was unaware at the time just how lucky I had been; Hermann Graf described it thus in his diary:

"Dickfeld turned his aircraft on course for home. He hadn't yet disappeared over the horizon when a considerable assembly of Russian aircraft appeared over the landing field from out of the east, with bombers above and somewhat lower a swarm of Rata fighters. Guns rattling, they swept in and fell upon us. The din was terrific. Bullets shredded the turf, bombs exploded; never before had they taken us so completely by surprise."

My bird's tiny motor sputtered away reassuringly, all sixty horsepower. Its tanks were good for about 450 kilometres, then I'd have to come down. With my lousy maps navigation in this huge, endless, snow-covered region was not a simple task. Rivers, usually prominent features, were frozen over, everything was white on white. Railway tracks, normally dependable reference points, were blown over with snow and unrecognizable. The notorious search for the needle in the haystack, what am I saying, in an entire hay barn, would have been easier than my futile efforts to hold the correct course. I had to use dead reckoning, which was no walk in the park. But my home and my wife and children drew me like a magnet. It was still bitterly cold, minus 38 degrees, but the three pair of long underwear, my woollen undershirt, the pullover, and the one-piece flying suit kept me warm, thank God! It was still three days until Christmas Eve.

I spent the night in a small Russian provincial town. The accommodations in the Wehrmacht hostel were excellent. I would gladly have stayed a few days but home was calling to me. Once again I found myself in the sky over God-damned Russia heading west. Finally, three days after my takeoff from the Sea of Azov, my home city appeared on the horizon. With the Oder beneath me I turned final for Gandau airport. The aircraft's tailwheel flew off as I touched down. At that moment I could have cared less, for I had done it! There was a joyous reunion with my loved ones. What a Christmas present!

Everything was normal there, or at least it seemed so to me. There was enough to eat and the stores weren't short on clothing, even though many things were rationed. Breslau had so far been spared the scourge of the "bombing terror" and was still an enchanting cultural centre. As a soldier one saw little sign of the war there. Perhaps they just pushed it aside, not wanting to believe that a great blood-letting was taking place beyond their city, the perversion of an apocalypse which would be remembered for centuries. I felt unsettled, even near our Christmas tree. How were my comrades making out far away on the "quiet" Don, in the ice and snow?

The airfield called: "There's no way you can go any farther in the aircraft, the right mainspar is broken, an old break. All that's holding the engine in place is two loose bolts. How on earth did you make it here in that pile of junk? Where did you come from? From Taganrog? Where is that anyway?"

And I still had to get to Berlin. My leave passed too slowly. Each day there were new bulletins from the Eastern Front but nothing of the Don and the Sea of Azov. I had to go back soon, but the question was how. I travelled to Berlin by train, hoping to catch a ride back in a transport aircraft. I was in luck, a Ju 52 was going to Kharkov. I made myself as comfortable as I could on crates of land mines destined for the infantry. The flight was very bumpy and the crates bounced up and down, but a short, uncomfortable flight was far better than a long, uncomfortable train ride.

Three days later I landed at our former playground with the unforgettable name: Kharkov. I had been feeling ill since the day before. I suspected that I had eaten something bad during a stopover in Vinnitsa. Soon I couldn't stay on my feet. There was blood in my stool. I had all the symptoms of amoebic dysentery. That evening saw me in hospital in Kharkov, deathly sick with a high fever. What a reunion with this big city. A Russian lady doctor gave me excellent care. She spoke excellent German and observed laconically:

"You'll be out of here in less than a month."

Stuffed full of pills and tablets I shuttled between the bed and the toilet. The hygienic conditions were catastrophic. Nina Bobrinova, the pianist from the Chevchenko Theatre, visited me, and her parents stopped by occasionally. Within two weeks I was back on my feet. By chance there was a Major Pape in the next room, likewise a victim of the amoeba. Well-informed, he knew my unit's current location. I could scarcely believe it; my JG was at the gates of the Caucasus. The name of the place was Mineralnye Vodi. How was I to get to "Mineral Water," more than 2,000 kilometres away?

"Damned Caucasus!"

I hitched a ride in a long-range reconnaissance aircraft. It was on its way to Stavropol and then Pyatigorsk, but the crew told me they would be happy to drop me off at "Mineral Water." After more than a month out of action I finally rejoined my unit. There were unfamiliar faces everywhere. Not until I saw Hess, my good spirit and mechanic, was I certain that I was really back. I also learned of the fearful losses which my unit had suffered in the meantime. Commanding officer Huberts was gone. Fred Burck had also been killed along with fifteen other experienced pilots and friends. The unit had a new commander and I became his adjutant. There were new pilots and new ground personnel. It was all hard to take. But that wasn't all. "Kreck" was gone. My personal things had disappeared without a trace in the course of the many moves, as well as my tent, sleeping bag, and air mattress. As usual Zierenberg knew nothing. I could have killed him. My inquiries were met by shrugs of the shoulders everywhere. No, this was no longer my fighter *Gruppe*. Afterward Dr. Sander had a look at me. That evening we were sitting in the mess tent; suddenly we heard a suspicious droning. There was a shout of "alarm!" and we ran outside into the fields, because as the New Testament said so nicely (or was it the Old) "blessings come from above." Light and heavy fragmentation bombs struck the airfield. There was an explosion directly in front of me. Clutching the earth, I received a heavy blow on the head. The bombs were still exploding all around me; I felt my way carefully along my skull and came upon something warm and wet. I had been hit. Machines blazed, ammunition exploded, the airfield was illuminated as bright as day. The rest of the bombers had no difficulty finding their target, it was as if we were laid out on a serving tray. It was strange, but I felt no pain. Then I discovered my mistake. In the panic I had landed in a melon field. A melon propelled by the blast wave from the bomb had scored a direct hit on my head. *Leutnant* Borchers had no such luck, a bomb fragment ended his young life. He was only twenty years old and had arrived just three days earlier. The technical officer, *Oberleutnant* Schwacke, was forced to place four aircraft on the loss list.

We were still receiving replacement aircraft however. Recently they had begun using women as ferry pilots, people such as *Flugkapitän* Melitta Schiller, Hanna Reitsch, Beate Uhse, and others. Mineralnye Vody lay directly before the foothills of the Caucasus Mountains. Early in the morning we could see the "alpenglow" of the flat-breasted Mount Elbrus and the bizarre Mount Kazbek, both snow-covered. Before us the Georgian military road led to Ordzhonikidze and Tbilisi. How many armies had passed over this historic road in the course of the centuries? Now it was our turn. Who would write our history? The new "old man," an Austrian, had a special mission for me.

"For more than a week a Soviet reconnaissance aircraft has been coming over the mountains from the south at about noon, you can set your watch by him. The army is concerned that he is providing the enemy with a steady flow of up to date information. You are to take care of him. *Feldwebel* Barowski will fly as your wingman."

Great, I thought, an interesting mission at last. I replied "*Jawohl, Herr Hauptmann,*" and left the command post. I was pleased that Barowski was coming with me, I liked him very much, especially his piloting experience, and I believed he liked me. It was good to be able to depend on someone, especially in such a dangerous area.

A Near Tragedy

It was eleven o'clock, time to get ready. Before takeoff we agreed to maintain radio silence, for the Soviets monitored our radio frequencies. The enemy reconnaissance aircraft was expected to appear behind the

Kazbek at about 1200. This bizarre, ice-covered giant was approximately 5,000 metres high. This day, however, its face was hidden behind tremendous cumulus clouds which billowed up to 10,000 metres in the deep blue sky above this charming, but to us strange land. We took off and gained altitude quickly. I looked at the dashboard clock; twenty-five minutes before he appeared. It was damned bumpy above 3,000 metres. Barowski hung to my left. I placed the oxygen mask over my nose and mouth and inhaled the pure oxygen into my lungs deeply. Wearing this strange device, which allowed us to survive at high altitude, we looked like people from another planet. The altimeter showed 5,000 metres. As a precaution I continued climbing to 6,000, because when the Ivan appeared we would need some speed in hand to catch him. I flew around a fat cumulus to look behind the Kazbek. We weren't far from Tbilisi, the capital of Georgia. The sunglasses kept out the ultra-violet rays. I had already cocked my weapons as a precaution; two machine-guns and a cannon were ready. Barowski pulled up alongside and by way of hand signals indicated that something was wrong with his engine. Dense, black smoke was coming from the exhausts. I pointed downward and he peeled off and dove away toward the deceptive, white carpet beneath us. Now I was alone. It was 1215. There wasn't a living soul to be seen anywhere no matter how much I twisted and turned in my seat. But then I thought I saw a shadow behind a towering thunderhead. At first I thought it might be an eagle, but what eagle flew at that height? I put my Me's nose down slightly and soon I was at 500 kph. I pulled around the cloud and there he was in front of me, the Soviet reconnaissance aircraft. He was right in the sun, but the profile was correct, it was a DB 3, no doubt about it. He spotted me and ducked into the nearest cloud. "Damn, he got away from you," I cursed myself. I half-rolled and dove. Soon there was 600 kph on the airspeed indicator. I raced through a tremendous cloud formation, heading south; if he was going to run for it I was certain he would head straight for home. I popped out of the clouds and there he was again, right in front of me. I pressed the triggers and my Me shook from the recoil of the guns. A stream of tracer reached out for the Ivan. Then the fellow broke right and my bullets went wide. My speed was too great and I pulled up over him to prepare for another pass. As I did so I was dismayed, paralysed, frozen! It was a German reconnaissance machine, a Bf 110. I hadn't realized it before. What was he looking for here, I asked myself? I reversed course and pulled up alongside him. The crew, pilot and observer, waved to me. I let go of the stick and folded both hands as in prayer, begging for their forgiveness. The two waved back generously. There was nothing left for me to do but peel away shamefully and fly home. I aged significantly in the few minutes before landing, by years I'm sure. The CO wasn't exactly enthused over my subsequent report. How could it have happened? The profile of the Bf 110 was similar to that of the Soviet DB 3, especially when seen only as a silhouette.

"Couldn't you have made sure first?" asked the old man?

Bf 109 E "White 5" of 3./JG 52 photographed by Leutnant Dickfeld at Mannheim in late 1939. The aircraft is camouflaged in the early war scheme of Black Green and Dark Green upper surfaces with Pale Blue under surfaces (RLM 70, 71, 65).

Leutnant Dickfeld in the seat of a 20mm Flak 30 light anti-aircraft gun. Mannheim, 1939.

Leutnant Dickfeld climbing into the cockpit of a Bf 109 E at Laachen-Speyerdorf, late 1939.

Starting the engine of Bf 109 E "White 2". Two mechanics of JG 52 crank up the aircraft's inertia starter and then jump clear when the engine starts.

An unidentified pilot in the cockpit of a Bf 109 E, note the Revi Reflector gunsight.

Bf 109 E-1 "White 4" France 1940.

Two further views of "White 4" (WNr. 5049), a Bf 109 E-1 of III./JG 52 photographed in France in 1940. This aircraft wears the colour scheme introduced in 1940, consisting of Black Green and Light Gray upper surfaces and Pale Blue fuselage sides and under surfaces (RLM 70, 02, 65).

Bf 109 E-1 "White 8" of 3./JG 52, photographed immediately after starting its engine. Querchamps, France, 1940.

"White 8" taxies out for takeoff at Querchamps.

f

Two Bf 109 Es of JG 52 photographed by Leutnant Dickfeld while in flight over France. Flying the nearest aircraft was Oberleutnant Günther Rall. Piloting the aircraft farthest from the camera was Oberleutnant Ehrenberg.

Günther Rall's machine once again. Note the later 70, 02, 65 scheme and the complete lack of unit markings.

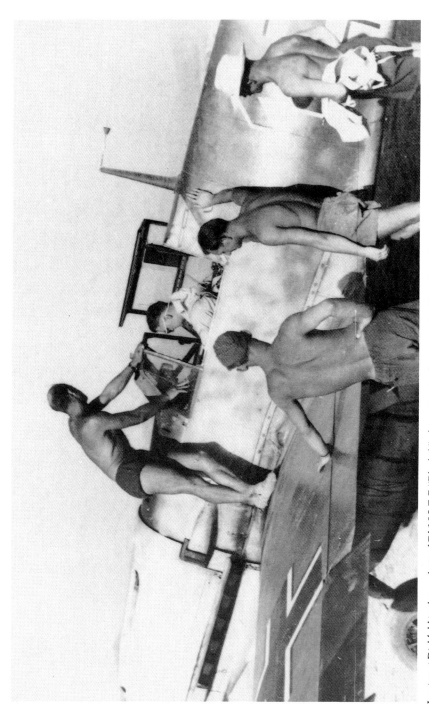

Leutnant Dickfeld in the cockpit of Bf 109 E-7 "Black 1" after returning from a sortie. Note the yellow engine cowling and auxiliary fuel tank beneath the fuselage. Molai, Greece, 1941.

Another view of Leutnant Dickfeld exiting the cockpit of Bf 109 E-7 "Black 1"

A group of JG 52 personnel photographed at Molai, Greece in 1941.

This page and overleaf, three views of the Bf 109 F flown by leutnant Dickfeld while serving as Gruppenadjutant of III/JG 52 in early 1942. These photos were taken at Taganrog in the USSR.

Leutnant Dickfelds Bf 109 F at Taganrog 1942.

A photo of Lt. Dickfeld with a canine friend in front of the same Bf 109 F. Note the III Gruppe emblem in front of the cockpit.

"White 11", a Bf 109 F of III/JG 52, photographed at Taganrog in early 1942. Unaware that the aircraft had been damaged by enemy fire, Oblt. Dickfeld walked away from the machine after landing. The aircraft subsequently caught fire and burnt out. A member of the ground crew was killed by exploding ammunition.

Leutnant Dickfeld looks on as an officer places the Knight's Cross around the neck of Feldwebel Edmund "Paule" Roßmann. Dickfeld and Roßmann both received the Knight's Cross on 19 March 1942.

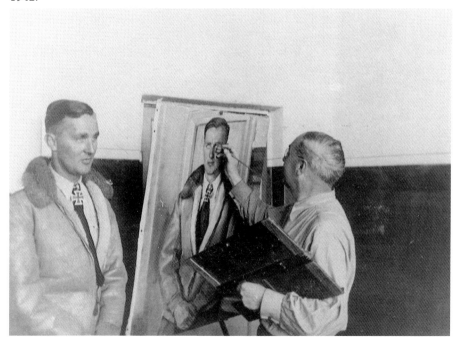

Adolf Dickfeld poses for portrait artist Professor Leo Poeten of Düsseldorf in the Crimea while wearing the Knight's Cross with Oak Leaves. The portrait now hangs in the Düsseldorf Museum of Art.

Leutnant Dickfeld with Knights Cross and Oakleaves, May 1942.

o

Leutnant Dickfeld with Hermann Graf in Rogani, 1942. Dickfeld wears the Knights Cross with Oak Leaves, while Graf wears the Knight's Cross with Oak Leaves and Swords, both of which were presented by Adolf Hitler personally at his Wolfsschanze headquarters on 19 May 1942.

Leutnant Dickfeld with Adolf Hitler in the latter's Wolfsschanze headquarters following the awarding of the Knight's Cross with Oak Leaves.

q

Newly promoted Oberleutnant Dickfeld.

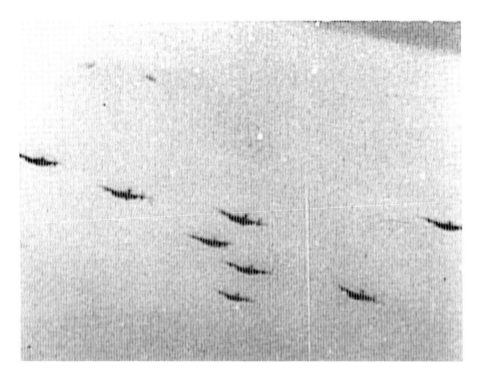

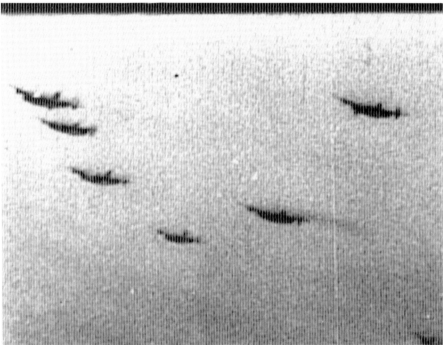

A German fighter closes with a formation of Consolidated B-24s. One of the aircraft has been hit and may be seen trailing smoke in the second photo.

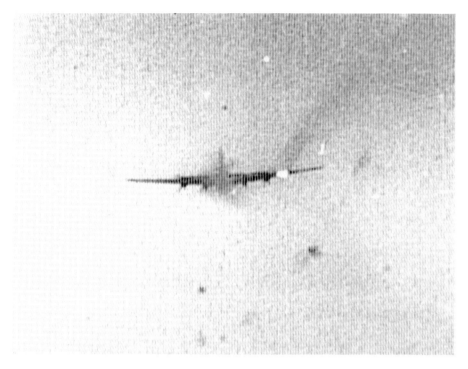

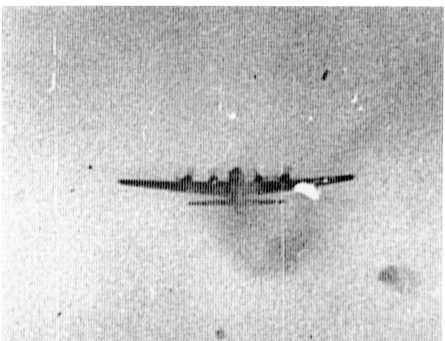

This page and overleaf, a German fighter closes in on a B-17, scoring hits on the starboard wing and fuselage. Mortally wounded, the stricken bomber rears up before beginning its long plunge to earth.

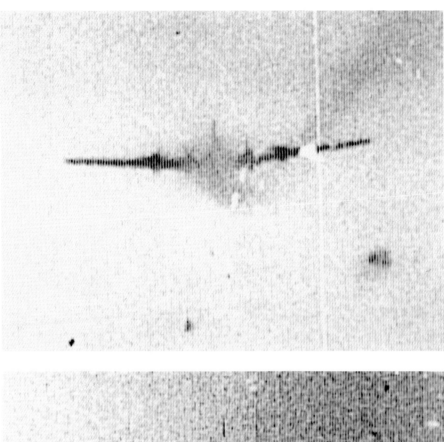

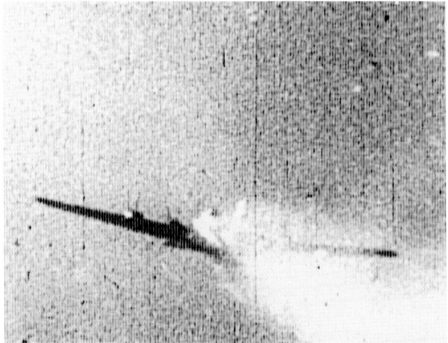

Camera gun sequence of the destruction of a B-17 continued from the previous page.

A badly damaged B-17 caught by the gun camera of a German fighter. Note the damaged horizontal stabiliser and the fuel leaking from the starboard wing.

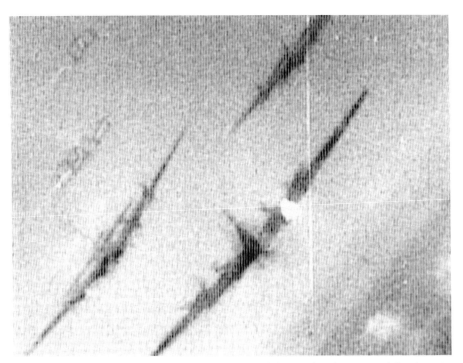

A formation of Boeing B-17s under attack by German fighters. The closest aircraft has been hit between the starboard inner and outer engines.

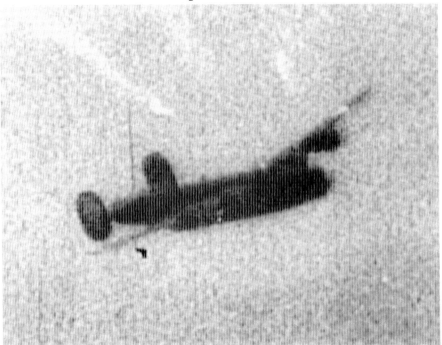

A German fighter makes a pass from the front quarter against a B-24. Note the smoke trails left by the fighter's tracer ammunition.

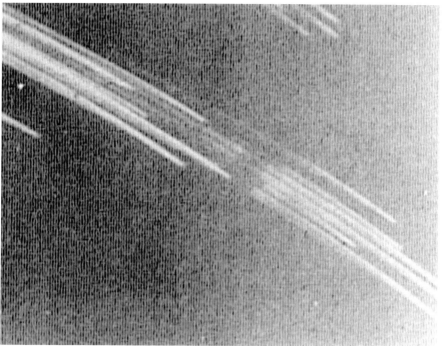

Contrails in the sky over Germany, as seen by German fighters climbing to intercept.

Adolf Dickfeld

Adolf Dickfeld with General Galland at Quedlinburg in 1944. The unidentified youth in the center had just won a Hitler Youth gliding competition.

y

Adolf Dickfeld

A Bücker Bu 181 *Bestmann* trainer aircraft modified to mount four 100M Panzerfaust Rockets for use as a "Tank Buster". Oberst Dickfeld flew operational sorties against Soviet armour in this type of aircraft.

aa

A group of II/JG 2 personnel in Tunisia, early 1943. Third from the left is Erich Rudorffer, who ended the war as a Major with 224 victories and the Knight's Cross with Oak Leaves and Swords. To the right of Rudorffer is Kurt Bühligen. One of the most successful German pilots in Tunisia, scoring 40 kills there, Bühligen ended the war as an Oberstleutnant with 112 victories and the Knight's Cross with Oak Leaves and Swords.

Send-off for Oberleutnant Dickfeld as he leaves II/JG 11 to take up his new post as General of the Replacement Luftwaffe. Jever, 1943.

The author, second from the left, with three unidentified members of JG 2 in front of the wine-Chateaux "Tindja". North of Bizerta, Tunisia.

How could I answer? That afternoon I learned whom I had come within a hair of killing. It was a crew from a long-range reconnaissance unit based nearby, and as fate would have it was the very same one which had kindly transported me from Kharkov. How embarrassing for me; I could have torn my hair out. That evening I took a Kübelwagen and attempted to repair the moral damage with a load of the finest Bavarian beer. Was that even possible, I asked myself on the return trip? Would I have been able to cope with it if things had turned out worse, to say nothing of the subsequent court martial and other unpleasantries?

Lost in No-Man's-Land

During the night it began to rain heavily. By morning our airfield resembled a large swamp. Flying was out of the question. Instead I busied myself with housekeeping chores and overdue letter writing. Fuel was scarce and provisions were running low as well. For days there had been nothing but tubes of cheese and sour, green Russian tomatoes which, by the way, had a funny taste. Perhaps Ivan had "innoculated" them with something special before leaving the lousy things for us. Who could say in this miserable war? Our special rations of chocolate had also been used up. Our long overdue deliveries of supplies did not keep up with the rapidly-advancing troops. Even Hamann, the organiser, was unable to come up with anything this time. Small wonder that we spent more time on the thunder beam with stomach trouble than in the air. Word arrived that a flying boat was to arrive the next day with a load of fuel. Where it was supposed to land was a mystery. There were no lakes far and wide, only a large river. We thought it must be a latrine rumour. The following morning, however, we heard a loud droning noise, then a great racket in the air. A huge, six-engined monster came roaring toward our field at low level. We had no radio contact with the aircraft. Helplessly the crew looked all around for a place to land. The flying boat flew away, then came back again, and after more than an hour of searching in vain the crew decided to jettison their cargo. The hatches were opened and each time the giant bird neared our field dozens of fuel canisters and supply boxes came raining down. Then the inevitable happened. The aircraft made an emergency landing on the steppe just beyond our airfield. First there was a crash, then a splintering sound. The engines were torn from the wings, and the fuselage was shattered into a thousand pieces. A huge dust cloud obscured the crash site and then all was still. Five slightly-injured Luftwaffe crew members climbed out of the wreckage. The solution to the mystery? The efficient general staff in Konstanta on Rumania's Black Sea coast had located a nearby lake on its map; unfortunately it had dried up fifty years earlier. What a huge strategic error; the Ivans would have laughed themselves silly had they known. It was a pity about the huge flying boat. The unfortunate crew was furious.

The next day brought another move, forward naturally. The whole circus took off and a few minutes later we landed near a lousy village on the Terek not far from Ordzhonikidze, even closer to the Caucasus. The huge massif of the Kazbek was so close that it seemed as if it might fall down on us. Not far away was Grozny, a significant oil centre and quite probably one of the main objectives of our advance. We were now also quite close to Tbilisi. I was able to fulfil a dream I had had since my youth. I had always wanted to go there, if possible as a Chechen Cossack Captain with a fur cap on my head, black boots of soft kid leather, and a cartridge belt over my shoulder. Also part of my outfit, of course, would be a *nagaika*, a seven-tailed, leather "cat" with which I could flay my riders if necessary. We roared about the area for days looking for something to shoot down but there wasn't a soul to be seen anywhere. I cruised over the steppe, usually at low altitude, into the no-man's-land which extended east to the Caspian Sea. Now and then there was a farm cottage, but there were no trees or bushes, it was a true desert. Only the devil knew where Ivan was hiding, our reconnaissance people had no idea. If we weren't on our toes we might be in for a surprise. There was always a strange feeling in one's stomach, for if they came at night we'd be defenceless. The Ivans would have laughed themselves to death over our defenses: one quadruple flak and the Walter pistols in our pockets. No, ground fighting wasn't our beer, so we always reconnoitred the situation before sundown to avoid being taken by surprise, for it was better to be safe than sorry.

Adventure at the Terek

For a change it rained all night. It was damp in the tents and we shivered from the cold, even in our down-filled sleeping bags. And then there were the stomach troubles. Morning came quickly, but luckily I was able to stay in bed a little longer. I heard the morning *Rotte* take off and then went back to sleep. It must have been about six when I stumbled out of my tent, drunk with sleep. Fog had moved in, I could scarcely see my hand in front of my face. The mess tent was filled with grumpy pilots, their mood quite in keeping with the weather.

"Who had the morning *Rotte* this morning?" I asked Franz Bienert, as he wolfed down a slice of bread with jam.

"I think it was Fw. Hanke and Uffz. Baldauff."

Bienert, both cheeks full, looked at me rather strangely. It was now 0615. The two pilots had taken off at four, so they should have been back long ago. Now I became concerned. If they hadn't come down at another airfield because of the fog then something must have happened to them. They might have been shot down in combat, but according to the reconnaissance people there was nothing between us and the Caspian

Sea. It was a paltry 140 kilometres, a short hop. Then the CO appeared. He looked mistrustfully into the fog and then turned to me.

"I should actually send someone out right away. As soon as the fog thins take off with Fw. Berendt and look for the two of them. They were on *freie Jagd* and I suspect that they lost their way in the fog and are out there on their bellies somewhere."

By about ten o'clock it had brightened up somewhat, so I had our two machines prepared for takeoff, and ten minutes later we roared out of the field.

"Yellow Four from White Thirteen, do you read me?"

Like a shot from a pistol Berendt replied: "*Viktor, Viktor!*"

We stayed at an altitude of about 500 metres and flew east. Before us was the Nogayskiye Steppe, which lost itself in the morning mist on the horizon. Beneath us the milky blue glacier water of the Terek followed a parallel course on its way to the Caspian Sea, accompanied by the snow-covered chain of the giant mountains of the Caucasus. Where the river turned northeast we discovered the remains of a narrow-gauge railway whose tracks appeared to disappear into infinity. My wingman weaved back and forth from my right side to my left. Exactly why he was doing this was a mystery to me, perhaps he was doing "morning calisthenics."

"Yellow Four, do you see anything?" I called.

"Aircraft in front of us!" called Berendt.

Then there it was, a Messerschmitt. There was no doubt about it, it was our "Yellow Seven." But how it looked! The canopy was gone, the landing flaps were down, and it was flying along slowly with two people in the cockpit. Crouched in the pilot's seat was Fw. Hanke and above him, half lying, half perched, was Baldauff. The slipstream whistled about their ears. Hanke gave a brief wave with his left hand. Baldauff was reaching over Hanke's back, holding firmly onto the windscreen with both hands. We made a steep turn and took up position to the left and right of the aircraft.

I keyed the microphone and called: "What happened, where is Yellow Nine?"

But there was no reply. In addition to the missing canopy Hanke's radio appeared to have been damaged, so there would be no answer. The three of us wobbled along at 250 kph, landing flaps down, heading for home. At this low speed we hung suspended in the air like ripe plums. I thought to myself that if the Ivans caught us in this "hanging party" we'd be easy meat. I gestured to Hanke to climb, for altitude and speed were vital to him and us. I didn't know why, but I had a queer feeling in my back. Suddenly tracer flashed past my cockpit. I looked back and was shocked to see two Ivans close behind, fast MiGs. I rammed the throttle forward. Then I sideslipped to the right, pulled up, and saw a third MiG fire a burst of tracer into Hanke's aircraft, which immediately began to smoke. I half-rolled and dove, and ended up right behind the lousy Ivan. The enemy aircraft filled my gunsight. A press on the firing buttons and he exploded in midair. Berendt had already set number two on fire and was about to administer the coup de grace to the last one. A brief burst of fire and the third MiG exploded in a ball of flame. In the meantime Hanke had executed a perfect belly landing in his "Yellow Eight." Both men appeared to have escaped unhurt; they raced away from the now blazing aircraft.

"Yellow Four, stay here," I called to Berendt, "I'll fly home and get the *Storch*. How much fuel do you have left?"

"*Viktor, Viktor,* enough for about 30 minutes."

Down below Hanke waved to us. I raced home. When I landed the CO asked for a detailed report. I gave him a brief account of what had happened and got the *Storch*. Moments later I was flying toward the stranded pilots, staying just above the steppe grass. I calculated that it would take 30 minutes to reach the downed pilots, much too slow for this emergency. I hoped I'd be able to find them, but the burning Messerschmitt should have been hard to miss. I had been in the air for ten minutes when I was overtaken by two of our aircraft, obviously on their way to relieve Berendt over the two downed pilots. Now nothing can go wrong. Nevertheless I began to grow uneasy. I should have been at the landing zone soon, but there was no sign of the burning aircraft or of Hanke and Baldauff. I circled about and saw neither Berendt nor the two Messerschmitts which were supposed to relieve him. I began to think that I might have lost my way. I checked the compass but there was no doubt that I was on course. However the terrain beneath me looked different. It was rugged with small valleys and hills. Then I spotted the burning Me in front of me; the fire was almost out by now. Where were the two pilots? There, below at the Terek, I saw two figures. It was our two pilots, no doubt about it. I turned right, lowered the flaps, and landed on the stony bank of the gurgling stream.

"It's a good thing you got here," called Hanke from a distance, "Baldauff needs help urgently, he's been shot through the arm."

The wounded man came closer. His face was chalk-white and he was close to unconsciousness. Hanke had bandaged his arm but he still seemed to be losing blood. I got the first-aid kit from the *Storch* and together we applied a dressing to Baldauff's arm. It was high time to pack both men into the airplane, because in the distance I could hear two cars approaching at high speed, probably Ivans. As soon as I lifted off two Messerschmitts took up station above me and escorted us all the way home. What an operation! While Doctor Sander tended to Werner Baldauff, in the command post Fw. Hanke described his odyssey.

"We made a normal takeoff, climbed to 3,000 metres, and set course for the Caspian Sea. There was nothing unusual below us. Now and then we saw a few trucks, trailing huge dust trails as they drove toward side valleys of the Caucasus. I thought we should take a closer look, so we descended, soon reached the trucks, and flew over them at treetop height. Naive as I was, I was thinking that they must be from a nearby collective farm and were probably hauling potatoes, when we came under massed rifle fire. I felt several thumps as bullets struck my machine. Baldauff's aircraft took a series of hits too, especially in the cooling system. A few moments later his cockpit was full of smoke, forcing him to jettison his canopy. We immediately turned toward the flatland where Baldauff was able to make a belly landing. Since the terrain appeared to be quite level, I decided to land beside him. The landing came off smoothly. I wanted to put Baldauff in the fuselage but the hatch was jammed and I couldn't remove it. All I could do was put Baldauff in my cockpit. I pulled the emergency jettison lever and the canopy came free. Baldauff climbed up and over me. He anchored one leg behind me and tried to grasp the windscreen hand grips with both hands. I opened the throttle and took off from the steppe without difficulty. It wasn't a moment too late, for a line of Soviet trucks was heading straight for us. Fw. Berendt can probably give you a better account of the rest."

Rought Trip to Tbilisi

I didn't know it then, but I was to end up deeper in the land of the Chechen than I would have liked. Dog-tired, I was just about to slip into my tent when the old man said to me:

"You have *freie Jagd* in the morning. Take Fw. Barowski with you as wingman and have a look around the Tbilisi area. Ivan is supposed to have based a new fighter wing there with brand-new MiGs. They're said to be a match for the Me. But take care, there is a large number of anti-aircraft batteries on the peaks around Tbilisi! Once we locate their base it will be our job to make it hot for the MiGs on the ground before they can get into the air."

I came to attention and saluted and after he had left threw myself down on my air mattress. I slept poorly, although the night was quiet apart from occasional artillery fire in the distance. Hess woke me at 0330 and informed me that my aircraft was ready to go. Apart from him and the sentry the entire shop was still asleep. Still half asleep myself, I staggered into the supply ten, but there was no coffee, no cook, nothing. I cursed the miserable fellow who was in charge of supply. Barowski was obviously still in bed too, so I sent the sentry to wake him. Finally there was movement in the camp. Barowski was unaware of his good fortune, totally unaware. The old man had probably forgotten to tell him. But now he was wide awake.

"What, we're going to Tbilisi, what are we supposed to do there?" he asked in disbelief.

I could tell by looking at him that it didn't suit him. But when you're at the front anything goes. The cook had rushed in in the meantime; our early departure had also caught him completely by surprise. We choked down our army bread, swallowed a cup of hot coffee and then it was time to go.

"Absolute radio silence," I told Barowski. "Ivan's supposed to have a large number of anti-aircraft guns in the mountains above Tbilisi. We'll make a single pass over the city from the north, try to find the new fighter base and then, depending on the defenses, head for home."

Barowski nodded silently. We walked out to our aircraft. The canopies were shut and locked and the mechanics began turning the starter cranks for all they were worth. Two powerful engines roared to life. We lifted off and disappeared into the morning mist. It was getting light on the horizon, but above the stars still twinkled in the firmament. I climbed rapidly, wanting to reach 6,000 metres as quickly as possible, for the Russian flak was damned good and nothing would have been more embarrassing than to be brought down that way. The first rays of the sun were beginning to fall on the bizarre, snow-covered Kazbek, an impressive five-thousand-metre peak. Had it not sounded so maudlin one might have called it alpenglow, but in Russian of course. Off to our right Mount Elbrus looked somewhat more flat breasted in comparison. Barowski hung beside me. I watched as he put on his oxygen mask. Since we were at 5,000 metres that was a good idea, so I placed my own mask over my nose and mouth. I drew the pure oxygen deeply into my lungs, which felt refreshing. The outside air temperature was minus 23 degrees and it wasn't much warmer in the cockpit. We didn't feel the cold in any case; we were well bundled up and the excitement took care of the rest. Actually one began to sweat much easier than he would have liked. The sky was almost cloudless, only a few thin cirrus in the area. Far below the Georgian Army Road was plainly visible as it wound through the mountains and then fell away to the south. A few Soviet supply trucks were working their way toward the front, perhaps we could have a go at them on the way home. I looked at my watch. We had been in the air twenty minutes already and had just reached the 6,000 metre mark. By my calculations the Kura Valley should have been right below us. Flak bursts interrupted any further deliberations. The Ivans were firing much too low. I gestured to Barowski and pointed down, he acknowledged with a nod of his head. To our right the Georgian capital appeared from out of the mist. We were right over the Mtatsminda, the tall hill in the centre of the city. The flak was more accurate now. Time to get out of this dangerous area. I pointed my thumb down, rolled my bird onto its back and dove away. My machine picked up speed rapidly. Soon I was at 550 kph and still accelerating. We dove into the valley and immediately afterward roared over the big city at 600 kph, heading northeast in the direction of the suspected enemy airfield. Tracer flashed past my cockpit; every anti-aircraft gun around Tbilisi seemed to have ranged in on us. It was funny, because they were used to firing at targets above them, and today they had to depress their guns and shoot down at us from the mountains. The fact that they were raining shells on to the city and its houses in the process seemed to make no difference whatsoever to the Ivans. We raced southeast along the Kura River and seconds later we saw beneath us rows of brand-new, Airacobra fighters, lined up as if on parade. They were American machines, painted frog-green with huge, red Soviet stars on the wings. We were by them too quickly, so we made a steep, climbing turn and headed back toward the airfield. I quickly turned up the brightness of my Revi. Then I flipped forward the safety catch and we began pouring streams of fire into the parade. It was a good thing I had had the armourer load my cannon with high-explosive incendiary ammunition. I saw Ivans running away from the aircraft and diving for cover. Our attack had been effective. Aircraft were burning, refuelling trucks too. Honestly speaking I didn't feel like making another pass. I was too scared and besides our fuel was getting low and I desperately needed to get to a latrine. (It was always the same in the morning!) So we climbed steeply into the blue, Caucasian sky, happy to have survived. The Russian flak pursued us, but the shells burst harmlessly in the blue sky above us. Not until the Kazbek with its bizarre notches came into view did I begin to breathe easier. I broke radio silence and called over to Barowski: "Wasn't that something!"

Instantly my wingman replied: "Those weren't Ivans, they were Americans, Airacobras!"

"*Viktor, Viktor,*" I answered, "they'll probably leave us in peace for a while now. Is everything alright with you?"

"I think I took a hit in the fuselage," said Barowski, "but otherwise everything is just fine."

The lad has an attitude like a butcher's dog, I thought. Just then my engine began to rumble. The revolutions fell off and the supercharger pressure dropped. It wasn't going to leave me in the lurch now was it, after everything had gone so well? The engine picked up again, but continued to sputter. The supercharger pressure climbed back up a bit, but there was definitely something wrong. A forced landing in the mountains was out of the question and bailing out wouldn't have pleased the Führer! We were still at 6,500 metres, I would have to try to glide home.

Barowski called over to me: "You've got black smoke coming from your engine!"

Had I been hit over the Soviet airfield? We were already over Ordzhonikidze and still at 6,000 metres, that was easily enough altitude to allow me to reach our airfield. Then, suddenly, there was a bang and the propeller stopped. Below me was the Malgobek Steppe. Should I bail out? No, better to make a belly landing somewhere, for there was no way of knowing where the wind might blow my parachute. Barowski hung beside me.

"Must you make a forced-landing?"

"Yes. Stay with me until I'm on the ground and then send the *Storch.*"

1,000 metres to go. I looked around and thought I'd found the right place. I didn't lower the undercarriage but dropped the flaps. I touched down, still going quite fast, close beside an empty stream bed. The flaps went flying and I raced over the grass on the radiators at an insane speed. The propeller was shot but I'd made it down safely. Barowski circled over me a few times and then I saw him disappear to the north. I was all alone, not a soul far and wide. All my hopes rested on Barowski and the *Storch*. I took a walk round my machine and discovered that I had been hit, and quite a few times. There were fifteen in the engine alone. The hits weren't from flak but from rifles. There were another dozen or so in the fuselage behind the armour plate. Man you were lucky, I thought to myself. My excursion to King Gorgassali's city might have been my last. Then I heard the lovely sound of the approaching *Storch*. It seemed to take forever before it landed nearby. Barowski picked me up. What did we do that evening? Drank ourselves silly, of course, what else?

In the Lion's Den

I reported my return to the old man. He looked at me rather strangely and then said, "I have news for you." Before I could say a word he continued: "The Führer wishes to speak with you, you're to receive the Oak Leaves from him. Congratulations by the way."

I was speechless for some time, but then it struck me. Man, this means leave, a full fourteen days of special leave. It wasn't until later that my thoughts turned to the Führer and the decoration.

"I'll speak to the transport *Geschwader* today. They can pick you up here tomorrow morning and then take you to the '*Wolfsschanze*.' It'll be a damned long flight, I'd estimate 2,000 kilometres, maybe even more. Do you have suitable clothes for the award ceremony and so on?"

"No *Herr Major*, all I have is what I'm wearing. Who thinks about such things when he gets to the front anyway," I replied.

The old man turned around and called *Leutnant* Habel, one of our recent "imports." When he appeared the CO said, "do you by chance have your dress uniform with you, we need to borrow it for *Leutnant* Dickfeld, the size might be right."

At first Habel wrinkled his brow, but then he nodded in agreement and said, "we can start the fashion show in my tent."

In fact Habel's uniform fit me perfectly. In a matter of minutes my appearance had become very stylish, almost like a senior officer. That evening a fast He 111 landed in order to fly me to the "*Wolfsschanze*" the next morning. It was clear that we still had to tie one on that evening. At the time I had no idea whatsoever where this ultra-secret "lion's den" was. All the He 111 crew knew was that they were to fly me to Breslau and wait there for further instructions. The mention of Breslau caused my heart to leap; I'd be able to see mother and the children sooner than any of us could have dreamed. I was damned nervous even before the operation actually got under way: the Oak leaves. Hermann Graf was to receive the Diamonds at the same time, so we got together in Breslau for a drink. There was no possible way to avoid the invitations and being passed around. All the waiting for the flight to Führer Headquarters was hard on the nerves and we spent a great deal of time talking to the devil alcohol. I am incapable of describing what drove the two of us to swipe a streetcar from the city's depot one night and rumble through the streets of Breslau. At first Hermann took the controls while I acted as switchman, then we changed places. In no time, however, the streetcar was full, for at every stop we picked up Breslau's night people, including a "chansonette" who insisted on singing a current popular song loudly and off key. I had no idea the thing had so many verses. The outing was intended to celebrate the occasion but it seems a little silly to me now. How we got the tram back to the depot undamaged I no longer know, all I do know is that I awoke with a terrific headache. By the way I still have the crank we used to start the thing. The mayor of Breslau, who allowed me to sign the city's golden book, closed his eyes to the whole affair.

Finally we received the call we had been waiting for: the pilot of the He 111 informed us that we were to take off for the *"Wolfsschanze"* at 0700 the next morning. By now relatively sober, we climbed into the speedy aircraft and a few hours later landed at Rastenburg, East Prussia. A staff car from the headquarters picked us up; our excitement mounted. The car stopped in front of a huge security installation, which was guarded by barbed-wire barriers. We got out and the guards checked our paybooks. Following a telephone conversation between the commander of the guard and someone somewhere, we passed the first barrier and drove for some time through a sparse birch wood past grey-painted bunkers squatting low to the ground. Then we came to the second checkpoint. Again we climbed out and again our paybooks were checked. Finally we were allowed to pass. After several more bends in the forest road we finally found ourselves in front of a large concrete block covered with camouflage nets. They were waiting for us. An adjutant, von Below I believe his name was, led us into a sort of reception room. Strangely no one asked us for the pistols dangling from our belts. I was thinking what lax security this was when suddenly there he was before us, the man who made the whole world hold its breath. There were just the three of us: Hitler and two poor "front swine." We stood at attention, our caps beneath our arms. He greeted us with a handshake and then presented us the decorations, which were in small cases. As if from far away I heard him speak of heroism, Fatherland and defending our homes. A photographer took photos as he spoke. The man, whom I had met before at the *Westwall*, still looked pale and thin. Almost softly, he asked us to sit down and shooed away the photographer with a wave of his hand.

"I know of your *Geschwader*'s accomplishments and can only pay tribute to all of you out there," he began. "You have a hard winter behind you. I know how difficult it was for all our men, but now we are moving forward again. I am confident that this year we will drive the Russians back beyond the Urals and reach the Turkish and Persian borders through the Caucasus."

Hitler gave us no chance to speak.

"How were you equipped for the winter? I repeatedly hear complaints on this subject from my front-line officers and that is why I have men like you visit me; for I am slowly beginning to doubt the reports that reach my desk. They don't reflect the true picture."

For what seemed like an eternity Hitler fixed his gaze on the portrait of Bismark behind us, the corners of his mouth twitching nervously.

Graf seized the opportunity: "*Mein Führer*, we were and still are badly equipped. We would have come off badly had our relatives not sent us warm clothing."

At this point I joined in: "Worst off all were the technical problems encountered by our ground personnel in getting our machines ready for action in the insane cold. They lacked almost everything necessary. Had it not been for their improvisation, their almost superhuman efforts, we two wouldn't be standing before you today. They are the true heroes of this winter!"

Hitler looked at me nonplussed. Then he found his voice and shouted toward the door: "Orderly!" A *Gefreiter* hurried in and snapped to attention. "General Bodenschatz is to come at once!" Then the Führer continued: "Bodenschatz is my liaison man to Göring. He has all the files on the Luftwaffe, including your *Geschwader*. I want to see what kind of winter equipment you received." The telephone rang. Hitler picked it up; the Luftwaffe General was apparently on the line. "Bodenschatz, as you know Graf and Dickfeld are with me now. Come over immediately and bring all the files on their *Geschwader*, especially those pertaining to winter equipment." Then he banged down the receiver. He seemed mildly agitated, this man who was responsible for our "travels" which had taken us almost to the ends of the earth. I wouldn't want his worries, I thought to myself. Then there was a knock on the door and in walked a tall, slightly greying General, a thick bundle of files under his arm. I didn't know him but I knew a little about him; he was supposed to be a close friend of Göring's from the First World War. He came to attention and saluted the Führer, then saluted us. Hitler asked him to sit and then had him give his report. Graf looked at me and I at him. As the General spoke our mouths fell open from sheer astonishment. What he described to Hitler from his files might have been fairy tales from *A Thousand and One Nights*! Hermann and I couldn't believe our ears. We were amazed to hear of all the winter things we were said to have received and in good time! Both of us repeatedly shook our heads.

Hitler became quite restive, then he stood up and, turning to us, said in a sharp tone: "I see from your expressions that this information can't be correct."

Then he turned to General Bodenschatz: "Thank you, you may go, I want to hear more now."

The General took his files, made a stiff about face and left the bunker room without saluting. Was that how Hitler reprimanded his Generals? No, I wouldn't have wanted to be one, I far preferred to have my rear end in the sky at the front. Visibly angered, Hitler stood up and gave us his hand.

"We'll see each other again at lunch," he said, then left the room quickly.

I wouldn't liked to have known what kind of thunderstorm subsequently fell on the General, but at that point it wasn't our problem. We were hungry, terribly hungry, and wanted to finally get to the Führer's "trough." A little later von Below, Hitler's Luftwaffe adjutant, appeared and invited us to table. We were led into a large room. Inside the leading figures of the Reich were already standing around the long table. I saw Admiral Dönitz, chief of the U-boat arm, General Guderian, the panzer commander, *Generalfeldmarschall* Keitel, and a large number of other officers. Göring and Himmler were absent however. Then the Führer came in. Everyone stood at attention behind their chairs, then he invited us to sit down. I estimate that there were 30 persons. Lunch consisted of a measly one-pot meal. I looked at Hermann and he looked at me. I knew at once that we were of the same opinion: pigswill! The Führer, a fanatical vegetarian, stirred his food deliberately. Everyone waited for the conversation to begin, but there was stony silence. Who could say where his thoughts were at that moment? Then he turned abruptly to Graf and said, "tell me, how do you get along with the Russian population out there? I hear repeatedly of good contacts. As well reports of betrothals between our soldiers and Ukrainian women, to say nothing of illegitimate children, have reached my desk. Do you think we should allow such things?"

"Dickfeld can give you better information about that," said Graf, "as military welfare officer he knows more about it."

I jumped in: "As far as I can assess the situation today, we've had only positive experiences."

"Yes, and who will pay for all this when the war's over," interjected Guderian.

Then Hitler banged his fist on the table so hard that the empty bowls rattled: "You, Guderian, and you, Dönitz, and you too, Keitel, no all of us, excluding Dickfeld and Graf of course."

Then the discussion lost itself in technical questions. Hitler wanted to know how the Russian flak was. Graf explained to him that it was extremely accurate, was definitely nothing to sneeze at, and that we suffered considerable losses to it, particularly during low-level attacks.

"I thought as much," observed Hitler, "I'm continually being told that the Russians are no good as artillerymen."

Then Dönitz discussed the submarine war. In spite of his optimistic prognosis for the end of American convoys to England, even we "windbags" noticed that he had his share of problems and we wouldn't have wanted to be in his shoes.

When, soon afterward, Hitler dismissed those at the table, *Generalfeld-marschall* Keitel came over to us, took us to one side and said, "Surely you're not full. Come with me to my bunker, I've prepared something for you there."

And indeed he wasn't exaggerating. We were finally able to eat to our heart's content and the vegetarian "Führer soup" was soon forgotten. Keitel was later hanged by the Americans at Nuremburg. A pity, his dessert was excellent! We flew back to Breslau that same afternoon. Graf went home to Lake Constance, I stayed with my wife and family.

Before my leave was over a telex summoned me back to the front. I travelled via Berlin and Bucharest where, as luck would have it, I was able to take possession of an Me. Heavy losses in pilots, especially in recent days, had made my presence appear urgent. In the few days we had been absent many of our comrades had either been killed, wounded, or were missing. There were many new faces. Proper greenhorns, no more than twenty years old and without any front-line experience, were supposed to replace veteran, tested pilots in this tough business. I reported to the "old man" as soon as I had landed.

"Now then, how was your visit with the Führer?" he asked moodily.

"Oh, quite interesting," I replied, "I met quite a few nice people, as well as some out and out idiots and sponges. I'm glad to be back. It's not exactly jolly at home right now."

I quickly got back into the swing of *Gruppe* life and soon I was back in the Russian sky, a decoration and many experiences richer. Later the decoration was to be the source of trouble for me and especially for my family.

To Say Nothing of Camels

Oh, before I forget, "Kreck" was back with me, having just returned from a brief visit to Italy. As had so often been the case, the crew of a transport aircraft found him behind some empty boxes after takeoff. His neck band revealed where he had come from and the name of his owner. But now he was back and, hypocrite that he was, acted as if nothing at all had happened, the gypsy! I was convinced that somewhere he was going to land in a frying pan someday. By the way our zoo was still intact. In addition to the dogs which most of our pilots kept, there were the monkeys from Kharkov as well as the parrots, all of which had survived. Late one afternoon we received a curious addition to the family. Our observer shouted down from his perch in a tree: "Horses approaching, but without riders!"

Immediately everyone became wide awake. Binoculars were produced and in fact some very unusual animals were approaching. They were not horses however. Someone guessed, correctly as it turned out, that they were camels. And sure enough, several minutes later they arrived, full-blown camels! They trotted over to where we had gathered and stopped, as if to say: "Well, we're finally among humans again, now do something with us."

They didn't know what to make of German and didn't seem to be familiar with the Russian we fabricated, perhaps they spoke a dialect unknown to us. We were left with sign language. They understood eating and drinking well enough and when Zierenberg offered them some potatoes they got down to business. "Kreck" tried to get them on their feet by yelping at them but they completely ignored him. The camels just looked down at him haughtily. Only when Doctor Sander tried to demonstrate his riding skills on one of them did they became angry. They spat at him incessantly and soon he was covered with stinking sputum. The doctor gave up his attempts to ride. The camels stayed with us overnight and showed no signs of wanting to leave in the morning. But getting rid of these unwanted spirits wasn't so simple. Then Hess had an idea.

"Let's tie one of our smoke flares to each of their tails. That should do something. Quite apart from the dense, red smoke hissing out behind them, the things will be quite hot on their tails! That would work quite nicely on some other species too," he remarked guilelessly.

"Right, that's the solution," said the CO. "Let's try it after lunch."

"Couldn't we put the monkeys on their backs too," asked Lossmann craftily, "there are seven of them. We'd finally be rid of this plague. I can't stand the smell of monkey shit any longer!"

A shout came from the command post: "Alarm! Boston bombers approaching!"

"All aircraft into the air!" cried the CO.

At the airfield perimeter our quadruple anti-aircraft guns began to bark. Then suddenly Russian fighters attacked at low level. In fact they were American aircraft, Airacobras; we had never seen them over our base before. Tracer ripped the crystal-clear morning. We jumped into our Messerschmitts and our "flying circus" roared into the air in a huge cloud of dust. The Airacobras had already disappeared at low level without scoring even a single hit. What madness! They'd come from God knows where, wasted a great deal of fuel, and then merely ploughed up the soil of the Caucasian steppe. They must have had a great fear of us when they made their attack. We heard the old man's voice croak in our headsets: "4,500 metres."

Boston bombers, they're American too, I thought aloud, how did they get them here to the Caucasus? But I had no time for further reflection. I was flying to the left of the "old man." We closed with the bombers. Flying towards us in tight formation, they were painted yellow with Soviet stars on their wings and fuselages. The "old man" climbed steeply and brought us into attack position. The bombers were now below us. Their dorsal gunners opened fire, much too early! Far from us their tracer slashed the magical, blue Caucasian sky. Then we attacked in line abreast formation. The first bombers caught fire and sheared out of formation. Parachutes hung in the sky. There was no stopping now. The Bostons were blasted out of the sky. Individual bombers sought safety in flight, but that meant their end. Not a single one escaped. The balance: 21 Soviet bombers eliminated, our own losses: nil. Not until much later did I learn that the Americans had sold more than 3,000 of these lame ducks to the Soviets, the poor swine!

What Misery!

Day and night Russian refugee columns passed over the road near our airfield. First they were fleeing before us Germans. Now, overtaken by our panzers, they were streaming back from where they had come. It was terrible to have to watch this misery. War is war, but we didn't want this type of war, me least of all. I just couldn't look away and often went over to pass out bread, cigarettes, and chocolate as our supply situation allowed. An old couple with a small rack wagon were unable to go any farther. Thousands of refugees passed them by without paying them any heed. The two old people sat helplessly in the ditch and with trembling hands tried to make a small fire over which to roast ears of corn. The steady rain frustrated their efforts, however. So I loaded the two of them into my car and took them to our mess tent. There were wide eyes all around, but they accepted my guests. Ziegenberg attended to the two old people. Our interpreter learned that they were originally from Taganrog and now wanted to get back there; it was a good 500 kilometres, and on foot at that. They'll never make it, I thought. Wasn't there a Ju 52 leaving the next day for Kharkov via Taganrog? I asked the CO about it and he gave his consent, provided the Ju 52 crew was in agreement. I made a telephone call and we were in business. The old couple had no idea what was happening to them. They just kept nodding their heads at all the amazing things going on around and with them. I made a place for them in my tent for the night; I slept in Hans Sander's tent. When morning came we took them and their pitiful belongings to the transport aircraft. I hoped they would make it home safe and sound, as the area there was thick with MiGs. I had lit a light inside me, unfortunately only one. That evening Hess and Zierenberg broke up the small wagon and used it for fuel in memory of the two old people. They had traded a can of real Russian tea for it, for fuel was scarce in the steppe.

That Was Something!

The camels, or should I say dromedaries, continued to hang around the airfield. They didn't bother us, but when even a single machine took off they panicked and scattered in all directions. This was likely to become a problem in the long run. Something had to be done. There was no way that Warnholz, the cook, wanted to slaughter them. No one knew what camel meat tasted like and anyway they might have some sort of disease.

"No," he said, "not me."

So our wish for a new dish went unappeased. Hess, who was a little on the sadistic side, saw a chance to try his idea. The seven camels were led in and lined up. The monkeys were brought out and tied expertly onto the "ships of the desert." One could tell by looking at the beasts that they smelled a rat. Every now and then one of the huge animals would turn its head and spit green mucous on its new "jockey," which the monkeys answered with loud chattering. Now Hess and his bright red smoke cartridges came into play. Carefully he tied one of the things to each of the camels' tails. Hans, the doctor, watched the proceedings closely to ensure that the rules of the game were followed, although camel racing wasn't yet an olympic discipline. The monkeys clung to the camels' humps. At the front of each camel was one of our men, holding onto the halter, at the rear another ready to light the fuse. Then our inspector gave the command: "On your marks, get set, go!"

The fuses were lit. Dense, red-yellow smoke hissed from the cartridges. At first there was dead silence, but then the camels raced off as if the devil had them by the collar. Unable to believe their eyes, the monkeys clung tightly to the camels' humps and were carried off. Soon the seven "racehorses" had disappeared in the distance. The only evidence of the equestrian event, which had been held in proper Georgian style, was the swaths of red-yellow smoke in the distance. The Ivans on the other side must have rubbed their eyes in amazement and then become justifiably suspicious. I could well imagine their reaction:

"This must be a new capitalist secret weapon, let's get out of here!"

The End of an Excursion

The weather was good, often too good. They rushed us into the air from dawn until dark, often seven sorties a day and sometimes more! This took a tremendous physical and psychological toll on us. Many promising pilots couldn't take it any more, and in order to avoid accusations of cowardice or shirking they feigned stomach or other problems. Mostly it was the young, inexperienced ones, the "freshly imported" pilots. They soon realized that there was more to this business than roaring about until the Knight's Cross was due, and that it required almost supernatural strength just to endure. Our ground personnel had it worst of all. Only rarely did they see anything of the fighting in the air; this day was to be the exception. It was shortly after lunch. We had had noodles with tinned meat, a meal I detested. I was lying in a deck-chair, daydreaming. Hess dozed in the shade beneath the wing of my aircraft. I must have fallen asleep myself, for a loud droning noise suddenly woke me. It sounded as if a large number of aircraft were nearing the airfield. I had just opened my eyes when about 20 MiGs roared overhead at very low altitude. The crews of our quadruple anti-aircraft guns must have been dozing too, because not a shot was fired. In short we had been caught flat-footed. More amazingly, however, the Ivans showed absolutely no inclination to attack and work us over, even though we were completely at their mercy. I jumped to my feet as if I'd been bitten by a tarantula and raced to my machine. Hess was already hanging onto the starter crank. I closed the canopy and took off alone. Even though it seemed safe to assume that the Ivans were long gone, I turned in their direction and then got a big surprise! The Ivans had reversed course not far from our base and were heading back. Once again they roared over the airfield and kept going, all except one. He lagged behind the others and in seconds I was on his tail. I pressed the triggers and the next second his cockpit was an inferno. Fire gushed out. His canopy flew away and the pilot jumped clear. A white parachute came down right in the middle of the airfield. Sideslipping to lose altitude, I landed immediately afterward. The slightly-injured Ivan was brought to me. His name was Alexei Richoletov, and he was a Captain and squadron leader. The Russian reeked of liquor. He thought his hour had come, for he asked our interpreter for permission to write a few lines to his mother before we shot him. At the time we were still unaware of how the Soviets treated captured German pilots. I explained to him that he would be taken to a POW camp and that it was not our practice to kill defenceless prisoners. It wasn't until long after the war that I learned how the Soviets had dealt with captured German fliers! It was quite normal for them to murder shot-down German pilots as soon as they were captured. The Soviet ace Vladimir D. Lavrinekov distinguished himself through his exceptional brutality and cruelty. Whenever he was able to catch a downed German pilot he strangled him with his own hands. (By the way he was decorated three times with the golden star of a Hero of the Soviet Union. For what?) Other Russian pilots are said to have personally liquidated their captured German opponents. It is safe to assume that most of the German pilots listed as missing in action were killed immediately after being taken prisoner and buried on the spot. Captain Richoletov didn't believe me when I told him I had shot him down. He stuck to his version of events, that our flak had brought him down. He simply shook his head and will probably never comprehend what happened to him. In any case he, as squadron leader, was completely unaware of our airfield. I would dearly

loved to have heard explanations offered by the other Ivans when they
returned without their squadron leader.

Deported!

We waited each day for new aircraft from Germany. Our Me's were
worn out, virtually flying wrecks, or perhaps I should say coffins. We were
almost at the point of fighting over well-maintained, fast machines. In
passing I heard Fw. Schnell say to Uffz. Werner:
"My White 3 is easily 40 kph faster than your Yellow 7."
This went on day after day among our pilots. Having a fast aircraft was
almost like having life insurance. I had Hess and his "Hiwis" give my
aircraft several coats of wax, for I had plenty left from my visit with the
bee-keeper. In return I shared with them my special rations, treats such
as real coffee, chocolate, cigarettes, and nuts and raisins. Their intensive
efforts had the desired effect; afterward my aircraft was easily 30 kph
faster. For days we had been awaiting the arrival of a replacement *Gruppe*
with new aircraft. Finally, at about noon one day, there was a loud droning
noise in the air and then they came, in textbook formation. As prescribed,
the "chief" was the first to land. He floated and floated, then the tail came
up, the nose went down, the aircraft swung, and flipped over in a huge
cloud of dust. The next machine dropped toward the runway. Suddenly
its nose dropped sharply, the aircraft swung, and flipped over in a huge
cloud of dust. I need not describe what happened the next six times. It
was a pitiful scene. Of sixteen brand-new Me's only eight survived, EIGHT!
All of the pilots managed to escape without injury. Our CO's false teeth
almost dropped out of his mouth as he watched this tragedy unfold. We
discussed the disaster at length and came up with the following theory:
the surface of the airfield was slightly undulating. The old hands landed
along the undulations or at right angles to them. However the replacement
pilots must have been completely unnerved, not only by the uneven
terrain, but by the crash of their CO as well. It was a good thing that we
didn't give such incidents too much thought or we wouldn't have been
able to sleep. Replacements had arrived, including a new *Staffelkapitän."
He was a fellow of silk and satin, a Siegfried from the Odenwald
complete with dragon's blood and the linden leaf. His name was
Hacker, but I never got a chance to get to know him, because the "old
man" called me to his tent in great secrecy.*
"I don't know how to tell you this," he began in his unadulterated
Viennese dialect, "*Leutnant* Hacker has brought good news. You are
very lucky. You have been transferred to a famous *Jagdgeschwader* on
the Channel Coast. Congratulations!"
What is this fellow up to, I thought, trying to cope with the news.
"Thank you very much, *Herr Major*, I realize that this is an honour,"
I replied. They want to get rid of you, I thought to myself.

"When is the earliest you can take off?" he asked warily. "If you like you can take Zierenberg with you."

Although more than anything I would liked to have punched him in the mouth, I answered politely and obediently.

"If there's transport available I can leave tomorrow, I'll take Zierenberg with me."

"We have an Me that has to go to Bucharest. You can take it; you should have no difficulty making your way from there."

Then I remembered Maria, who had made a name for herself as a chef, especially on account of her borscht soup. I could take her with me as well. I had just received a letter from my wife telling me that she had her hands full with the children. Maria would be like a gift from heaven.

"Would you mind, *Herr Major*, if I take Maria from the kitchen home with me, provided she agrees of course? My wife could certainly use the help."

"Yes, yes," he answered quickly, "of course you can take Maria with you. I've been wanting to get rid of the unit's 'Hiwis' for a long time anyway. You never know what trouble-makers might be among them. Zierenberg can look after Maria."

All I could say was: "Thank you very much, *Herr Major*."

I summoned the two. Maria was speechless when I told her that she could come to Germany if she wished. Enthusiastically she agreed to go. It would take the two of them more than four weeks to get to Dresden, Zierenberg's home town. From there to Gohrisch and mother was only another half hour. Yes, "home to the Reich" by train, especially from the Caucasus, was no joy ride in those days.

The time had come to leave "my" unit. I had been suspecting it for a long time but didn't want to admit it. The last evening was excruciating. I sat and drank beer with Hans Sander. The "old man" didn't put in an appearance, which was just as well, I never could stand the man from the beginning! Long before midnight I had gathered together my few belongings, it wasn't much. I took "Kreck," who usually stayed with Zierenberg, into my tent and by morning I was ready to leave. It was with relief that I heard the deep roar as Hess warmed up the Messerschmitt's engine. A brief handshake and I was "dismissed." Hans Sander came over to the aircraft and passed "Kreck" into the cockpit. I took off without turning to look back. Soon the Kazbek disappeared behind me. Elbrus lay hidden behind a fat cumulus cloud. A pity, I would have liked to seen it one more time. (By the end of the war JG 52 was one of our most successful fighter units with more than 10,000 kills to its credit, at the cost of almost 700 pilots lost.)

By economizing on fuel I was able to reach Krasnodar, but there I had to land. I refuelled, walked the dog, and took off again. I couldn't believe my eyes; they had secretly fashioned a wound badge for "Kreck" out of tin. It hung about his neck like a second dog tag. I reached Sevastopol and then Bucharest, where I had to turn in my aircraft. From there I had to continue by train. For days I sat there, my rear end getting sore, until finally I reached my destination, an airfield not far from Calais.

"I have surprises for you," said the new *Geschwader-Kommodore*, "one good and one bad, which would you like first?"

"It doesn't matter to me," I replied.

"Very well then," he replied, not without an ulterior motive, "let's begin. The good: you're only staying here for three days; the bad: you're going to Tunisia as acting commander of my 'Second.' "

I almost fell out of my chair. I realised straight away that the working conditions were very different here. The new "old man," highly decorated, was cut from different cloth than my smooth Viennese from the Caucasus. And he had to be, because here over the Channel the enemy, young, dare-devil Britons, were not only equal to us but often superior. They were not to be taken lightly and with their Spitfires they were our equal technically. I spent the first evening in a tasteful chateau with my *Staffelkapitäne*. What a difference from our lice-ridden tents in the mud and filth of Russia. It was sort of a feeling-out session. First they sized up the newcomer who, as they saw it, came from the deepest back woods, knew nothing about aerial combat, and who was "so old," already past thirty! He ought to be sent home to sit by the stove with mother rather than be dumped on us without ceremony. And what sort of flying experience did he have? After all the Ivans fell out of the sky in fright at the mere sight of a Messerschmitt. I tell you it's not going to work. At least that's what I read in their faces. I wasn't exactly comfortable, but war is war, orders are orders, and we'd have to get along. The next morning I got another surprise. Conversion! My unit had received a new and completely different aircraft type for its battle with Rommel. The new single-seater was called the Focke Wulf 190. Farewell fine-limbed, sensible, thoroughbred Bf 109. The new aircraft was a solid, heavy machine, stronger and more robust than the Messerschmitt. It had better weapons, new electrics, in short everything about it was very foreign, including its handling characteristics. But what could I do, I had to fly the thing. After the third circuit I had the bird well in hand.

Preparing a fighter *Gruppe*, with all its flight and ground personnel, for departure took a great deal of time. On day three, however, the whole mahalla set out. Our initial destination was Tours on the beautiful Loire, away from the daily bombing and strafing attacks by the Tommies. The city had an almost peacetime atmosphere. The population, as far as we could tell, was not unfriendly. Bars and other establishments provided our soldiers with what they expected from them. The only problem concerned provisions; there were shortages of everything. *Major* Dreier had a secret tip: the best mushroom omelets were to be found in the establishment run by Madame Duvalle: the "Bor d'Elle," Rue de le Paix. As a result the place was frequented by many people. Some were there for the omelets, some to offer a helping hand to the madame, and perhaps some to enjoy both. In spite of what you might think, I was only keen on the omelets, especially with plenty of pepper. But we poor front swine had to be patient. Madame had her old, long-established favourites. The atmosphere was very familiar, with plenty of hand kissing and so on. I, however, lived by the following motto: If my Führer gives me the opportunity to visit other lands and peoples, then the cultural aspect must come into its own. Wherever I was, I made every effort to absorb as much of the local culture as possible. I used the last autumn days to view several of the magnificent castles on the Loire. The war had left its mark, but these relics of the bourgeoisie were still impressive. But soon it was time to say farewell to the chateaus and the Loire, to madame and the omelets. X-Day had come. Thirty-six machines took off on a misty morning. We passed over Marseille, the Cote d'Azur, Naples (Vesuvius was in the midst of an eruption at the time), Reggio di Calabria, and then Sicily. Not far from Mount Etna, near Caltagirone, our "swarm of hornets" landed in a side valley. We weren't to stay unemployed for long. Someone somewhere had decided that Malta, that history-rich island which was such a thorn in the side of the Axis, could not be allowed to remain in English hands and had to be taken. It would be no more than a walk in the park together with our Axis brothers the Italians, or at least that's what the General Staff thought. We heard that German and Italian bombers were flying from Catania day and night, dropping their deadly loads on Malta. But not for much longer. Just at the time we arrived the Tommies succeeded in getting a huge convoy consisting of aircraft carriers, battleships, and other filthy things through to Malta. From then on the fight became much harder. When we took off on our first mission against Malta we saw from a distance swarms of British fighters hanging in the sky like flies, only not so harmless. Everywhere we looked there were Spitfires and Hurricanes; there was no point in allowing ourselves to be drawn into a fight. From that point on Malta became a mass grave for the German bombers, which fearlessly attacked the island in an attempt to soften it up for invasion. We frequently battled our English opponents in the air, but the air had gone out of this business. There were rumours that they had a device over there which detected us as soon as we took off, for how else could one explain the immediate presence of the Tommies high above the island? One morning, just before sunrise, we crept up on the island just above the waves. To our amazement we saw that they were already in the air above the cliffs of Hal Far. Strung out as if on Jacob's ladder, in flawless formations as well, they were bent on working us over. We were ready for a fight. Since there was no point in crawling around at low level, we climbed to 6,000 metres. The Tommies dove on us. A mad dogfight broke out: Focke Wulfs behind Hurricanes, Spitfires behind Focke Wulfs, and so on. Tracer and lead slashed the sky. Since this was leading nowhere I broke off the circus and dove for home. Buhlmann had a strange feeling in the back of his neck and quite by chance turned to look behind him. He found himself staring down the guns of a Hurricane. At first he thought it was a hallucination. He looked again and by then the Tommy was almost within firing range. Buhlmann banked his aircraft steeply and turned hard to the right, a maneuver with which he had always been able to evade an attacker. It worked this time too. Seconds later he was sitting on the Tommy's tail. When the Hurricane filled his reflector sight he opened fire. The tracer wandered precisely into the fuselage of the Hurricane. Seconds later pieces flew off the wings and tail, the canopy sailed away, and a shadow catapulted out. A white parachute drifted slowly over the sea toward the coast.

We were sitting in the supply tent having supper. Outside a car pulled up. We heard Italian voices, then the flap opened and a young Englishman in full array looked in, behind him an Italian Carabinieri. We were speechless. Then the Carabinieri spoke:

"We fished him out of the water. He's supposed to be on his way to a POW camp but he insisted on seeing you. Was it you who shot him down?"

The young Lieutenant was in dress uniform, long blue pants, low-cut, black shoes. He was also still soaking wet. He had probably imagined the "damned Jerries" somewhat differently. We offered him something to eat but the Italian complained loudly.

The Tommy looked at my wristwatch and said, "actually I'm supposed to be standing in front of the museum in La Valetta right now, my girl is waiting for me."

We could see the concern on his face. Why had he pursued us at all, especially when he was all alone?

"It was my first sortie and I wanted badly to shoot down a Nazi. My mistake, sorry."

I liked the young man, he was one of the smart Britons. Actually the carabinieri was supposed to take him with him, but a bottle of French cognac solved the problem.

"I'll pick him up again in three days," he said gullibly.

I invited the young man to stay with us for three days. His entire face beamed and he promised not to run away while enjoying our hospitality. He wouldn't say which airfield on Malta he came from, but he was worried about his girl. As a result we set in motion an action which could only take place in such a crazy war as this.

"How would it be," I asked him casually, "if tomorrow we dropped a letter for your girlfriend so that she doesn't worry about you? Your unit would also be interested to know that you are in the best of health, to say nothing of your parents."

He thought it over for a long time, but finally he showed us the position of his unit on the map, an airfield of which we were unaware. We also learned why they were always in the air waiting for us as soon as we left the coast. He called the system radar. Only if we approached low over the water would the system fail to detect us. What a revelation! That same night the information was sent to the *Fliegerführer Italien* in Taormina. It was to spare us many losses in the future. The man was a gem without knowing it. The same evening he wrote three letters. I read them, nothing to complain about! At dawn three Fw 190s took off, the "mail" in a special pouch. Flying low, they reached the northeast tip of this interesting island unmolested. They roared over the hornet's nest, taking the occupants completely by surprise, dropped the pouch and raced for home. No alarm, no anti-aircraft fire; the surprise must have been complete. Richard Palmer felt at home with us. There was a small drama when the carabinieri turned up to collect his booty. Richard wanted to stay with us and we would gladly have kept him, but the Italians had jurisdiction over all prisoners captured on their territory. We parted with heavy hearts. I never heard anything about his subsequent fate. Perhaps he sits in his rocking chair today and tells his grandchildren about the "evil Nazis" in Sicily.

"To Say Nothing of Rommel"

Soon it was time to say farewell to Etna and its valleys, with their grapevines, pine woods, gnarled olive trees, relics from the past, and charming people. After barely three weeks we gypsies were once again in the air, this time over the deep blue Mediterranean. Our first destination on the African continent was Bizerta, a Tunisian port city. The airfield was large, with room for several *Geschwader*. There was also an airship hangar. Our quarters were in a hotel in the centre of the city. It was almost deserted. There was just a lone elderly man at reception who handed us our keys. Bedding? None! I soon fell asleep on the bare mattress. It must have been about midnight when I was shaken from my bed by a tremendous crash. The city and harbour were being bombed, British bombers leaving their calling cards. There were fires and explosions not far away. Flames were visible from a great distance. Sleep was out of the question. Remorsefully we moved into tents at the airfield.

Those were hectic days. Unit after unit arrived from old, venerable Europe. The transports brought supplies for Rommel, soldiers and weapons, to Tunisia, and took wounded home to Germany. Only the dead were allowed to remain. The brown African soil refused no one, friend or foe. The days were hot; ground crews fried eggs on the wings of our aircraft. The nights, however, were very cold. Lacking sleeping bags and blankets, we shivered in our tents. Our bowels rebelled against unfamiliar bacteria, viruses, and other African "pleasantries." One could see the afflicted at night, running from their tents in hopes of finding a place on the "thunder beam." Placed under the commander of another unit, we were left with little room to exercise our initiative. There was no sign of Rommel; he was said to be on his way to the pyramids. The rainy season had begun and our machines sank into the mud, in some cases almost to the wings.

Deliveries of supplies continued. Six-engined *Gigant* transports, which flew in gaggles of up to a hundred, spewed forth companies of paratroops and mountain infantry onto the single runway. How long would this continue, we asked ourselves. Where were the Tommies?

"Alarm!"

The *Vierling* flak had already begun to fire and filled the air with streams of tracer. We jumped into our fighters and raced into the air one after another. Then we saw them: Marauders with Spitfires above, a whole mahalla, at least 100 machines. Below to my left the first bombs were already exploding. Their aim was damned good! The British fighters were on us before we had formed up. A wild dogfight broke out; everyone had one or two of these damned British on his tail. I was hit several times straight away. It was a good thing my engine was air-cooled, otherwise I'd have been long done for. There were twelve of us against eighteen Spitfires, but we slowly gained the upper hand. Gebhardt and Radtke had already reported kills, the bombers had long since disappeared. We were far superior to the Tommies at low altitudes, so we strove to keep them there. Gebhardt was shot down but managed to bail out of his Focke Wulf. The end of the story: six Spitfires destroyed, three Focke Wulfs written off. Back at the airfield they hadn't got off quite so easily. Aircraft and ammunition were still burning and exploding. The single runway was pitted with bomb craters and it was only with great difficulty that we brought down our "hornets." One of our best pilots had been killed on the ground in the hail of bombs. He was to have gone on leave the next day. The neighbouring *Geschwader* had suffered equally. Worst of all, a dozen *Gigant* transports had been caught up in this disaster. At that moment it was impossible to say how many of them had been lost. The old airship hangar had been the scene of a bloodbath. For weeks Italian deserters had been gathering there in hopes of finding a way home. We warned them repeatedly to avoid the place, for it was easy to see that when the Tommies came they would find it difficult to ignore such a huge target.

Only recently an Italian Major had said to me: "We'll stay, for the Madonna of Palermo, to whom we have dedicated our altar, is watching over us."

Hats off to such faith, but the many dead and wounded spoke a different language. It was to be weeks before all the victims were recovered from the completely-destroyed hangar. To stay there any longer would have been complete madness, so I searched out another airfield. In the steppe-like plain it didn't take long to find one. I soon came upon a harvested corn field, close beside a farm, which could serve as a temporary base. The Tommies wouldn't find us right away, or at least that's what I hoped. It took only a few hours for the entire circus to move. We had gained time to lick our wounds. Thanks to the efforts of our outstanding ground personnel we were operational immediately, which was vitally important. The owner of the farm, a bearded old Arab, was very cordial and invited us for tea that evening. His wives, four in all, wore their finest apparel as did the children, of which there were eight or nine, perhaps more, I'm not quite certain. The conversation was conducted in French, which the old man spoke very well. We struggled to get by with our schoolboy French. It wasn't much, but at least we understood one another. The man had never sat in an aircraft, so I invited him to join me the next morning for a circuit in the unit's *Storch*. None of the "ladies" had any interest in participating in this adventure. The next day the solemn old man appeared as expected. I sat him behind me and strapped him in tightly. Then we took off. In the mirror I could see him praying, his hands folded. Then he began to sing, loudly and clearly. I believe it was verses from the Koran. As he sang he looked down enthusiastically. The women and children waved but he gave them not a glance. What could have been going on inside this man? After landing he hugged me and kissed me on both cheeks. We had made a friend.

In the afternoon the alarm was sounded: bombing raid on Bizerta! A *Schwarm* took off and was soon involved in a furious air battle. It was our first encounter with the "Amis," or Americans, who had joined the battle in this area with their P-38 Lightnings, twin-engined fighters which we had not encountered before. It was an easy guess that their bomber formations wouldn't be far behind. Rumours swirled about that they had shipped their bombers in giant convoys into the southern Sahara, in order to reassemble them there. I found such stories difficult to believe; after all they could have simply flown their long-range bombers there.

"Tomorrow morning at 1230 you and your *Gruppe* are to be over Pantelleria at 3,500 metres, where you will wait for a group of Me 323 *Gigant* transports coming from Sicily. From there you will escort them to Bizerta."

I received the orders over the phone from our *Kommodore*. We saw him only rarely, and then usually in the midst of an air battle over Tunisia. That evening I called the pilots together and explained to them the trip to Pantelleria. The island, which lay west of Malta, was Italian territory and thus gave us a place to make an emergency landing if need be. We took off from our "ploughed field" at noon, eighteen aircraft, and climbed quickly to 3,500 metres. Soon we were off Pantelleria. It was 1230. I scanned the sky to the north but there was nothing to be seen. We began to get nervous, but finally they appeared on the horizon. Endlessly slow, they neared Pantelleria like a huge swarm of bumblebees. We flew toward them. They were without fighter escort, which seemed mad in this dangerous area. We took up station beside and above them as they flew towards Bizerta. I counted 110 of these six-engined "furniture vans." Each contained 120 fully-equipped infantry, reinforcements for Rommel. I was just thinking to myself, "my God they're lame, we'll soon be out of fuel," when Spitfires and Lightnings began pouring down on us from a great altitude. The first transports were already burning. German soldiers leapt from the inferno into the sea without parachutes. The sky was one great chaotic scene. We became involved in furious dogfights. Although we succeeded in shooting down several Tommies and Americans and driving off the rest, our losses were considerable. Eleven of the huge transports crashed into the sea in flames with their soldiers. There were no losses among the fighters and we escorted the rest of the transports in close formation to their destination, Bizerta.

We learned that we were to receive a visitor, an *Oberst*. He was the *Jagdfliegerführer Italien*, but we had no idea what he wanted with us. Perhaps he wanted to accompany us on a mission or play Santa Claus, with many gifts and so on. This soon proved to be wishful thinking, however. He landed with his two escorting Messerschmitts at lunchtime. We waved him over to our dispersal and invited him and his escorts to lunch. He declined however, stating that he had too little time. He had to fly back to Italy straight away, but first he wanted to talk to us fighter pilots. I assembled my boys and we received a lecture on love for our Fatherland, loyalty to the Führer, revenge against the enemy, and hatred, especially of the Americans, which left us stunned. We were speechless; had we done something wrong up until now, we asked ourselves? The *Oberst* disappeared again as quickly as he had come. We watched the three machines until they disappeared over the Mediterranean horizon. The men dispersed slowly, shaking their heads. As far as I was concerned the entire event was scarcely worth mentioning. This man later lost his life over Germany in combat with Flying Fortresses. He was a Prussian, a fighter, defending his homeland as the law demanded.

Who Will Write Your Heroic Saga?

It seemed as if the rainy period would never end. Our machines sank ever deeper into the mud. We were scarcely able to take off and land. It was all our ground crews could do to keep in working order the aircraft, equipment, weapons, and all the other things they were responsible for. They were the real heroes of this terrible event. But who was there to give them their due apart from us pilots? After all it was we who lay side by side with them under the hail of bombs, crawled through the same muck with them, and shared the "thunder beam" with them at night when our bowels began acting up. We shared coffee, chocolate, cigarettes, and whatever else was in our extra flight rations with them, but it was too little, much too little! We watched, partly in amusement, when out of hunger they fried potato pancakes in motor oil on the wings of our aircraft, which had been heated by the pitiless sun. We were hard on them when they were brought up on a charge for stealing butter, coffee, sausage, or cheese from the supply chief's stocks. Unfortunately the supply chief thought up a special measure to deal with coffee thieves. He placed a large scorpion in a sack of coffee and then spread the word, apparently with success. What kind of people had we become?

Flight Through Hell

The Tommies had found us. We had already endured our first night raid. All the bombs missed us and our friend the farmer, but they would be coming back, as certainly as the "Allah el Akbar" in the Bizerta mosque. The enemy's intelligence service appeared to be functioning efficiently. We had to get away from there as quickly as possible, away to another field. I found just the place not far from a jade-green lake. Its name was Achkel, and it was full of fish, turtles, and other creatures, such as delicious wild ducks for example. Tall trees and thick cactus hedges provided passable camouflage. A teletype from Taormina summoned me to the *Fliegerführer Italien* and so I saddled up my "war horse." It was a short hop across the Mediterranean. A *Storch* was waiting for me in Catania and in a few minutes it delivered me into another world. High above, between Etna and the coast, lay the former monastery of San Dominico, now a hotel. Bruno Loerzer, *Generaloberst* and *Pour le Merite* flier of the First World War, greeted me cordially. We already knew each other from the Deutschland flights of previous years. He called to me across the long room and then clapped me on the shoulder:

"Dickfeld, who would have thought we'd meet each other under these circumstances. But come inside."

He and his staff lived damned comfortably. There was a breathtaking view of Etna from his office window. We had lunch, after which they came to the point. An *Oberst* whose name I have forgotten began to speak.

"Several days ago the Americans landed in the Algerian port of Bone, close to the Tunisian border, with an armada of warships and aircraft carriers. Not only have they unloaded troops, but fighter and bomber aircraft as well. We know this from radio reports sent by Arab informants. Already three of our reconnaissance aircraft have failed to return and we desperately need more accurate information. A special Bf 109 equipped with cameras and a long-range fuel tank is standing by in Trapani, ready to go immediately."

As he spoke the *Oberst* looked at me strangely. Then the *Generaloberst* jumped in:

"Can you or one of your pilots take on this vitally-important mission?"

What else could I do but mumble, "I'll do it of course."

At this the *Oberst* who had done the talking said, "it would be best if you take off from Trapani at noon tomorrow. It is exactly 900 kilometres there and back."

I thought he must be mad, but I wasn't about to commit suicide. Taking off at noon would mean running into the open knife of the massed anti-aircraft fire of the Allies.

"If it's alright with you, I would prefer to take off from Trapani while it's still dark and, coming from deep in the interior of the country, race over Bone at first light. That seems to me to be more tactically sound and likely to succeed."

Loerzer wrinkled his brow then said, "I leave it up to you how you proceed, naturally. I believe it's time to take you back to Catania. The *Storch* is waiting. Good luck, *Hals- und Beinbruch*. I expect you back tomorrow evening safe and sound and with good photographs, we need them badly."

I saluted and walked to the small strip, which was no larger than a handkerchief. Soon I was back in Catania and shortly afterward I landed my Focke Wulf at Trapani. They were expecting me. A Kübelwagen with a yellow pennant led me to a hangar, inside of which was waiting "my" Bf 109. A technician explained the details of the brand-new equipment. All weapons had been removed, as had the armour plate which normally protected the pilot's back. Instead there was a huge fuel tank hanging under the aircraft's belly, which increased my range considerably. The technical officer explained the functions of the unfamiliar buttons and Bowden cables. They controlled two still and one movie cameras.

"It's best if you start the things before you're over the target. And don't forget to jettison the auxiliary tank first, otherwise it won't work as the cameras are located near the tank. How high do you intend to approach the objective? I hear that a high approach is best."

"No, I intend to fly over the entire business as low as possible," I answered. It was obvious to me that he had no idea whatsoever where I was going and what the mission involved. It was better that way.

"Oh, then we'll have to reset the cameras," he observed sullenly.

"Yes, I guess you'll have to," I replied, "anyway that's not my problem."

"When do you plan to take off?"

I looked at my watch and made a quick calculation. "Takeoff at 0430, but I would like to be at the aircraft at 0400. Where can I spend the night?"

"We have a Luftwaffe soldiers home quite close by. I'll take you there and pick you up at let's say 0330."

Dead tired, I fell into the quilts and slept without dreaming. My alarm woke me at 0300. The hot coffee from the thermos did me good. The dry crackers were no replacement for fresh buns, but they were better than nothing. Then there was a knock on the door. The technical officer picked me up and a few moments later we were standing in the dimly-lit hangar. Capable hands pushed the Messerschmitt through the hangar door. I arranged my flying kit, put on my parachute, and plopped myself down in the narrow seat of the Me. I fastened my straps and gave the thumbs up signal. Two men began turning the starter crank. I selected both magnetos "on" and pulled the starter switch. The power plant which was to catapult me on my long journey roared to life. I gave the signal that I was ready to taxi. The technical officer got into his Kübelwagen and drove ahead of me to the takeoff point. Before commencing my takeoff roll I ran the motor up to full revs and it sounded healthy and powerful. I shut the canopy, my knees trembling like aspen leaves. Was it the cool morning or was it excitement? I wasn't sure. A final wave, full throttle, and I lifted off into the darkness toward an uncertain day which was a still long way off. Seconds later I was already over the Mediterranean; deep black, it was scarcely visible. Now and then the water reflected the light of the stars from the magnificent firmament. My course led right over the port of Bizerta and then across the interior to the Medjerda Mountains, south of Bone. If my calculations were correct, I should arrive there right at dawn. But many minutes had to pass first. I climbed to 5,000 metres to save fuel; I might need it later. Strange how lonely it seemed to be there above, although I knew that the air was full of metal around, above, and below me. The engine droned a powerful, sonorous song, which for me was endlessly soothing. I had been under way 30 minutes now. I should have been able to see the coast, but it was almost impossible to make out. Bizerta was almost certainly totally blacked out, the recent bombing raids by the Tommies had driven home the need for it. Thus I had no chance of making out this distinctive reference point. I flew by compass only. Its illuminated points showed me the general direction. But then I detected a fine outline below me, the boundary between the sea and the coast, it could only be the Gulf of Tunis. It was odd to think that down below my comrades were still sleeping. If they only knew that I was in the air above them. But I had no time for further musing. I had to descend, had to work my way up to the Medjerda Mountains at ground level if the whole affair wasn't to come apart. In the east, to my left, there was the beginning of a soft pink glow, paper-thin, almost invisible. No doubt, the new day was beginning. The first contours became visible beneath me. The engine continued to sing its reassuring song. Nevertheless I was agitated. Was I on course or had I had I erred somewhere? It didn't bear thinking about. No, I was on course, there was Mateur with its railway crossing. Now it was only a few minutes to the mountains. If I was spotted too soon I'd have to abort my mission and probably wouldn't reach home alive. Soon I was over the railway line leading directly to Bone. Ass-drawn carts jogged off the road into the fields. Damn, I had arrived late! It was bright as day, the sun had come up. I flew over an airfield crammed with Spitfires. Time to jettison the auxiliary tank, it was almost empty. A tug on the release handle and it tumbled toward the earth. By now I was at treetop height. The first houses of Bone appeared in front of me. I switched on the cameras, a green light indicated that they were working. The lens had been adjusted for 100 metres. I climbed; beneath me was the harbour. What I saw there left me speechless. The port was crammed with ships of every type, aircraft carriers, battleships, transports, landing craft. I could scarcely comprehend it all in the few seconds available. Then the first tracers came up, they had spotted me. In a matter of seconds every one of the ships was blazing away at me, the air was filled with lead. Then I cleared the harbour and pushed my Me down until it was just above the water, almost touching the waves. But I had got away in one piece, undamaged. A feeling of triumph filled me, but only for a few seconds. More tracer flashed past my left wing. Out of one eye I saw Spitfires hanging behind me, firing. I broke away to the right and switched on the water-methanol injection. My Me raced away from the Tommies at terrific speed. Somehow Cap Serrat passed me. Bathed in sweat, I hung suspended over the blue Mediterranean at 5,000 metres and inhaled the pure oxygen deeply. My hands and knees were shaking. The cameras were still running; in the excitement I had forgotten to turn them off. I found that I had some difficulty holding altitude. Moreover my aircraft wanted to veer to the left. Perhaps I had been hit after all. But there was Trapani. I ripped the oxygen mask from my face and shouted out loud, for I was still alive and able to see the sun, the sea, the trees, the flowers—what a happy feeling!

I'm not exactly sure how I landed, but I recall the words of the technical officer as I stood in front of the hangar:

"They sure got you! Half the elevator is gone and there are a good 15 hits in the fuselage. Hopefully the cameras are still intact."

At that point I wasn't the least bit interested in the cameras or the hits in the fuselage, not at all. With shaking knees and in a blue funk, I dropped into an easy-chair. A kind soul helped me to a shower, what an act of kindness! Someone woke me from a deep sleep; Bruno Loerzer was on the phone:

"Congratulations! When are you coming?"

Half asleep, I didn't know where I was at first, but then I roused myself and said: "I think I can be in Catania by 1100, *Herr Generaloberst!*"

"Good, good, I'll send the *Storch*."

Still dead tired, I slammed the telephone receiver down onto the cradle. Still damned wobbly on my legs, I wolfed down several slices of bread and was soon back in my old, faithful Focke Wulf. The undamaged cameras were stowed behind me and I took off for Catania. Etna puffed smoke in welcome, and soon afterward the *Storch* lifted off for Taormina with me aboard. Again I found myself facing them, Generals, Colonels, Captains, in short the highest of the high. But it was the orderly with the champagne bottle whom I was most interested in. Word soon leaked out that the photos were excellent. Our leaders were dismayed, indeed even speech-less, at the enemy concentration. There were pensive faces all round. Talk of fourteen days special leave rang in my ears, but soon I was on my way back to my unit.

Still Deeper into the Sahara

Achkel Lake with its green waters greeted me at sundown. Everyone was still alive, there had been no losses during the days of my horror trip.

"You're wanted on the telephone," called Wunsch, "it's the *Kommodore*."

He handed me the receiver.

"Can you hear me? Glad to hear you got back in one piece. I have news. Tomorrow you and the entire *Gruppe* are transferring to Kairouan. You're needed there urgently. We suspect that the Amis are moving out of the Sahara toward Tunisia. Infantry can no longer hold the area."

My jaw dropped. "*Jawohl, Herr Major*" was all I could say. Man, Kairouan was far to the south in the middle of the world. That evening we sat over red wine and tried to picture Kairouan, of which we knew damned little. There was supposed to be a mosque there, together with veiled women and plenty of children. Oh yes, there were also the Kairouan carpets, but that was the extent of our knowledge. Brandt observed that Kairouan was supposed to be the Mecca of Arabian North Africa. Mohammed's sabre was in the dome of the mosque.

"Where did you learn that," I asked in astonishment, for until then he had given no indication of his education, although he was an excellent fighter pilot.

"Yes," he observed smugly, "some have it and some don't."

Was he referring to me? The next morning found us standing in the rain, anxious and annoyed. Everything was sopping wet. We couldn't wait for the sun and soon the entire unit was in the air. The ceiling was only 200 metres, but that was sufficient for a low-level flight to Kairouan. We arrived in just under an hour. I circled over what passed itself off as a landing strip. I had my doubts and left the others to wait above while I landed. But the ground was firm and my pilots came in to land one after the other.

"This is a serving tray par excellence," I observed to one of the pilots. "I'll be amazed if the Tommies leave us unmolested here."

An infantry *Leutnant* came by to brief us on the situation.

"This is the end of the line," he said, "South of here is God knows what. No one knows what's going on there. We are only 23 men and are pulling back, for if they come out of the desert we can't stop them. I recommend that you maintain standing patrols to keep on top of the situation. The Amis are said to be advancing from the south from the Beni Abbes oasis, a rumour to be sure, but the Arabs are usually well informed. Good day, gentlemen."

Then he and his Kübelwagen disappeared behind the nearest hill. We all made gloomy faces, for if they came by night we'd be helpless, like stewing hens in aspic. The first Fw 190 soon took off on a scouting mission to check the situation to the south. After landing, Brandt reported no sign of life anywhere, also no vehicle tracks or other indications of enemy activity. Before dark I flew another reconnaissance patrol and came back with the same results. Having learned the hard way, our tents had been pitched far from the airfield and the aircraft. It was a good thing, for that very first night we heard the familiar droning high in the sky and then the bombs began falling. One stick after another came down, but the whole "salad" fell among the dunes behind the city. I would liked to have moved again the next day, but the terrain around Kairouan was highly unsuitable and so we stayed. Arab workers dug slit trenches for us, for we were more than helpless against low-level attacks, at least at first. They came racing over the nearest hill and were upon us before we could get our rear ends out of our easy-chairs. We had to get a radio-equipped reporting team into the hills. Soon five men trotted off with everything they'd need, especially water. This measure was soon to pay handsome dividends. It wasn't quite noon when the first report came in:

"Reconnaissance aircraft approaching, height approximately 4,000 metres, coming from 270 degrees."

Two Focke Wulfs raced into the air to put an end to the fellow's business. But he smelled a rat. The huge dust cloud left by the two fighters should have been enough to convince even the stupidest reconnaissance flier that his premature end might be at hand. He therefore turned tail and our two pilots returned disappointed.

That night rain clouds moved in from the mountains. It became bitterly cold and we shivered in our thin tents. In the morning there was dense fog, which gave us an opportunity to have a look around the city. I couldn't miss the mosque of the sword and in fact it was a treasure of Islamic architecture. In the huge hall, somewhat off to one side, sat a group of women. They wore no veils and were weaving huge carpets. A guide informed me that they were adulteresses who for a period of time had to weave for the mosque before all the men who came to pray. The sentence could be as long as a year, depending on the severity of the case. I thought to myself that if all the adulteresses in Berlin, for example, were forced to weave here, the mosque would be too small. An addition would have to be added and the moslem men would have to "kowtow" out of doors. But they would have had carpets en masse! Oh yes, the women. The guide secretly offered us women, for our temporary or indefinite use. The price was one to fifteen goats each, depending on their quality. None of us had goats, so this unique arrangement never came into being, what a pity! In my mind I saw myself in the midst of my harem, a turban on my head, Sulaika at my left, the water pipe at my right, and of course the other harem girls all around me. I guess it wasn't meant to be. A pity, *Inshalla*! There were rumours, however, that some members of the ground personnel had secretly taken advantage of the offer. I hoped they wouldn't catch anything, but as far as I was concerned they could "catch" whatever they wanted as long as the aircraft were kept combat-ready. There was supposed to be a brothel somewhere behind the city, but I considered it all to be a story from *A Thousand and One Nights.*

It wasn't yet ten o'clock, we had to hurry. The sun would be out soon and so we raced back to the airfield. Not a moment too soon. Our mountain observers had sounded the alarm:

"Low-flying aircraft approaching, Lightnings!"

They were P-38s, fast, heavily-armed, twin-boomed fighters, Americans of course, and they were soon upon us. It was too late to get into the air, so we dove for the slit trenches. Cannon shells smashed into the ground, tracing ammunition flitted about, literally hundreds of fragmentation bombs fell, rolling along the ground before exploding, and bursts of machine-gun fire sawed the desert sand. The Amis denied themselves a second attack. Our quadruple anti-aircraft guns did great work. One Lightning went down burning not far from us and exploded in a huge wall of flame, a second disappeared beyond the hills trailing black smoke. However our own losses were nothing to laugh at. *Leutnant* Behr and a mechanic had been killed, three others wounded seriously. The runway was full of bomb craters and three machines had been reduced to wreckage. If this kept up we'd be out of business within a few days. I telephoned our *Kommodore* but got nowhere. We were to stay in Kairouan for now and eventually change bases. It seemed we never learned. What we needed was better, faster information, that's all, we could do the rest ourselves. I have to state that our logistics were simply awful.

It was midday, with not a cloud in the sky, perfect weather for a bombing raid, I thought to myself. Then the mountain observers called in:

"Bomber formation at high altitude, approximately 4,000 metres, heading for the airfield!"

"Alarm!"

We climbed into our machines and took off unmolested, finally! Two flights of four Fw 190s each raced toward the gaggle of bombers. They were Martin Marauders, English, 18 aircraft. Brandt and Riedel were already behind them. They opened up with everything they had. Two Tommies sheared out of formation after the first attack. Both were on fire and soon afterward they broke up in midair. Parachutes hung in the sky. Having grown nervous by now, the formation turned away into the desert. It was at this point that my *Schwarm* caught up with them. We poured tracer into the machines flying in the rear of the formation. They caught fire, first one, then two. Brandt and Riedel were back again. I saw them fire once more. Two more Marauders caught fire and exploded. Before I was able to carry out another attack the rest of the Tommies had disappeared over the horizon. There was no point in pursuing them.

The Only Thing Driving Us On Is Revenge

Whether pilots or ground personnel, we all had difficulties with our bowels and stomachs. At night, when the thermometer sank to zero, we writhed in pain. Normal food had long been out of the question. Our daily "litany" consisted of tea and zwieback plus "Aplona." Added to this was the strain on our nerves from the constant bombing and strafing attacks. When we slept at all it was due to adequate doses of Tunisian red wine of which, Allah be praised, there was a plentiful supply. How can this go on, I often asked myself in the night. Of course, I was fighting for my home, to defend my fatherland, to bring an end to the bombing terror against our civilian population by the Anglo-Americans. That morning I had received mail from home. Mother and the children were still alive, however the roof had been burned off our house in Berlin, the work of English incendiary bombs. Our next door neighbours were no more. An aerial mine had brought down the boarding house. Twenty-one people, women and children, including the Richters and their four little girls, had fallen victim to this terror. My men received similar bad news each day. I was seized by an unconscious rage. Eager for revenge, I awaited the coming day. I'd show them! In aerial combat, man against man, one still felt a sense of chivalry, although by now even this was little more than a facade. But a surprise low-level attack, when the enemy felt safe and secure, that would give them something to think about. I vowed to strike back at the enemy. Before me lay recent aerial photographs. They showed a newly-built airfield. It was only thirty minutes flying time from us and crammed with American fighters, the Lightnings which had been making our lives miserable in recent days. I counted 32 machines. The airfield was guarded by 12 batteries of wicked American quadruple anti-aircraft guns. But then my heart leapt. The Marauders, which had inflicted such heavy losses on us, were based at a neighbouring airfield, right beside the first. I'd light a fire under their tails too! That same evening we discussed our tactics for the coming morning's attack. Everything that could fly would take part. The armourers were instructed to arm our guns with high-explosive and high-explosive incendiary ammunition. That would rip their arms off right up to the collar and make things hot for them, especially since a little phosphorous went a long way. Our tactics were simple, we would take off at dawn. One of us would act as lookout and stay above the others. We synchronized our watches: takeoff at 0545.

Restless, I tossed and turned on my air mattress all night; sleep was out of the question. I was hot, racked with fever. Chaotic visions of people burning in Berlin woke me repeatedly. Nevertheless, I didn't hear my alarm clock when it went off. It wasn't until the man on watch opened the tent flap that I got up. I jumped to my feet as if I had been bitten by a scorpion, only to collapse immediately. I was unable to stand. Still half-asleep, the doctor came into my tent, examined me and observed:

"If you ask me it's an attack of malaria. Where could you have picked that up?"

0500, damned rubbish! Outside the ground crews had been busy for some time preparing the aircraft.

"It would be best if you remained lying down; you can't take off like this."

What took place afterward was described by Brandt in his diary:

"It is 0530, we walk to our machines. The mechanics help us in. The usual radio check is cancelled. We maintain radio silence and taxi out for takeoff, we're a considerable swarm of hornets. It's just beginning to get light in the east; in a few more minutes the sun will release its fireworks on the horizon. Schwarm after Schwarm takes off. We immediately drop down to just above the ground. I fly in the first Schwarm, the map on my knees. We climb over a medium-sized mountain and then drop back down into the valley. It's now quite light, the sun's first rays are already lying on the mountain peaks. Are the Amis and the Tommies awake yet? Only a single pass and then straight home. We intend to hit them both in one go, the Lightnings and our special friends the Marauders. Five minutes to Tebessa. We climb over one last hill and there they are, as if on a serving tray, our friends from the other side. The second Schwarm moves up beside us. I flip forward the safety catches on the control column and then the eight of us begin to dive. In front of me two Lightnings are taxying for takeoff, probably the early morning patrol. They don't have a chance; a tremendous explosion tears them apart. Seconds later we're over the Marauder field. They're all still asleep. We spray tracer into three fat bombers. Again there are fires and explosions. But where are the dreaded quadruple anti-aircraft guns? We've already passed over the entire salad. Making a shallow left turn, I see spreading fires and explosions; it must be hell on earth down there. We're gone in seconds. I count the aircraft. With the exception of our lookout, everyone's there. Now I break radio silence:

'White 2 from White 1, where are you?'

'I'm above you, good work!' observes wooden eye, our watch-dog.

We come back safely, but it takes a long time to relieve the crackling tension which is in us."

By noon I was back on my feet, though still shaky, and learned of the blow that had been struck against the Amis and the Tommies early that morning.

"Tomorrow or the day after at the latest they'll come and give us a going over we won't forget," observed Bönig casually.

"All we can do is disperse the aircraft and build blast pens," I added.

Radtke joined in: "The Arab workers have their hands so full already that I don't think we can expect them to do this too."

A distant droning interrupted our palaver. It was the daily English reconnaissance aircraft, flying at about 6,000 metres. There was no sense in sending a *Rotte* after him. By the time the fighters reached his altitude he'd be long gone.

"But now he knows what's here. A whole bunch of lovely, new Focke Wulfs for them to chop up."

"You're right," said *Unteroffizier* Will, "they'll send Spitfires with nice little bombs and other lovely things."

The night passed quietly, but nevertheless I was unable to sleep.

The events of the past days and weeks went through my mind.

"What are we looking for in this lousy, God-damned desert anyway?" I asked myself. "We're on the Atlantic, in the Caucasus, at the gates of Cairo, at the edge of the Sahara. Who's going to occupy and hold all of this? We are after all no more than 70 million, including grandmothers, grandfathers, and babies. Of these about 8 million are under arms. How quickly will this huge area swallow up these occupiers? Who would keep a check on all these subjugated peoples? But give up, ignore my duty, run away, no not me."

I clenched my teeth. It would turn out alright, surely our leadership knew what it wanted. Nevertheless doubts remained.

The morning began well. The Arab workers went on strike; they wanted more money. I called the *Geschwader*. Not approved! Was I supposed to pay for the blast pens out of my own pocket? We desperately needed this protection for our "mills," if our losses weren't to climb further. I had to get Bruno Loerzer, the *Generaloberst*, involved. Why hadn't I turned to him sooner? It was clear to me that jumping the chain of command would mean big trouble with the "old man." Getting Taormina on the line was easier than I thought.

"Loerzer here."

The connection was terrible.

"What do you want?" he asked back. "You said blast pens, is that correct? And you want money for blast pens?"

"Yes, *Herr Generaloberst*, for my units for their Fw 190s, which will be smashed to pieces otherwise."

"But that is a matter for the *Geschwader*," he said.

"But they don't want to give us anything, *Herr Generaloberst*," I shouted back.

"In God's name have the things built and send everything to me."

There was a click on the line and I was one dressing-down and 25 blast pens richer. There wasn't much going on in the air that day. The weather was good but there wasn't an aircraft to be seen. Lunch wasn't exactly the best. There was fish and that was enough to drive me from the table.

"Alarm!"

We hurried outside and jumped into our machines. The first engines were already running, but mine refused to start, now of all times! Brandt and his *Schwarm* lifted off but I remained stuck on the ground. The bombers were almost over us. Finally the beast started. Canopy shut, full throttle, I was the last to take off. To my dismay I saw a carpet of bombs racing towards me. A huge explosion tossed me upwards and to one side. My aircraft was flipped upside down. I hung there in my straps, head down, close to the ground. The canopy was shattered, the full fuel tank torn open. Gasoline gurgled out of the tank and poured over me. One spark and I'd be a pillar of fire. I closed my eyes tight. More than anything I wanted to release my straps but I was held fast as if in a vice. Gasoline fumes threatened to asphyxiate me. I felt blood running over my eyes, a lot of blood. Good God, wasn't anyone going to help me? They're still sitting comfortably on their asses in the slit trenches, I thought to myself. I could clearly hear the singing of the English bombers in the distance, as well as the barking of the guns of our Focke Wulfs. Why wasn't I unconscious? I couldn't move my hands, what was wrong with them? Then I thought I heard voices. I wanted to call out but I couldn't. All that escaped my throat was a gurgling sound. I felt dizzy. Was this death? Must I die? Good God, crawl out of your slit trenches and help me! Then they were there, standing by my machine.

Someone shouted, "cigarettes out!"

Another said, "he's done for."

"Crawl under and have a look," said someone else. A face appeared before me. It was Borchers, my armourer. My eyes were wide open now. He stared at me.

"He's alive," he shouted, "lift the machine."

Then I lost consciousness. When I came to I was lying on a table. There were people around me and I heard French being spoken. A doctor in a white smock said something to me. My mouth was swollen, I wasn't able to make a sound. Where are you? What have they done to you? Apart from my left eye, my head was completely covered in bandages. Then I recognised *Feldwebel* Hinrich; he was standing beside me wearing a concerned expression.

"Can you hear me?" he asked in a sonorous voice.

I nodded my head.

"You have head injuries. They've just sewn you up. Your right eye is damaged and your left knee is broken, but the doctor thinks you'll pull through."

Then I slipped into a deep unconsciousness. When I came to again I was still lying in the French doctor's Arab hut. I was able to speak again, they must have rinsed out my mouth and throat. My adjutant was sitting on a stool beside me.

156

"Thank God that you're awake again, I was worried about you. I'm supposed to pick you up and take you to Karthago in the *Storch*, do you think you can make it?"

"What does the doctor say?"

"He says that it's alright provided you're on a litter."

"Agreed!"

Soon they lifted me from the table and strapped me in tight. They had some difficulty balancing me in the narrow, slow-flyer, but soon we were on our way low over the desert sand. I must have lost consciousness again, because when I awoke I found myself in an operating room, surrounded by doctors.

"Can you hear me?" one of them asked in German.

I nodded weakly.

"You're in Karthago. We're sending you to Rome." The voice sounded far away. "We can't do any more for you here. You have a fractured skull."

When I came to again I thought I must be dreaming; I was lying on my stomach in the glazed nose of a Focke Wulf *Weihe* looking down at blue sea water. The aircraft was racing low over the water toward an island. Before me was the familiar sight of smoke-belching Mount Etna. The *Weihe* climbed slightly and then glided past the grey flank of the huge volcano. I would very much liked to have pinched myself to see if this was real or just a dream, but my bandaged hands prevented me from doing so. Then I heard a voice in my right ear:

"Can you hear me? Are you awake?"

I nodded my head. I recognised the voice, it was *Feldwebel* Harnisch.

"We're flying straight to Rome, they couldn't do any more for you in Karthago. The Luftwaffe hospital in Rome has been alerted. Everything will be alright."

But Rome, too, passed me on. Finally I landed in Berlin. My new address: the Reich Sportsfield Hospital. I was shocked by what they told me there:

"We can repair the damage to your eye, but the skull fracture and the fragments in your head and leg will take time."

They had pulled my scalp forward and sewn it up with a large number of stitches. The kind sister said that I shouldn't look in the mirror at first.

The weeks passed quickly, interrupted only by bombing raids on the capital. When the bombers came I was taken into the basement on a stretcher. All the tokens of human affection I was shown allowed me to get back on my feet sooner than expected. Although I was on crutches I was still eager to get back to my unit, which was engaged in a desperate defensive battle in Tunisia. But I was far from well and it was much too early. The fortunes of war had abandoned Rommel. The English from the east and the Americans from the south and west were making life difficult for our troops. Tunisia could not be held. My unit transferred to Sicily under dramatic circumstances. As many ground personnel as possible were flown out in the cramped, single-seat Fw 190s. By removing the radios and leaving the ammunition behind, it was possible to cram in as many as three members of the ground crew. The fighters flew low and fast to Trapani, hoping that they weren't caught. It was a helpless feeling for the pilots, but they returned to Tunis to take out as many people as possible. In spite of their best efforts hundreds of men from my unit had to be left behind. Poor fellows! They soon found themselves facing captivity in the hands of the Americans. It was certainly better than being captured by the Russians, but that was small consolation.

A Dreadful Slaughter

I learned that I was to be transferred to a *Geschwader* on the German Bight. Every corner of the German Reich was ablaze, it had become a playground for Allied fighters and bombers. They attacked day and night, giving the nation no rest. Equipped with the latest versions of the Bf 109, my and other fighter units faced what was probably the most difficult task in this life and death struggle of our people. We had little with which to oppose the vile terror being inflicted on our population day and night by the English and American bombers. We had been bled dry in men and machines. It was possible to set one's watch by the appearance of the bombers over the North Sea in the morning, on their way to attack our country. On this particular day we had been sitting in our machines since dawn. It was a magnificent autumn day and in recognition of this there was excellent jazz coming from the airfield loudspeaker, although our leaders would surely have frowned on such an idea. We had our headsets half on. In one ear we could hear "Some of His Days," and in the other, "report from our picket boats: in southern England Boeing Fortress wings are preparing for a mission into Reich territory. Likely arrival off the coast, about 1045!" It was going to be another busy day.

It was now shortly before nine. My two aircraft mechanics dozed beneath the wings. They had had a late night, not getting to bed until about one. My aircraft's radiators and tail assembly had been damaged and had to be changed. Over Bremerhaven I had been hit 21 times by a Boeing I was attacking. Yes, one needed nerves of steel or he wouldn't last long. One never knew if he'd still be among the living after the next mission. We had got drunk the previous evening, like every other evening, just to forget what had happened yesterday, what had happened today, and what was likely to happen tomorrow. A morning hangover was almost normal. Last evening replacements had arrived to take the place of those killed, wounded, or posted missing the day before. Nineteen young pilots, among them my long-time friend Helmuth Meckel. I was especially happy to see him again, but being young and inexperienced in combat he had little chance of survival. He was full of zeal and I couldn't have restrained him if I'd wanted to. He had a wife and children at home and he was soon to die.

We had had a problem for days. There was a herd of deer at the edge of the forest, tremendous animals, I estimated about twenty of them. They browsed there in the evening and early in the morning, oblivious to the aircraft landing and taking off, and it was easy to see that it was only a matter of time before one or more of them was "mowed down" by us. I was of two minds about the whole business. One said: think of the pilots and machines. An accident is unavoidable if one of them gets under the wheels of an aircraft. The other said: here is an opportunity to get some meat, for we were already badly short of rations. I wrestled with the problem for some time until fate stepped in. One of my pilots, *Feldwebel* Rudolph, landed just before dusk, his aircraft shot up, with a tailwind, and from the wrong side. He had too much speed and overshot the runway, striking the herd of deer. Four does were chopped into pieces by the big, three-bladed propeller, almost ready for the oven. Two others were hurt badly. Rudolph finished them off with his 7.65mm pistol. The aircraft itself suffered no further damage. The news spread like wildfire and soon a pack of Kübelwagens and motorcycles was racing to the scene, led by the chief cook. There was enough for three *Staffeln* and a *Stabsschwarm*. The disagreeable part came the following morning. The quarter ranger responsible for the deer turned up, booted and spurred, and demanded the return of his animals. He threatened to report us to the police, to have us court-martialled, and so on. This went on for some time until I was able to talk him out of it. In the end he realized that we didn't give a damn about his complaints anyway. Finally he left with his tail between his legs. Actually I felt rather sorry for him.

Each day young, inexperienced pilots (not just from our unit) were killed in the skies over the German Bight. Day after day we urgently needed replacement pilots and aircraft. It was a terrible blood-letting. One afternoon more replacement pilots arrived from the fighter schools, very young and inexperienced. I looked past them, feeling rather guilty, because I knew that scarcely any of them was likely to survive the next three days. One of the boys was a small, wiry Austrian. He had brought his accordion with him and he played Viennese music with striking perfection. I wondered to myself if he would last even a few days with us. I could certainly use him to help relieve the burdens and cares of a day in the sky over the murderous sea. We were spellbound as we listened and watched him play. Should I spare him from combat and keep him on the ground indefinitely, just because he could play Viennese music? No, he had to die just like all the others, damn it to hell!

Anti-aircraft fire in the distance, surely English Mosquitoes approaching over the German Bight. They were probably going to Berlin, as was usual in those days, to drop their huge aerial mines which were capable of blowing up whole blocks of houses containing women and children. We were powerless against them. Unequipped for night flying, we had to stay on the ground, besides they were faster than we were and flew at great heights. An unconscious rage seized us in the face of this situation. It was almost miraculous that they hadn't hit us! They knew about our base as certainly as the amen in church. It was late and I still had paperwork to finish. I also had to write letters to wives and parents, in which I informed them that their husband or son had been killed that morning in a heroic battle against the enemy for Volk, Fatherland and Führer. How that made me sick. It strained my nerves. Every day I asked myself when it was all going to end. But then when you heard that cities like Bremen, Kiel, Hamburg, and others had been attacked again and that thousands of innocent women and children had been burned alive in the wreckage of their houses, you were seized by rage again and swore to extract a measure of vengeance against the enemy on the next mission. Dead tired I fell into bed. It must have been about two in the morning when a terrific explosion woke me from a deep sleep. The large window in my room blew in with an ear-splitting crash. In the hall I heard running feet and shouts. Apparently my pilots next door had been caught as well. I ran out of my room, stepping over broken glass and pieces of wood. In the corridor near my door lay a girl, apparently a friend of one of my pilots. She had been badly injured. Blood poured from her mouth and nose. Dr. Pohl, our *Geschwader* medical officer, was already kneeling beside her. Suddenly a completely bewildered-looking *Leutnant* Wächter was standing before me. He had been hit too. His face was smeared with blood and he had a gaping wound in his head. He had only arrived that evening. Now the war was over for him, without combat, without the Knight's Cross. That was it. In the morning we inspected the damage. The mine had blasted a two-metre-deep crater out of the ground barely 20 metres away from us. The full force of the blast wave, and with it thousands of steel fragments, had struck our quarters. Five of the new pilots were out of action, our quarters unusable. We took what was left of our belongings and moved into tents at the edge of the airfield. Our aircraft had escaped damage; the ground personnel got away with a scare.

I had a terrible headache and was feeling simply awful when what I had been expecting, indeed fearing, came.
"Cockpit readiness for the entire *Geschwader*."
Enemy units were crossing the English coast, course 130 degrees, or straight for us. We had about 30 minutes until we were ordered to scramble, time enough to give the Viennese musician from the night before, whose name was Erich Handt, a brief lecture on how to act in the coming air battle. He was surprised when I selected him to be my wingman.

160

"Stay with me no matter what happens," I explained to him, "fire only on my express order. Believe me, it's your only chance of surviving your first mission against the Flying Fortresses, to say nothing of the Ami escort fighters."

We climbed into our machines and waited for the order from the command post. Walch and Dudek, my faithful ground crew, hung about beneath the wing of my Me, waiting morosely for what was to come. The dreaded red flare hissed over the airfield from the command post. It was time. Immediately afterward the order came through my headset: "Scramble!"

Canopies snapped shut and the mechanics cranked for all they were worth, until finally the engines started. A total of 23 Bf 109s lifted off into the misty sky over the North Sea; it was all that a once-proud *Geschwader* with an authorised strength of 120 machines could manage. My *Schwarm* was the first to take off. My knees trembled, making it hard for me to control the rudder. Weaving slightly, I lifted off. I had been drinking the night before and now I felt sick to my stomach. In position on my right was Lt. Handt, he had got off the ground without trouble. Behind us I saw the machines of Fw. Kuras and Lt. Balinger lift off from the grass surface. The command post called:

"Boeing Fortresses and Liberators, height 6,000 metres, about 500 machines grouped into ten formations. Above them escort fighters, about 150, at 7-8,000 metres; mixed Spitfires, Lightnings and Thunderbolts. Fly a heading of 290 degrees."

My God, I thought, we're supposed to take them on with a mere 23 fighters? But there was no time to debate the issue. Looking back I saw the rest of my unit's aircraft. Far below they were climbing toward our attack altitude of 9,000 metres. Hopefully we'd be able to reach this altitude before the whole bomber armada was upon us, or things could get hairy. We had to climb above the fighter escort, otherwise our first attack, if we got an opportunity to attack at all, was bound to fail. We had had our oxygen masks on for some time. As a precaution I cocked my cannon and machine-guns, just in case one of these "gadflies" should get the jump on us. The information supplied by our picket boats and submarines off the English coast was reliable. Rarely did they lead us astray.

Suddenly Handt screamed, "In front of us, they're coming right toward us."

I lowered my sunglasses over my eyes and there they were. Trailing long, white condensation trails behind them, they looked like a swarm of hornets. My motor wasn't running properly, revolutions were down noticeably. I hadn't noticed until now. Meanwhile we had passed 8,500 metres and were still climbing. It was a good thing that the sun was behind us. There was a chance we wouldn't be spotted too soon and would have an opportunity to carry out at least one attack. It was sheer madness to attack from behind in the old way. We should have begun training for

161

frontal attacks, for which I had long been pleading, as quickly as possible. But such thoughts were of no use now. Finally, we reached 9,000 metres. Erich Handt was hanging bravely beside me, gesturing forward excitedly. I had spotted them too, eight Spitfires heading our way. They broke towards us and in seconds we were involved in a hairy air battle. Four against eight, this doesn't look good, I thought to myself. If only I didn't have the new pilot with me. But now I couldn't keep an eye on him any more, I had to look after myself.

"Run for it!" I called to him.

Handt disappeared into a fat cumulus cloud. I got the first Spitfire in my sights. Tracer flashed past my cockpit. I hauled my Me into a steep turn to escape the deadly fire. Too late, bullets smacked into my fuselage. I hoped the tank hadn't been hit. There was no time to think about it. Another Spitfire raced toward me from in front. Tracer smacked against my armoured windscreen, shattering on the bullet-proof glass. For a fraction of a second I saw Balinger and Kuras below and to my left, in a clinch with three Tommies. "My" Spitfires appeared to have dived away, so I descended. Suddenly there was a Lightning in my sights. All I had to do was press the triggers. It caught fire immediately and then exploded in a ball of fire. Below a white parachute descended toward the choppy, grey North Sea. Far below the rest of our Messerschmitts were attacking straggling Flying Fortresses. Four of them were already on fire. Parachutes swung toward the water. I was right over Helgoland. Continuing the dive I came upon another Boeing. Its bomb bay doors were already open; the first bombs came tumbling out. The rear gunner immediately began firing at me with his twin machine-guns, so I dove away and poured cannon shells into the bomber's fuselage from below. The Ami began to glow inside like a traffic light and then exploded in an inferno. I dove away. It was high time too, my engine was just about finished. I had about 650 kph on the clock and swept toward land. I had no wish to come down in the drink, with a water temperature of nine degrees it wouldn't have been a pleasant swim. It soon became obvious that I wasn't going to reach my home airfield. The engine began to smoke and then the propeller stopped. Beneath me was a field. I left the undercarriage up but lowered the landing flaps. I crashed through a pasture fence at terrific speed. It broke apart like brittle winter asparagus. Then a ditch appeared before me. My aircraft flipped over and I ended up hanging upside down in my straps. Blood ran over my face. Then I heard voices.

"I wonder if he's still alive."

"Lift up the rear end of the fuselage," said another, then a face appeared before me.

"Hurry up, I have to get out before the crate catches fire," I shouted. Then I lost consciousness. When I came to I was lying in a meadow. There were people all around me. Someone was bandaging my head. I had some cuts and bruises, but nothing worse. That afternoon I was sewn up by medical officer Pohl. How much more of this could my skull take? That evening I was back in the *Geschwader* tent and learned more about what had come of the morning's engagement. The enemy had lost eleven Flying Fortresses plus seven escort fighters, but what was that against the massed power which was deployed against us. We had lost "only" five machines together with their pilots, including my *Schwarm* leader Kuras. Also missing was Lt. Balinger. Four weeks later they found him dead in his tiny life raft in the mud flats off Nordeney. He must have died a thousand deaths before, wounded and alone, he finally died of thirst. Lt. Handt returned that afternoon, his parachute under his arm. A Lightning had shot him to pieces while I was busy with the Fortress. He was forced to bale out of his burning crate at 7,000 metres and was pulled out of the water near Borkum by the crew of a fishing boat. Apart from a few bruises he was unhurt, but the experience had aged him several years in a few seconds. There would surely be no *Beautiful Blue Danube* or *Vienna Blood* tonight. I took him off flying for the next few days, then we'd see.

It is absolute rubbish when "story tellers" now claim that our successes were due to the stimulant Pervitin and that they had "pumped us up" before takeoff, in the same way that athletes of some nations use anabolic steroids today. I never witnessed this practice nor did I make use of it. As well none of our doctors would have thought of offering something like that.

The Amis Make Our Lives Difficult

That night I had a terrible headache, a relic from Rommel's African adventure. It was still there in the morning. Dr. Pohl gave me some aspirin, but they did little good so I stayed home that day. I had plenty of work to do trying to catch up on the paper war, what with reports, letters, and so on. At about nine the usual routine began: cockpit readiness followed by a scramble. They raced into the air, a total of eleven machines against several hundred Amis and Tommies. I watched them disappear into the clear, blue morning sky. Lt. Handt was with them, his second combat mission. Will he make it, I wondered? I had no time for further musings. I leapt into a nearby slit trench as explosive bullets began ploughing up the airfield. Lousy Mustangs, at least a dozen of them, swept across the airfield, but most of their bullets were wide of the mark. Apart from a barracks in flames at the edge of the airfield we suffered no damage. We had got off lightly, but they'd surely be back again just as soon as they received a dressing-down from their CO. For their high-altitude reconnaissance aircraft were usually on the spot to immediately deliver photographs confirming their success or lack thereof. There must have been a lovely scrap over the North Sea, in any case there was a great mix-up on the frequency between our pilots. They had made solid contact with the enemy. One of them, it sounded like Lt. Koppe, reported shooting down a heavy bomber, a B-24 Liberator.

163

"It's breaking up, it's breaking up! They're bailing out!" he shouted hysterically.

I believe it was his first. Then an unfamiliar voice came on, it had to be the fighter control centre in Stade. The man called to the fighter pilots engaged in the desperate struggle high above:

"Close in, close in!"

Then someone, I think it was Fw. Roskop, answered in a sonorous voice. He shouted down furiously: "Come up yourself, you idiot! You sit in your concrete bunker and let us get killed up here!"

All the pent-up fury and desperation had broken through. Only someone who had been up there himself knew how it felt and how difficult it was to keep one's nerve in this hopeless battle where the odds were stacked against us. They came back in ones and twos, in total five machines from the eleven which had taken off. Three had made emergency landings elsewhere, but the pilots were unhurt. Two had gone down in flames into the North Sea, Lt. Koppe and Uffz. Bienert. One was missing. It was *Leutnant* Handt. The others had seen him collide with a B-17, which had then exploded in a ball of fire. Tonight I would write to his family to express my regrets. How I hated that! The next day I received a call from the Wilhelmshaven naval hospital:

"Early this morning air-sea rescue brought in a pilot with severe burns. He was fished out of the water near Helgoland. From his clothing, or what's left of it, it looks like he might be from your unit. He has no identity disks on him. He's unconscious and delirious, but he keeps mentioning Schwechat."

It was then that the penny dropped. Wasn't Handt from Schwechat near Vienna?

"Yes," I said to the sister on the other end of the line, "yes, that could be our Lt. Handt. When should I come over?"

"Tomorrow morning would be best, shall we say at about 9 o'clock? Then we'll know more."

There was a click and the kind soul on the other end of the line was gone. It was a good thing I hadn't written his parents the day before; I had simply been too busy, too empty and exhausted. The naval hospital was some distance away and it took quite a while to get there. The air raid sirens began to wail just as I arrived. Nurses carried wounded into the air raid shelter on litters. The scene was one of confusion and I found myself penned up with hundreds of doctors, nurses, and patients. My search for Lt. Handt would have to wait until the all-clear had been sounded. But then I saw something that, as hard-bitten as I was, still took my breath away: a human form, completely swathed in bandages except for one eye, still breathing, moving slightly, but unresponsive. He was easily identifiable by the remains of his flight suit, it could only be our man from Vienna. It seemed to me pointless to stay with him any longer. The attending physician observed laconically:

"I doubt we can pull him through. With second and third degree burns over his entire body he has little hope."

So I left, feeling depressed. I did however inform his parents that evening that their son was still alive and would pull through; what a liar I was! It was difficult to believe that he had survived. The following is his version of events: while attacking a B-17 he was wounded in both hands by return fire. He lost control of his aircraft, which then flew into the Boeing at full throttle. It wasn't until a week later that he regained consciousness. He remembered nothing of crashing into the Boeing, opening his parachute, falling into the North Sea, or being fished out of the water. Understandably he also remembered nothing of my visit. Soon he was sent back to Vienna. I was to meet him again after the war in very different circumstances, but more about that in my next book.

Shot Down!

Rumours swirled about the fighter arm that in the future we were going to use rockets to attack the bomber formations in an effort to obtain better results. I felt that such stories were just that, rumours, and in fact most of them proved unfounded. But just imagine it: a climb to high altitude, perhaps 10,000 metres, then the release of your rockets into the midst of the Amis from a safe distance and they fall from the skies in dozens. It sounded too good to be true! We repeatedly heard stories of miracle weapons. There was supposed to be a V 1 and even a V 2, which were going to level London. I never saw one and remained sceptical. In the last four months our fighter arm had lost 1,000 pilots, about 50 in every incursion by the enemy and usually the best ones. I was certain of only one thing: if losses continued at this rate, with the irresistible bomber streams over our country day and night the end wasn't far off. Then God have pity on us! But each morning you got out of bed and attempted the impossible. With clenched teeth and trembling knees you took off again into the apocalypse, into the icy skies over the North Sea, which already had your name on its death list. All that remained was for your name to be crossed off.

Whenever there was time now we practised frontal attacks using models. This was our only chance of surviving. The huge, four-engined bombers had scarcely any defences to the front, at most a single, puny machine-gun. Behind, beneath, and to the sides they fired at us poor swine with 12 heavy weapons. It was easy to figure out how quickly we'd be shot down. The new method did have one disadvantage however; attacker and target raced towards one another at almost 1,000 kph. Firing time had shrunk to fractions of a second and if one's reactions weren't lightning fast then you were into the American bomber and you can imagine what took place then. Finally X-Day arrived; we were going to try out the new

165

tactic. I had decided to take only "old hands" along with me; I wasn't about to sacrifice the youngsters, they would have enough to do. I wasn't exactly well myself, but it simply had to be done if the enemy wasn't to go on effectively and relentlessly terrorizing our defenceless civilian population. There were only eight of us, all experienced men, highly decorated, even if we had been thrown together from every theatre of the war. They were daredevils, men I could depend upon. Yesterday the weather had been miserable. Sea fog had kept us on the ground: time to go over everything once more. Today the sun shone, the sky over the North Sea was cloudless. We gathered for breakfast at 7 o'clock. The command post issued the first report from the English east coast:

" Enemy bomber wing tuning its radios. Takeoff by this unit expected at eight o'clock."

I stood up and made a quick calculation: they'd be off our coast at nine, unless they flew a completely new course. We would see. I hastily ate another slice of bread and swallowed the rest of my coffee. Who could say where and when we'd have our next breakfast. Around me pale, tired faces; I went over the attack plan with them once again. Then it was time. The red flare which rose high into the air above the airfield finally put an end to the dreadful waiting. That was the worst, the period between cockpit readiness and the scramble. One sat there, wanting more than anything to climb out and perhaps escape one more time, perhaps hold onto one's puny life. Too late! The mechanics were already turning the starter cranks, eight canopies were closed and locked shut.

I was first to take off, sweeping across the airfield with Fw. Eckhardt on my left and the rest behind me. We lifted off, the sand flats already beneath us.

"Enemy approaching from 275 degrees," reported the command post. "321 Boeing Fortresses, 84 escort fighters, mixed. Combat altitude 5,500."

They're damned low today, I thought, and then there they were, above us!

"Shit! They're here much too soon, nothing to do but attack from behind as usual!" I grumbled into the radio.

We were just climbing through 4,000 metres when the first Amis jumped us. A Thunderbolt got on my tail but he missed me. I could see the muzzle flashes as he fired, but the tracer whizzed past my cockpit. I pirouetted upwards at full throttle and lost the Thunderbolt. Beneath me my seven pilots were engaged in a wild dogfight. Fw. Eckhardt was also there; apparently he'd had to break away from me. The air battle drifted northward. Helgoland had already disappeared on the horizon behind us. Beneath me a burning Spitfire smacked into the dark water. The Tommy inside had apparently failed to get out, as I saw no parachute. Suddenly Bartsch was beside me, gesticulating wildly with both hands. His radio was probably out. He pointed in front of us and I saw two Boeings, apparently trying to sneak away. But they weren't getting away from me! Their bomb doors were still open; they had probably just finished dropping their deadly loads on Bremen.

What a feast! After them! We were now at 4,000 metres and had both Amis right in front of us. I signalled to Bartsch that I would take the one on the right, so he immediately turned toward the bird flying on the left. The two Fortresses were flying close together and constituted a considerable amount of firepower. The Boeings had a crew of twelve and each of them now turned ten heavy machine-guns towards us and began firing, even though we were still much too far away. There was no point in attacking from behind now. Finally we had an opportunity to test our new tactic. I swung out far to the right, Bartsch to the left. Then we climbed into the sun, pulled ahead of the Amis and, with a half-roll and dive, began a joint, head-on attack. They must have lost sight of us, because they weren't flying as close together as before. That made things easier. My cannon had automatically cocked with a fat plop and I had turned up the brightness of my reflector sight. I throttled back slightly to increase firing time. I couldn't pay any further attention to Bartsch, the attack required my full concentration. "My" Ami appeared out of the mist, as big as a barn door. I pressed the triggers and my burst of fire went straight into the bomber's cockpit. I clearly saw the pilots slump forward. For an instant I saw fire inside the B-17 and then I was diving away. Not a moment too soon; I had come within a hair of ramming him. I pulled out a thousand metres below and turned slightly to the left. To my consternation I saw that "my American" appeared to be undamaged. The beast was still flying as if nothing had happened. Its speed was reduced but there was no sign of any damage or fire. Meanwhile the second Ami seemed to have disappeared. Perhaps Bartsch had finished him. I wasn't about to allow "mine" to get away so I prepared for another attack. I climbed back up and a moment later was right behind the Boeing, not 50 metres away. The twin tail guns were pointing straight up into the air, so I had nothing to fear. I moved in closer; my Messerschmitt was tossed about by the bomber's propwash. The gunner was slumped forward, apparently dead. But all of a second the guns swung around and fired a long burst at me. Numerous explosive bullets struck my aircraft, the cockpit filled with smoke and biting steam. I hauled my Messerschmitt around, gasping for breath. Bright flames began pouring from my engine.

"Get out!" I screamed to myself.

I unfastened my straps and pulled the emergency canopy release handle. The plexiglass hood flew away, the slipstream whipped into my face. I rolled the burning aircraft onto its back and dropped clear. I let myself drop for some time, turning over several times. I wanted to get away from the blazing inferno. Then I pulled the release handle. There was a crack and a jolt, and a shock went through my body as if it was being torn into pieces. I swung beneath my parachute, which spread its billowing white folds above me. I looked just in time to see my burning

Me disappear into the mirror-smooth sea. Meanwhile "my" Ami escaped on the horizon. Its left, inner engine was burning brightly, while the right, inner motor was trailing black smoke. Would he make it to the English coast? I doubted it. I was still 2,000 metres up, time to prepare for my "splashdown." I pulled the belt of my life vest tighter. The sea came up toward me quickly. A few metres to go. With a press of the central button I released myself completely from the parachute. I fell faster, then hit the water. I went under, swallowed some water, and came up again, the huge canopy over my head. I went under again, losing my fur-lined boots, came up again, and finally got my hands on the compressed air bottle for my life jacket. There was a plop, the vest filled like a balloon, and suddenly I found myself bobbing on the surface. It was then that I recalled that I also had my small life raft. It was tied flat on my back. I searched desperately for the raft's compressed air bottle. The huge canopy was still lying over me, I had to get free of it. I pulled and pulled, my God a parachute had a lot of lines! Finally I was able to see the sky above me. I fumbled for my flare pistol, found it, and fired my ammunition into the air. Then I began searching for the packet of dye. Once opened and poured into the water it created a patch of colour intended to ease the task of the air-sea rescue service. But I left it, for who'd be looking for me so far from Bremen and Helgoland? It struck me that this was my second time in the drink, but it was different on the channel. The air-sea rescue service was better organised there. It was damned cold. I shivered and my teeth chattered. Finally I found the compressed air lever. There was a hiss and the life raft swelled up beside me. Hauling myself in took the rest of my strength. Dead-tired, I fell into a deep sleep. When I awoke it was pitch black. My wristwatch showed 2030, it was a miracle that it was still working. I was terribly thirsty. Back at the base they'd be in the mess, drinking. Perhaps they'd think of me with a shrug of the shoulders, but then I'd be written off. Who would tell my wife? What difference did it make anyway? The sea was unusually calm. There should have been a bar of chocolate in my flight suit, emergency rations, but when I felt my pockets all I found was my small 7.65mm pistol. You don't need that yet, I thought, better leave it there. Would it even work after being soaked in sea water? I was able to pull my parachute out of the water and laid it over me. It had floated at my side the whole time like a faithful dog. I wasn't so cold now, even though my rear end was sitting in sea water. My angora underwear seemed to be proving itself. There was a loud droning high above me, fresh bomber squadrons on their way to the Reich. I must have fallen asleep again. It was just after midnight when I woke up. Clouds had moved in and waves began tossing my tiny boat to and fro. An object I couldn't identify was floating beside me. A type of bag, it was being tossed from wave to wave. It submerged, then resurfaced. I was too tired to be curious and I had no desire to paddle over to it with my hands. I kept reminding myself that I shouldn't drink any sea water, it would only make me thirstier. Wouldn't it have been better to die a quick death in the air than to perish slowly here? Everyone thought that it was a good way to die, you felt nothing when the enemy got you cleanly. One lost consciousness immediately and when you crashed somewhere below; all the fear, the distress, the desperation was long behind you. I fell into a deep unconsciousness. When I came to it was beginning to get light and soon the first rays of the sun were shooting over the agitated water. My tiny boat held out bravely, but without its drift anchor it would have tipped over long ago. My wristwatch had become waterlogged and wasn't working any more. The dark object was now drifting close beside me and I realized to my horror that it was the body of an American. His green parachute was drifting just beneath the water's surface. The body was pushed closer to me with each wave, as if it wanted to say to me:

"Take me with you, take me home, my parents are waiting for me!"

On his pale face was a peaceful smile. His long, black hair hung over his pale cheeks and his eyes were closed. He must have been quite young. On his right wrist was a silver chain. On the small plate I read Eric Swanson, L.A. His blue flight suit was torn. Blood welled out. On his breast I saw a tattoo, a red and blue eagle. To my horror I now realized that there were other bodies floating around me, I counted twelve in all. It was probably the entire crew of a Flying Fortress. With a sense of relief I realized that they couldn't have been killed by me, as if that could be an excuse! A shiver went through me. I wasn't happy, no I was horrified. Panic seized me. I had to get away, away from the bodies. I began to paddle like mad with both hands, but they appeared to be following me. Then finally they were gone, I lost sight of them and I was alone again. Exhausted and my strength gone, I fell asleep. When I awoke the sun was shining down on me pitilessly. It was at its zenith therefore it must be close to noon. In spite of this I was terribly cold, my whole body shook. My thirst was terrible. Why wasn't anyone helping me? Had they written me off already? What was the good of all the rescue equipment, the raft, the life vest, the warm underwear, the pocket compass, the packet of dye, the signal flares, and all the other rubbish if they were just going to let me die? Then I heard a droning in the distance. Far away an aircraft flew past and disappeared into the mist.

"Open the packet of dye now, make a pretty, yellow, fluorescent patch of colour in the murderous sea," a voice said to me, "make it as a farewell gift to a pitiless world. Then take your 7.65, hold it in your mouth, point it up, pull the trigger, and then it will all be over. Just don't die of thirst, don't end up like Lt. Balinger."

Then a feeling of deep, inner peace came over me. I tore open the packet of dye, and in a few minutes I was floating in a huge, fantastic display of colour. The powder mixed with the sea water in an orgy of colour. If I hadn't been so miserable I'd have been enthraled, but at least I was distracted. A long swell began to bob me up and down. Up, down, up, down, how long would I have to endure this? Then there it was again: engine noise. Your senses are deceiving you, you're hallucinating, I thought. I squinted as I looked into the sun from where the noise was coming, and suddenly a huge, thunderous, black shadow passed over me. It was a Dornier *Wal*, one of our air-sea rescue flying boats. I shouted like a madman and waved my arms. The flying boat turned, came toward me and set down on the water beside me with a huge bow wave. I don't remember how I got on board or the takeoff. Not until they poured hot tea with rum into me during the flight home did I really come to, but my legs still felt like lead. But then unconsciousness took me under its wings once more. When I came to again I was lying on my stomach in a bed. I heard voices.

A female voice said, "I think he's waking up!" Then she turned to me: "Can you hear me?"

I nodded my head.

"You're in the Wilhelmshaven naval hospital. Your *Kommodore* will be here soon."

And then he was standing beside me, the "old man," who in reality was quite a young man.

"How are you? It was lucky that they fished you out of the water, it was pure chance that they found you. I have news. The naval hospital says that your back injuries are too serious to be treated here. They're sending you to a special clinic."

"What kind of injuries?" I asked in amazement.

"You apparently struck your back on the tail while bailing out. Several vertebrae were damaged."

Up to that point I hadn't noticed anything. But the unerring X-ray machine knew more; it now became clear why my legs felt as heavy as lead. I prayed I wouldn't remain paralysed. Adieu *Geschwader*, adieu comrades, adieu faithful mechanics, armourers and radio technicians. I was transferred to the Reich Sportsfield Hospital in Berlin. This was the same hospital where a certain Herr Rommel had sent me not long ago. The doctors and nurses were the same. There was a warm welcome all round. The daily routine in hospital was a tiresome affair. I was confined to bed most of the time and all movement was severely restricted. The hospital staff pushed me around in a wheelchair. They fussed over me to the point that it was becoming an embarrassment. I sought something to do and finally learned the meaning of mercy. Later I was allowed to do some paperwork in the ministry, with the secretaries and so on, until my wounds had completely healed. At night I cowered in the air raid shelter with the women and children. It was here that I learned what war was all about, war against the defenceless. That was the worst! Outside in my Messerschmitt I could kill the enemy or he could kill me, but here I was a nothing, very, very small. What did I know of bravery? In the shelters our old people, women and children endured the terror bombing without complaint, not for Führer and Fatherland but for the next day, for a piece of bread, some hot soup or a cup of coffee. One felt damned miserable sitting in the shelter with the civilians, decked out in full uniform and decorations. I was just as scared as they when the British bombers dropped their deadly loads indiscriminately, but I couldn't let them know how wretched I felt. No, I had to get out of there, out of the air raid shelter, out of Germany, away from the lousy headquarters with its parasites, shirkers, and party functionaries.

That's All I Can Take

I'd never heard of Döberitz until I became involved with the place in the course of my official duties.

One day Loerzer, who was my CO at the time, said to me, "Go and have a look around Döberitz. There's supposed to be a First World War archive there which has all the documents concerning my *Geschwader* (Loerzer served in the same *Staffel* as Göring and Richthofen). I don't want to see them lost in an air raid." Loerzer continued, a hint of a Berlin accent in his voice: "Drive over there and try to bring back all the documents. We (by this he meant Göring and himself) will take them to Karinhall and store them there. But move quickly; we can't be sure that Döberitz will even be there tomorrow."

I replied with the usual *"Jawohl, Herr Generaloberst"* and was dismissed. The next morning found me on the road from Berlin to Döberitz. At about noon we were forced to take to the ditches when a group of American Mustangs began strafing the road. Now covered with dirt and mud, I climbed back into my ancient Mercedes 170 and finally reached Döberitz airfield, which by then was burning brightly. The main building had been destroyed. Various hangars were burning and now and then there was an explosion; in short it was no place to be searching for an archive, especially since I had no idea where to begin looking for the damned thing. I stayed off to one side, for my experience in the ditch had left me somewhat hesitant. Then a group of transport aircraft approached from the north and swept over the trees at the edge of the airfield. I counted five Ju 52s. They circled the burning airfield and then the first began its approach to land on the crater-filled surface. They avoided the holes skilfully and soon five undamaged mills were sitting at the northern edge of the airfield. Having become curious, I drove toward the aircraft. The doors of the aircraft flew open. I could scarcely believe my eyes; nurses jumped down from the aircraft. Each held a huge wire basket filled with empty baby bottles and wore a somewhat perplexed look. In the meantime I had reached the aircraft and entered into a conversation with the pretty, young women. Only a few of them spoke English, much less German. I learned to my astonishment that they were Norwegian. Then, from inside the aircraft, I heard the sound of infants bawling, many infants. A German NCO, the pilot of one of the Junkers, told me that there were about 120 babies in each aircraft. What I was told next bordered on the unbelievable. In the final days of the war the SS, who believed strongly in the concept of the nordic race, had taken steps to ensure that all children born to Norwegian women with German fathers were taken out of the country, provided that is what the mother desired. Homes had been prepared for these children in Czechoslovakia.

"We've already flown from Oslo to Prague eight times with our five machines. We 'refuel' with milk here in Döberitz and then continue on," observed the pilot, "but as far as I can tell there won't be much milk to be had today."

Then the man in charge of the operation, a *Hauptmann*, came up to me and said, "can you tell me where we can collect the bottles of milk which have been prepared for us as well as the provisions?"

"I'm sorry," I replied, "but I have nothing to do with stores at this base. I just happened to be here and saw you land."

"Yes, well we'd better get going again before the next attack comes," observed the *Hauptmann*. I believe this will be the last 'baby' shipment." Things aren't the best in Norway."

"How many babies do you have on board today?" I asked cautiously.

"There are exactly 498. As well there are 41 nurses, almost all Norwegians, with their children. They either can't or don't want to stay in Norway. They're afraid that they'll be pursued after the war because of their friendliness towards the Germans. Others hope to somehow, somewhere find the fathers of their children."

The officer saluted then called to the nurses and crews to get back aboard the aircraft. Not long afterward the five Ju 52s lifted off from Döberitz' grass strip and soon disappeared behind a dark wall of cloud. Years later I learned the fate of these pitiful creatures, five-and-a-half thousand of them all told. Following the occupation of Czechoslovakia by the Red Army the homes were seized and the children taken to the Soviet Union. Their subsequent fate is unknown to this day. One story alleges that they were murdered on Stalin's order and buried in mass graves. Another tells of secret facilities where the children were raised to be dedicated Soviet soldiers before being expended in various conflicts. When will the Soviets finally open their archives and provide some information on the fate of these unfortunates? I have my doubts. By the way, no organisation has made a concerted effort to unravel the mystery of these children, very strange! Plenty of money is being made available today for similar efforts, multicultural human rights organisations have been founded, financed by generous stipends, but in this case the fate of thousands of human beings has been swept under the rug. The standard excuse: "Oh well, it was only five-and-a-half-thousand German-Norwegian bastards anyway!" In any case, Göring's archive, which I had to thank for this experience, most probably ended up in the bin. In any case I never heard any more about it.

Areopag

The Brockhaus encyclopedia describes it briefly and concisely as follows: "Areopag, the hill in ancient Athens and the tribunal named after it." A teletype message reached my desk: I had been ordered to Gatow to attend a two-day discussion being held by *Reichsmarschall* Göring. It was no secret that the "fat one" and his Luftwaffe had been at odds for some time. It wasn't that I hated him. He had his merits to be sure, but they were all in the past. But in our time, the present, it would have been better if he had taken his hat and left. Not many of us bothered any more to conceal our views over the coming disaster. Now the "fat one," who had long ago fallen from Hitler's graces, was slowly growing uneasy. He sought scapegoats and who best fit the bill? The pilots of course! In his opinion it was they who allowed the enemy to fly deep into our territory. They were cowards and bore the sole responsibility for the ceaseless attacks on the Reich by the Amis and Tommies. It was an assembly of the most highly-decorated men in the Luftwaffe. Were they to avert the coming catastrophe? Were they to be made responsible for the unforgivable, irretrievable mistakes made by the highest levels of command? It almost seemed so. Then he strode in, or perhaps better, waddled in, the man who had once been the most powerful man in Germany after Hitler. Dutifully we stood up when he walked in and waited until he jovially bade us to sit down. Then he let his massive body drop into a much-too-small easy chair.

"Man, he's grown fat," whispered Baumbach, who was sitting on my left.

I, too, couldn't conceal a certain amount of amazement. The last time I had seen him in France one could have said that he was somewhat "overgrown," but now! He gave us no time to catch our breath, rather he came straight to the point.

"Gentlemen," he began, "this is to be no ostracism, rather an Areopag. I ask you, the bravest, to tell me what is wrong with our arm and what in your opinion should be improved. I will not tolerate criticism of my person however, just so that we understand each other."

And then he began. He brazenly shifted the blame onto us for everything that had gone wrong thanks to his failings and those of others. The population couldn't understand why there was no resistance while their cities were wrecked day and night. We were failures. At the same time he refused to listen to any criticism of the decisions made by the Führer, for example to employ the world's first jet fighter, the outstanding Me 262, as a bomber and not as a fighter. Any further discussion was pointless. Then he lost himself in generalities and before we knew it he had hurried out and turned over the discussion to a bomber General. Then a row broke out. An *Oberstleutnant* came right to the point:

"The 'fat one' must go!"

On the one side were the dedicated National-Socialists, on the other those who held a somewhat different view. There was no precise border between the two camps, it shifted as opportunities arose. Soon Baumbach and I returned to our room. Over a bottle of excellent Burgundy, God knows where he got it, we tried to forget what we had just experienced. It was pointless to participate in further discussions. I didn't stay around for the second day of the conference, instead I made my way back to burning Berlin. It was clear to me that in the face of all this misery an end would soon have to be brought to this catastrophe, a catastrophe for which the generations to follow would have to suffer for a long time.

The Road to Nowhere

The Red Army was advancing irresistibly, Eisenhower's cross-channel invasion was making considerable progress. I was ordered to attend a secret meeting in the Air Ministry. An illustrious gathering of Generals, scientists, designers, and leaders of industry had been brought together to stave off what could be staved off. On the table lay a program for a new jet fighter, the people's fighter. It was called the Salamander but is better known as the He 162. The second jet fighter after the Me 262, it was to help put a stop once and for all to the Allied bomber streams, which had become unbearable. It was already five minutes to midnight, but none of us dared express this sentiment. It was as if we were all paralysed by the spectre of the imminent loss of the war. But now fate was to be averted one more time. Built by glider manufacturers with simple means and cheap materials, thousands of the new people's fighters were to bring about a turn in the war. For once the enemy's superiority in the air had been broken there would again be progress on the ground. At least this was the opinion of the assembled panel of experts. I knew that courses were under way at various gliding schools with a view toward preparing young pilots for such a fighter. *Generaloberst* Keller, a Pour le Merite flier of the First World War, was quite bent on throwing himself into the breach, confident that he could turn out more than 2,500 Volksjäger pilots per year from his gliding schools. I was impressed by the program too, although I must say that there was scarcely enough time, given the huge Allied bomber fleets, to put sufficient numbers of aircraft into the air, to say nothing of pilots. The well-known fighter General Galland considered the whole affair to be utter madness and the facts were later to prove him right. Hitler gave his blessing and one of the last armaments programs of the war got under way.

In February I flew in my Bf 108 *Taifun* with Hanna Reitsch to Rechlin, the Luftwaffe testing centre, to evaluate the He 162 and make an assessment of the new fighter. I must admit that I felt rather uneasy, for there had already been several accidents involving the new bird. I had no desire to meet my end in such a way with the end of the war so near at hand. I received my initial briefing on the aircraft from Bär, with whom I had flown against the Americans and British in North Africa. This "people's fighter" certainly appeared to have an impressive performance. It was supposed to be capable of 725 kph at an altitude of 6,000 metres and could easily reach 1,000 kph in a dive. Its armament was nothing to sneeze at either. The new MK 108 cannon was capable of firing sixty 30mm high-explosive shells per minute. One hit was enough to tear a considerable piece out of a Flying Fortress. After only one flight it was obvious to me that this thing was still a long way from maturity. Even an experienced pilot had his hands full just getting the machine back on the ground in one piece, and that without any interference from the enemy. What hope was there for a young, inexperienced glider pilot?

A War Crime?

A call came from the outer office:

"*Herr Oberst*, a *Hauptmann* Noack is here to report to you, he says he's been posted to the Merzhausen gliding camp."

I recalled that he had been recommended to me by the personnel office the week before.

"Let him come in, Frau Werner."

There was a knock on the door and a Luftwaffe *Hauptmann* hobbled in. Walking on crutches, he straightened up and announced:

"*Hauptmann* Noack, transferred from the 3rd Parachute Battalion to the General in Charge of Replacements Luftwaffe."

I stood up and shook his hand. His face had been marked by war. His cheeks were sunken and his fine, blond hair made him look even paler than he was.

"Please sit down. Where did you lose your leg?"

"On Crete, during the capture of Malemes, near the city of Chania," he answered, visibly moved.

"Oh I know Malemes too, the grave of more than a hundred Ju 52s. I was there soon after its capture. We must have almost run into each other, where were you in hospital?"

"I was flown out the same day, first to Athens and later to Berlin."

"Yes, Noack, I have you in mind for the gliding camp at Merzhausen, north of Frankfurt am Main. I desperately need people for my gliding schools. The front is releasing almost nothing, yet the air ministry is screaming for trained glider pilots. The blanket is too short everywhere, and inexperienced men are of no use to me there."

Noack laid his crutches against my desk ceremoniously: "But I only have the 'Silver C' in gliding, is that sufficient?"

"Yes, just barely," I replied, "But the most important thing to me is that the young people are handled properly. I'm not impressed with the gliding instructors there. If you can just make them toe the line I'll be satisfied."

"*Herr Oberst*," continued Hptm. Noack, "I have a request. I would like to bring my wife and two small daughters to join me. They're in great danger in Bremen from the constant air attacks."

I just had time to give my consent before Frau Werner stormed into my office without knocking and called to us:

"Large formations approaching Berlin. They're already near Magdeburg, they'll be here in a few minutes!"

Then the sound of sirens rang out through the halls. Noack and I made our way to the well-equipped air raid shelter in the basement of the air ministry. We had scarcely arrived when heavy steel doors slammed shut behind us. When I looked around I found that we were part of a select circle. I saw *Feldmarschall* Milch, of whom Göring had recently said: "I decide who's a Jew in my ministry!" *Generaloberst* Loerzer, my CO, was also there. There were Generals everywhere one looked. I felt puny and insignificant among so many prominent figures. Soon we heard the first exploding bombs, they weren't far away. The room heaved as if on the open sea. The Amis appeared to have brought along especially heavy bombs that day. Hptm. Noack on his crutches became quite still. I had just finished saying that it would all be over soon when there was a tremendous crash. A hissing, grey cloud of dust spewed into the shelter room through the tiniest cracks. The light began to flicker and then went out for a while. There reigned a paralysing, yes even eerie silence.

When the light came back on *Generaloberst* Loerzer turned to me and said, "I bet you'd feel better at the front than in this miserable cellar."

"I believe you're right, *Herr Generaloberst*," I replied, "I'd gladly be back with my unit but only recently you turned down my transfer."

"Well, what isn't yet, can still be," observed the affable man, clapping me on the shoulder.

Then there was another shock and we were almost knocked out of our socks. A blast wave ripped one of the steel doors from its hinges. Noack and I were thrown against a wall. The blast caught the Generals too. There had obviously been a hit on the RLM. At first there was deathly silence, then someone pulled himself together and called into the large room:

"The gentlemen are requested to hand in their wardrobes for cleaning on the first floor."

There was an outburst of laughter which broke the tension, then the sirens sounded the all-clear. The damage was obvious when we went upstairs. A 1,000kg bomb had crashed through the roof and all the floors. It had ended up in the cellar right beside the air-raid shelter, a dud. If it had gone off we'd all have been done for. This realisation made me weak at the knees. I took Noack by the hand and we staggered upstairs. But my office had vanished! All that was left of my place of work was a huge hole. Frau Werner stood beside me, speechless.

"I think we can all go home. Tomorrow is another day," I told my staff. "Noack, you should drive to Bremen as quickly as you can. Pick up your family and get them to Merzhausen as quickly as you can. report to me from there."

Noack thanked me profusely, then he was on his crutches and gone. These were the last words I was able to exchange with this brave man. His life took a very different turn after that, as B. Kunze described in his book *und vergib ihnen nicht, oh Herr!*:

Gerd Noack had his hands full in Merzhausen. He had scant opportunity for glider flying, and the paper war kept him so busy that he had little time for his wife and his two- and three-year-old daughters. He saw them only in the evening and in the morning at breakfast. It was September 26, 1944, a beautiful autumn day, the gliding program was in full swing. A steady stream of gliders were launched into the air by the cable winch, before landing a few minutes later on the grass strip. An air-raid advisory had been issued. A penetration by strong American air forces was expected. Noack immediately cancelled all flying activities, which was a common occurrence in those days. The young glider pilots took cover and by the time the first condensation trails became visible in the sky everyone was in the slit trenches except the crew of the quadruple flak stationed at the airfield perimeter. Noack was worried about his wife and his two daughters. They had left early for the Taunus meadows in order to pick a bouquet for papa and were supposed to return at about noon. In the sky countless formations of Flying Fortresses moved east, escorted by Thunderbolts and Lightnings. The gun crew's spotting team reported:

"Enemy bearing 105 degrees, staggered at various altitudes between 4,000 and 6,000 metres."

Hptm. Noack, who was sitting in the trenches with the others, felt sure that the raiders would pass them by. Then he saw his small family at the airfield perimeter, waving cheerfully, their arms laden with flowers. Suddenly a Thunderbolt approached at low level. The pilot saw Noack's wife and children and opened fire. All three were riddled with bullets and killed. At the same time the quadruple flak on the airfield perimeter opened fire. It hit the American fighter, forcing it to crash-land a few kilometres beyond the airfield. Hptm. Noack, half insane over the deaths of his wife and children, jumped into the nearest Kübelwagen and raced to the scene of the forced-landing. There he found the American pilot, who had climbed out of his aircraft unhurt, and shot him dead on the spot. The man was loaded onto a truck and taken to the cemetery, where he was buried. So far, so bad! The war ended, Gerd Noack remained in Merzhausen and began studying at Frankfurt University. It was now 1946. By chance a US Army team searching for fallen American soldiers came upon the grave of the Thunderbolt pilot in Merzhausen. One of the residents of the village pointed out the unsuspecting ex-*Hauptmann* to the Americans in exchange for ten cigarettes. A few hours later Gerd Noack was arrested on his return from Frankfurt and was taken to Landsberg. Only weeks later an American court sentenced him to death by hanging for war crimes. He received the familiar red clothing of the condemned and waited for his end. Months passed. One day he seized an opportunity to escape by hiding in a large garbage container. On a grey November afternoon he was transported out of Landsberg fortress prison along with the other garbage containers. He was free! That night local farmers helped him out of his "red death shirt" and secreted him out of the area. Noack wanted to reach the Russian-occupied zone as quickly as possible. He thought he would be safe there with his parents. But his disability made travel difficult. The Americans had taken away his prosthesis in Landsberg, and without it walking was all the more difficult. Nevertheless he succeeded in reaching the border between the two zones. The first snow had fallen, making the going difficult in the mountains. He had already crossed the green zone and thought himself safe, when he was stopped by a West German customs official.

"Stop, or I'll shoot!" shouted the man in the green uniform. The customs man came up to Noack: "What are you doing here, don't you know that this is the zone border?"

"Dear man," Noack pleaded to the border guard, "I have just escaped from the Americans in Landsberg prison. Please let me cross over to the Russian zone to my parents."

But the German official refused. Noack wasn't about to let himself be stopped now. As he prepared to slide down the snow-covered slope the West German fired. Gerd Noack was hit in the thigh. The customs agent pulled the seriously-wounded man back onto the American side and alerted the nearest police outpost. Noack was taken to a hospital and when he was well enough to travel was transported back to Landsberg prison. Three days later *Hauptmann* Noack was strapped to a stretcher and hung on the gallows!

I don't know what I should say about the affair. Where does the law end? Where does mercy begin? How would you have dealt with that vile and cowardly American pilot if he had just taken your loved ones, your defenceless wife and children, from you just for his own amusement?

The Oder Front Ablaze

Finally I was released from my duties behind my desk. I had proposed a new method of attacking Soviet tank formations by night. *General-oberst* Loerzer approved my request for a return to front-line duties following a practical demonstration at a gliding field near Berlin. The operation has gone into the history books under the name *Sonderkommando Falke III*. The Ivans were already in Pomerania and were moving fast towards the Elbe and Berlin. There wasn't much time left to halt their advance. Standard Bücker 181 training aircraft, hundreds of which were sitting about uselessly at the flying schools, were converted to carry

Panzerfaust rocket-launchers. Four of these weapons were installed beneath each wing. I carried out the first test with the new weapon on a captured T 34 tank which had been parked at the edge of the airfield. I scored four direct hits on the very first pass, which I made from a height of 20 metres. The first *Staffel* was formed as a night harassment *Gruppe* a few days later. A few days later a desperate action by this very unit enabled thousands of refugees from the east, women and children, to cross the Oder in safety and thus escape the Soviets. But the unit's losses were heavy. Of the 121 aircraft which took part in the operation only 39 returned, most of them damaged. The Ivans however lost more than 200 tanks and other vehicles that night. I was only permitted to fly one night sortie. I returned with fourteen bullet holes in my aircraft, inflicted by infantry fire, but I believe that I destroyed at least two T 34 tanks. However what was that in the face of such overwhelming numerical superiority? I had scarcely begun to reaccustom myself to life at the front when Loerzer summoned me back to the RLM.

Shadows over Karinhall

In the afternoon I received a telephone call. On the line was *Major* Hering of the Luftwaffe personnel department.

"The Reichsmarschall would like to speak with you this evening. Report to Guardhouse I at the main entrance to the Karinhall at 2000."

"Do you know what it's about?" I asked back.

The *Major* said, "I can't tell you, but it seems to be urgent and top secret as well."

Then he hung up. I got ready and set out for Karinhall in plenty of time, for there was the nothing the "fat one" hated as much as tardiness. I passed through Berlin's northern suburbs without any problems. Some distance from Schorfheide, however, I was stopped. Military police had barricaded the road. One of them said to me, "See that you get out of the area quickly, *Herr Oberstleutnant*, we have advance warning that enemy bombers are approaching Berlin."

My papers and uniform got me through quickly. There were additional checks at the main gate to the Karinhall. They took my paybook and went away to speak with God knows whom on the telephone, but then the "Gordian knot" was loosened. Someone was coming to pick me up in a car. A VW Kübel came roaring up to me from out of the pine forest.

A *Hauptmann* Börner introduced himself and said, "They're already waiting for you."

"But it's only 1900," I replied, "I was ordered to be here at 2000."

We arrived at the main house and I was led into a large, dimly-lit room where *Generaloberst* Loerzer was waiting.

"Where have you been Dickfeld?" The *Reichsmarschall* is getting impatient."

179

"*Herr Generaloberst*, I was instructed to be here at 2000," I replied. Looking at my watch, I continued, "it's now exactly 1915."

"Yes, yes, but there's an air raid alert and the *Reichsmarschall* wants to discuss something with you before the attack."

The big folding doors opened and in HE came, dressed completely in dove blue. He gave me his rather clammy hand, on which there were many rings, and asked us to sit.

"Have you flown the He 162?" he asked.

"Yes, *Herr Reichsmarschall*," I replied, "Bär checked me out on the aircraft at Rechlin."

"And how does the bird fly?"

"If I'm to be honest, *Herr Reichsmarschall*, I would have to say that it does not come up to expectations."

My response touched a sore spot. Göring looked as if he was about to blow up but he calmed himself after remaining silent for some time. Loerzer looked at me disapprovingly and then the "fat one" said,

"How can it be that such a celebrated aircraft is torn apart in this way by my front-line officers?"

"It's because of the incomplete development of the aircraft, the materials used in its construction, and the way the program is being rushed through, *Herr Reichsmarschall*, at least that's my impression."

Göring opened his desk drawer and pulled out a huge cigar box. On the lid I read: "*Reichsmarschall* Brand." Then he opened the monster and invited me to help myself. I wasn't eager to comply, being a non-smoker, but I wasn't sure if I should refuse.

Göring apparently noticed my discomfort however and said, "You must be a non-smoker."

"Yes, *Herr Reichsmarschall*, I have never smoked in my life, I have no idea how to go about it."

Then he turned to Loerzer and observed: "He wants to be a hero but he can't smoke. One can't be a man if he doesn't smoke, don't you agree Bruno?"

The latter nodded reflectively. At this I summoned up my courage and said, "There are other ways of proving my manhood besides smoking cigars."

This remark seemed to catch Göring off guard. At that moment the air raid alarm was sounded in Karinhall and he suddenly seemed to be in a hurry. He got up from his chair and as he left he said to Loerzer,

"You can continue this with Dickfeld later."

Before I knew what was happening Göring had disappeared through the folding doors. I still didn't know what the whole affair was about.

Loerzer turned to *Hauptmann* Börner: "Go to the common air raid shelter with Dickfeld. We'll meet again after the all-clear has been sounded."

Then he, too, disappeared as if the earth had swallowed him up.

"The *Reichsmarschall* has a private air raid shelter for himself, his wife and daughter, and his closest friends," said Börner. "We're supposed to go to the room for personnel but I know something better. We'll stay here until everyone has taken cover and then when the air has cleared I'll show you something, agreed?"

Outside in the hallway there was the sound of running feet, everyone was rushing to the air raid shelters. We remained seated for a while, then Börner led me down the stairs into the cellar. We walked down several long passageways until we came to a steel door. Börner unlocked it and switched on the lights. To my amazement I found myself in a large room which consisted of nothing but a huge miniature railroad, with dozens of miniature trains, railway cars, tunnels, stations, and so on. I was speechless.

Börner broke the silence: "So, now we play trains for a while."

He installed himself in a raised seat which was equipped with a huge control panel and in no time the first locomotive had pulled out of a train shed and onto the installation. He started up more trains and soon the whole room was buzzing and humming. Last of all he carefully steered a brand-new train into the system. Outside Berlin's anti-aircraft guns were pounding away. At that very moment men, women, and children were dying while we sat in the Karinhall cellar playing with trains, far removed from reality.

Börner said to me, "When the all-clear is sounded we'll shut the whole thing off, leave it standing, and vamoose back upstairs."

We'd been playing for some time when an air force guard came in and called to Börner: "*Herr Hauptmann* I've been looking for you, the *Reichsmarschall* wants you at once. He's already rather upset!"

Börner jumped up as if he'd been bitten by a tarantula and switched off the system. Then the two of us hurried upstairs, passing through a fitness room which was packed with every imaginable kind of training equipment. I arrived in the conference room just as Loerzer walked in.

"It must be hot in Berlin," he said, "there's almost 300 bombers this time. You'd better stay here for the night. It would be difficult getting through and we can continue our discussion in peace. The *Reichsmarschall* won't be coming though. We'll see him again in the morning."

Loerzer sat down. The two of us were alone. Then he began speaking again.

"You annoyed the *Reichsmarschall* greatly with your criticism of the He 162, for he has received only positive reports until now. Nevertheless he would like you to form a *Geschwader* with this fighter as quickly as possible. Ihlefeld already has orders to equip JG 1 with it. Even if you don't agree with this bird you should bear in mind that the machine's aggravating shortcomings are being rectified at the production level. Hanna Reitsch has thrown herself mightily into the effort."

"*Herr Generaloberst*," I began, "I am aware that this is a great honour, but I am thinking of the pilots who will have to take this 'projectile' into the air, I'm thinking of the maintenance personnel who have no sort of training on the machine, I'm thinking of the vastly superior enemy who already commands our skies to such an extent that it's almost impossible for us to get into the air at all. It will be very, very difficult to achieve ad hoc success, to say nothing of the scant amount of time available to me. Nevertheless I am ready to follow the wishes and orders of the *Reichsmarschall*."

Visibly relieved, Loerzer poured two glasses of French cognac. We clinked glasses and he said to me, "I expected nothing less of you Dickfeld. Now then, *Hals und Beinbruch*. We'll discuss the details tomorrow morning."

Hauptmann Börner came in and informed Loerzer that Göring wished to see him. I was dismissed. I had no thought of spending the night there, who knew how things looked at home after the attack? On the return trip I drove through the inferno of burning Berlin. On arriving home I breathed a sigh of relief; my house was undamaged and my family was safe in the air raid shelter.

". . . .Oh God, Forgive Them Not"

Winter had arrived in Berlin. The streets of the battered city were ice-covered and treacherous. I was sitting at my desk in the Air Ministry when Frau Werner put through a call to me. The line was poor but I recognized the voice of my mother. She was calling from Breslau and sounded very agitated:

"Son, get us out of here before it's too late! The Red Army is at the gates of our city. This evening Hitler declared Breslau a fortress! We must all stay inside and no one is allowed to leave. Do you know what that means for us, for more than 100,000 women and children, if the red hordes capture the city?" I didn't know what to say at first, but I composed myself immediately and shouted as loudly as I could:

"Mama I'll come right away, I'll get you out. Don't leave your apartment until I get there."

Dismayed, I crashed down the receiver and went into the outer office.

"Frau Werner, which vehicle do we have available at the moment? I must get to Breslau right away!"

"But *Herr Oberst*," she replied, that's more than 400 kilometres and that in the ice and snow and over the heavily damaged autobahn! How are you going to make it?"

"I don't care, I've got to save my relatives before the Ivans come, no matter what the cost."

Afterwards I hurried down the corridor to my chief's office. I rushed past his indignant secretary, straight into the "holy of holies." I knocked on the door and seconds later was standing in front of his desk. Loerzer looked up at me in amazement.

"*Herr Generaloberst*," I said excitedly, "my mother just called me from Breslau. Tonight the Führer declared the city a fortress, no one else is allowed in or out. I must save her before the approaching red hordes break in!"

"First calm yourself," said my warm-hearted superior, "it's clear that you must try something."

"*Herr Generaloberst*, I have an Opel *Kapitän* ready to go. Might I be allowed to take it and a few days leave as well?"

"Agreed," said Loerzer. I could have hugged him. "But don't let anything happen to you, I still need you!"

I vacated his office so quickly that I heard his last words from a distance. I even forgot to salute. Everything after that is a blur. I raced down to the motor pool. A *Feldwebel* informed me that the Kapitän was in the garage being converted to burn wood gas.

"No wood gas," I said angrily, "I need high test fuel, as much as it will hold. Man, I have to get to Breslau straight away."

The *Feldwebel* shook his head in disbelief: "To Breslau? It was closed this evening. And the autobahn, it's had it, and then there's the ice and snow."

I looked straight at the man; he obviously felt I was insane.

"And high-test fuel is only available on orders from on high," he added.

I'd rather not say how I managed to organise my "high-test," my car, and a small trailer, I might still end up behind bars. In any case I left Berlin at 0400, direction Cottbus and Breslau. Visibility on the autobahn was virtually zero, especially with the car's shielded headlights. I passed military columns, trucks, tanks, horse-drawn artillery, and much more in the blowing snow. I drove by Cottbus at about 7 o'clock. It had grown lighter by then, outside it was very cold. It was a good thing I had brought enough fuel in the trailer to get me there and back, for there would probably be nowhere to get gas in Breslau. Beyond Liegnitz I was stopped by military police.

"Do you have authorization to drive to Breslau?" asked a well-bundled-up *Feldwebel*.

"Of course I do," I said to the man and passed him the orders I had cut myself. He saluted and I raced onward. The autobahn was full of holes, but passable. I was now only 18 kilometres from the entrance to Breslau. Once again I was stopped and checked, this time by the SS. The same procedure followed and then I got on my way again. Then I was stopped again. I came up to an anti-tank barricade manned by infantry. A *Hauptmann* came toward me.

"You can't go any farther here, you'll have to turn around," he called while still some distance away. But the man didn't know me. I climbed out and walked up to him:

"Come to attention and take your hands out of your pockets before you speak to me! Who are you anyway," I growled at him.

At this the man pulled himself together and reported.

"Now open the barrier and let me pass before I take an even greater interest in you!" I roared.

And lo and behold a miracle happened. He called to his men to open the heavy log gate and I drove into Breslau, past burning houses and down shattered streets, straight to my mother's house. She was waiting on already-packed suitcases and threw her arms around my neck.

"Son I can't believe you made it!" were her first words. "But we have to go and get your sister Ruth and her children as well as her in-laws, they're waiting for you too!"

In the meantime another snowstorm had begun. One could barely see the hand in front of one's face and the thermometer had fallen to minus 21 degrees Celsius. It took some time for me to collect all my passengers and stow the luggage. Just as we were about to climb in, heavy Soviet artillery fire began, forcing us to retreat to the cellar. Powerful explosions nearby caused the house above us to shudder. It was after midnight when the firing finally abated. It would have been madness to set out then, so we waited until dawn. Luckily the car and trailer were undamaged. The Opel sagged to its knees under the heavy load; there were, after all, seven of us. We drove through the burning city and at about 9 o'clock arrived at the anti-tank barricade. To make matters worse the forces manning the position now also included some "golden pheasants." First we were stopped by a local Nazi party leader.

"You can't get through here," the fat sack said at my window. "Orders from the *Gauleiter*. Breslau is a fortress and you can only get through with the permission of *Gauleiter* Hanke."

I was seized by a towering rage. "Can you get in touch with your *Gauleiter*?" I screamed at the man. Then I climbed out and walked with him into an earth bunker next to the barricade. The party man cranked the field telephone for some time and, finally, I in fact ended up speaking to the most powerful man in Breslau at that time. I heard a dry voice at the other end of the line:

"Hanke here. With whom am I speaking?"

"This is *Oberst* Dickfeld, a wearer of the Knight's Cross with Oak Leaves in the Luftwaffe. I would like to ask you to instruct your people to let me and my relatives pass, I have to be back at the Air Ministry in Berlin this evening, *Feldmarschall* Göring is expecting me."

To be sure I was lying shamelessly to the man, but what difference did it make in those days?

"Very well, put the *Ortsgruppenleiter* back on the phone," I heard him say.

Then I walked back to my car. The infantry didn't make a fuss this time and the barrier opened for me for the second, and I hoped last, time. Meanwhile the snowstorm had begun again and I skidded as much as I drove in the direction of Berlin. To my dismay I realised that the sides of the road were littered with hundreds of bodies, women, old men, and children, even babies still in their carriages. Apparently they had perished the previous night while trying to escape from the "glorious" Red Army. Then I saw a hand waving from the snow-filled ditch on my left and I stopped the car. I went over and pulled a young mother up out of the ditch. There was a baby in her arms. It was so slippery and she was so weak, that I had to drag her across the icy road. We lifted both of them into the car and not a moment too soon, for immediately afterward the autobahn was blocked by an SS Tiger unit coming the other way. We were unable to move forward or backward. The tanks moved into position and a few minutes later began firing. We were stuck in the middle of a battle. A *Leutnant* came running over to us and led us to shelter inside an armoured personnel carrier. The hatch slammed shut and we were sitting in darkness. Outside it was an inferno. All around us the batteries fired salvo after salvo and now and then we heard shells exploding, obviously from Russian guns. The children screamed and I have to admit that I wasn't feeling very well myself. Thank God I couldn't see the others' faces. This all went on for about 30 minutes, then the hatch opened again. The *Leutnant* acted as if nothing had happened and brought us back out into the light of day. Curiously my Opel was undamaged, although a number of shell fragments had struck the trailer. The SS unit drove on in the direction of Breslau and we were able to resume our journey. Finally, eight hours later, we arrived home safe and sound. And what of the mother with the child? She and her son stayed with us for several weeks, then she met her fate in the terrible events of the last days of the war.

The End

The formation of the still nameless fighter *Geschwader* was to present me with considerable difficulties at the outset. Arriving at Merseberg I found a tossed-together collection of convalescent pilots, scarcely fit for operational flying and with no knowledge whatsoever of the new *Volksjäger*, and ground personnel who possessed not the faintest glimmer about the He 162. It was exactly as I had imagined it would be. The unit's aircraft complement: zero! They tried to pacify me by telling me that they'd be coming from Vienna in a few days. The Americans and British flew overhead day and night, completely unhindered, strafing and bombing everything they saw. In their search for targets they even attacked farmers behind their ploughs, it was outright murder. In recent days the Americans had even stooped to shooting bailed-out German pilots as they hung helpless beneath their parachutes. I was forced to stand by powerlessly before the people to whom I had promised an opportunity to soon strike back at the enemy. After days of waiting the first *Salamanders* arrived, five in all. For a unit whose authorised strength was normally 120 it was pitiful, no laughable. One of the machines was written off in a landing accident, reducing our strength to four. Nothing happened to the pilot, however. Thank God! I was going to need him! Seven more of the precious birds landed two days later. We were now almost up to *Staffel* strength but still lacked ammunition, fuel, and so on. It seemed to take forever to assemble everything we needed, but finally we were ready to begin operations with a total of nine *Salamanders*. On closer examination it was found that two further He 162s were unfit to fly. The glue on the leading edge of the wings was letting go, which could have led to very unpleasant consequences in flight. Sabotage or defective glue? That was the question. I approached the first mission with a great deal of trepidation. Luckily bad weather kept us on the ground for the first few days, time for the ground personnel to become familiar with their new charges. It was still dark when I received a phone call from Berlin. It was *Generaloberst* Loerzer:

"Dickfeld, can you hear me?"

"Very well, *Herr Generaloberst*," I replied.

"How far have you got with the formation of your unit; when will you finally be ready for operations?"

I was dumbstruck. The unit was still in the midst of formation, there could be no talk of operational readiness.

"*Herr Generaloberst*, after a great deal of effort I have assembled a total of nine *Salamanders* and even on these the glue in the wings is slowly letting go. How are we to fly a mission then? If all goes well and the weather cooperates, perhaps in one or two days."

Then there was a click on the line. Loerzer was gone and I was left with all my worries.

The next morning brought crystal clear weather. I sauntered about the machines as dawn was breaking. Hopefully the Amis wouldn't destroy our precious aircraft before the first air engagement. I was looking forward to taking the He 162 into action if the opportunity arose. I summoned Lt. Bartz, who was to be my wingman.

"Bartz, the Amis will be coming today, as certain as the amen in the church. How many flights have you made in the He 162?"

"A total of seven, one of them a crash-landing at Vienna-Schwechat on account of the weak undercarriage," he said, visibly startled.

"You've no combat experience, but I'd like you to accompany me today, agreed?"

I could see that he was afraid, but each of us had to take the plunge sometime. (If only he'd known how unwell I felt at that moment!)

Hesitantly he replied, "*Jawohl, Herr Oberstleutnant.*"

That was all he said; he looked right past me. What must he have been thinking? I could have chosen someone else, but I had a feeling that the man had potential. I had no intention of taking the other operational machines with me, first I wanted to see for myself how the new bird performed. There would be plenty to do for those left behind, I was certain of that! By now it was 9 o'clock. The local warning service reported enemy units approaching central Germany. Bartz and I ran to our machines. It was a good thing that the Heinkels were armed with the new MG 151 cannon. They had an enormous rate of fire, which should allow us to land a few on the enemy's nose. Unfortunately the He 162's endurance, barely 30 minutes flying time, was damned limited.

"Scramble!"

The dreaded red flare hissed over the field. There were butterflies in my stomach and my knees shook against the control column as we taxied out. Very, very carefully I pushed the throttle lever forward so as not to wreck the turbine on takeoff. The *Volksjäger* began to move. This bird was damned lame on the ground! But there was no time for further thought. After what seemed like an eternity I was able to lift off, quite close to the end of the runway. Bartz managed to get off the ground safely as well; he maintained position skilfully off my left wingtip. The Amis seemed to be under way earlier than was their habit. Then our command post checked in:

"Enemy formations approaching the Hannover-Braunschweig area."

I turned sharply toward the north. We reached 5,000 metres quickly. I wanted to avoid being surprised by American fighters so I clamped the oxygen mask over my face and continued climbing. Condensation trails began forming at 5,500 metres and at 7,000 metres we were above the leading bomber formations.

"Do you see fighters anywhere?" I asked Bartz.

Instead of a reply, tracer flashed past my cockpit. Behind me was a fat Thunderbolt. I was looking right into its guns and at that instant I was able to calculate when its next burst would end my life. Just as I had done many times before, I hauled my aircraft into a climbing right turn. I rolled my Heinkel onto its back, pulled through, and ended up sitting right behind the American fighter doing more than 800 kph. My cannon made a fat "plop" as I cocked the guns. I don't think the enemy pilot saw me at all. I closed in quickly: 300 metres, 200 metres, 100 metres, 50 metres. The P-47 seemed near enough to touch. I bounced around in his propwash, the white stars on his wings filled my gunsight. I pressed the triggers and a stream of 20mm shells left my guns. For three seconds tracer poured into the Ami. Pieces flew off and banged against my fuselage. First he began to smoke, then flames spurted from his engine. More pieces struck my wings and then the P-47 was blown to pieces in a huge ball of fire.

The pilot failed to get out, I saw his body slumped over in the cockpit. A piece of white parachute cloth tumbled earthward beneath the blazing inferno. I turned away. Where was Bartz? I couldn't worry about him while the dogfight was under way. I called to him but received no answer. The frequency was jammed with the chatter of other units. Damn! I hoped he hadn't been shot down. With only minutes of fuel left I had to head home. When I approached the airfield I saw Bartz' machine lying at the edge of the runway, thank God! It looked to be in pretty bad shape though, Bartz had probably come to grief while landing. As I turned final my machine began drifting sharply to the right. I was unable to hold it on course and touched down hard on the grass surface. There was a rending and tearing sound. The landing gear sheared off and the next thing I knew I was sitting in a heap of wire, metal, and plywood, all that was left of my Heinkel. How I managed to escape unhurt is still a mystery to me. Bartz had suffered the same fate. His undercarriage had failed too, but he managed to make it to the edge of the airfield with his damaged aircraft. The two of us were in the air again the next day and Bartz, the raw newcomer, was able to shoot down a Thunderbolt. However this was the beginning of the end for the fighter unit in which so much hope had been placed. The Americans were already on the Rhine. Spitfires, Lightnings, Thunderbolts, and other aircraft kept a constant watch over our airfield and we were unable to take off. They would have jumped us immediately and with their speed advantage in the dive we wouldn't have stood a chance. Our aircraft were simply too slow during takeoff and landing and it seemed pointless to fly under these circumstances. Curiously Loerzer didn't call again. Had he realised that we were in our death throes?

Shouldn't I have been compelled to recognise, in view of the situation, that the war had been lost long ago, shouldn't I have realised then that it was senseless to prolong the war even by an hour through our missions? I often asked myself that question in those days. But I couldn't go back. Not for myself and not for my men. I was too filled with hate, with rage, with a feeling of powerlessness, too filled with the desire and the hope for revenge!

Orders arrived that all serviceable machines were to be flown, if possible, to Marienehe. At dawn I took off for the flight to the Baltic with the remaining five machines. The airfield had been carpet-bombed a few minutes before our arrival and it was with great difficulty that we landed our Heinkels safely between the burning hangars and aircraft, past fresh bomb craters. All went well except that Lt. Bartz' aircraft collapsed after the turbine was shut down, probably on account of the glue. He really had bad luck, poor fellow! After the surrender he succeeded in escaping to neutral Sweden. A few weeks later he and thousands of other German soldiers were handed over to the Soviets by the Swedes contrary to the Geneva Convention. Together with tens of thousands of other German prisoners of war, Bartz was starved and killed in Siberia. I think of him often.

Looking back, I realise now that the production of thousands of *Volksjäger* fighters would have been madness, the war simply could not have been won. It is seldom mentioned today, but this actually shortened the suffering, especially of our sorely-tried civilian population. Perhaps we were even spared a German Hiroshima. The American president Truman voiced such a notion. Such thoughts were beyond us. We had survived, untouched by the perversion of the apocalypse.

Bitter Laurels

The Soviets were at the gates of Berlin. They had already crossed the Oder near Frankfurt. The bridgehead, defended by old men and children, had fallen to elite Soviet troops. The Hitler Youth and the *Volkssturm* were forced to pay a high price. A few of them escaped with their lives to go into Soviet captivity, where they then died in misery. All around me in the RLM the devil was loose. The building was being prepared for a fight, everyone with a head and at least one hand was assigned a role in the defence. Fate had something special in mind for me, however. I was to be allowed to leave Berlin with my people for Lübeck, but I doubted that we'd get through. Rumours swirled about the RLM like angry hornets: the Soviets had already closed the ring around Berlin and no one could get out. Nevertheless, during the night I prepared five vehicles for a breakout. Our direction was clear, it had to be north. If the Ivans had closed the ring there too, we would simply look for their weakest spot and drive through. We stowed weapons, including machine-guns and *Panzer-faust* anti-tank weapons, and a large quantity of ammunition in the vehicles. On our route lay Karinhall and Schorfheide. I knew my way around there and the devil would have to have a hand in it if our convoy didn't get through there. Surely the Ivans couldn't have sealed off the area that tightly yet. It was about four in the morning when we left the RLM parking area. We quickly skirted various anti-tank obstacles and reached the northern edge of Berlin. There were problems with the SS in Bernau. A keen, young *SS-Scharführer* informed us that *Reichsführer* Himmler had issued a general ban: no one else was to leave Berlin, everyone was to stand ready to take part in the defence of the Reich capital. They had no idea who I was. I gave the man in charge such a hard time that he finally gave up and let us continue on our way. Göring's personal order (bearing his real signature), which he had given me for just such a situation, had its effect. The order stated that "*Sonderkommando Falke III*" under the command of *Oberst* Dickfeld had orders to break through to Lübeck by the shortest possible route, by force if necessary, in order to carry out a secret command matter. We must have made a martial impression in our vehicles, especially since my people were waving around machine-guns and rocket launchers. At about ten o'clock we reached the southern edge of the Schorfheide, a huge wooded area outside Berlin. Not far away was the entrance to Karinhall, Görings beloved hunting lodge. I preferred to avoid turning up there again, especially since the master had probably long since headed for the hills and it was possible that some left-behind General might find a special "use" for us. We had been driving down a tree-lined forest road for about ten minutes when we were suddenly stopped by a Tiger tank. The hatch opened and the head of a young *Leutnant* appeared:

"You can't go any farther here, the Ivans are only 100 metres ahead of us, it appears to be a patrol. We're just about to take care of them. If you can wait a few minutes we'll have done them in. Then you'll have a free road. Where are you going? To Lübeck? You'll never make it!"

But before I could reply the hatch slammed shut again and the Tiger began to move, its tracks rattling loudly. Soon afterward we heard bursts of fire, then all was quiet. We waited a while and followed the tank tracks. Along the road we found the bodies of seven dead Russians, but there was no sign of the Tiger. We felt our way along slowly and by about twelve we had reached the northern edge of the Schorfheide. When we emerged from the forest we were stopped by members of the *Volkssturm*.

One of them asked: "Have you seen any Ivans? There should be eight of them. We surrounded them but they escaped."

"You can rest easy, seven of them are lying dead in the forest, not 300 metres from here, you can collect them," I answered.

They gave no sign of wanting to go and check. I had no time to get angry with them; we had to keep moving and it was exactly 150 kilometres to Lübeck. I thought we should be able to make it by evening if we weren't chopped up into little pieces by American fighters. But our progress was slowed by numerous columns of refugees and it was about midnight when we finally arrived in the relatively undamaged Hanseatic city. Now we parted ways. My co-workers, well equipped with discharge papers, set out on difficult journeys to their home towns, most of which wad been completely destroyed and occupied by the enemy. Fate had been more than kind to me. My BMW and I found temporary shelter with a member of the Swedish embassy. We knew each other from Berlin, where I had often been his guest and he mine. In the basement of the old villa on Travemünder Allee they had set up a bed for me and laid out civilian clothes. My uniform went into the furnace. I had no idea that military clothing could burn so well. A few days later a Wehrmacht Kübelwagen rolled into the front yard. A man climbed out. I couldn't believe my eyes: it was Heinrich Himmler, the most eagerly sought-after "top Nazi." I had no idea what Himmler and he spoke about on the floor above me, but I did know that the British were at the gates of Lübeck and that things were likely to get hot for the *Reichsführer* when they arrived. After a long discussion he left the embassy as unobtrusively as he had arrived. Only hours later he took his own life with a cyanide capsule.

I was now the official embassy driver, and I delivered gift parcels to the port of Lübeck day and night in my BMW. Tied up there were two concentration camp ships, filled with Norwegians and Danes, which the English were supposed to allow to sail to unoccupied Flensburg prior to the occupation of Lübeck. I can still see the big ships leaving the harbour. Only a few hours later they were attacked and sunk by British bombers. After years in the camps, more than 2,000 people died only days away from their liberation. The fateful order was given by an English Air Marshall infamously known by the name "Bomber Harris."

Lübeck was captured by the English with little fighting. They drove up to the Swedish embassy and asked for an interpreter. I was moving up minute by minute: now I was an interpreter! What an irony of fate! Now I had become the fox and the Tommies the geese! They sealed off Travemünder Allee with a tank in order to capture the German troops fleeing into Lübeck in their thousands before the Red Army, hoping to escape capture. I stood beside a Sergeant, who together with his soldiers took the German soldiers prisoner and disarmed them. I could understand that, but I was dismayed by what happened next. In no time at all they had "relieved" every prisoner of his possessions. Rings, watches, neck chains, money, it all went into a steel helmet. When it was full they dumped it into their tank and started all over again. I lost a great deal of respect for the British notion of fairness. I managed to enlist the aid of a German civilian. I sent him to meet the incoming German troops and warn them of activities of the English "highwaymen." I also had him warn female Wehrmacht auxiliaries to take to the woods before reaching our checkpoint, perhaps sparing them an unpleasant fate.

I simply couldn't and wouldn't abuse the hospitality of my host any longer, especially as I was worried about my family in the Soviet-occupied zone. So we parted ways. I steered my BMW, with Swedish markings, sufficient fuel and packed with gift parcels, into an unknown adventure. I was going to attempt to find my way home across the zones occupied by the Tommies, the Amis, and the Ivans. I carefully stowed my 7.65mm pistol, loaded and cocked, just within reach beneath the steering wheel housing. Who could say whether I might not need it again at some point! Then it was time for me to leave Lübeck. I drove through completely-wrecked Hamburg in the direction of Lauenburg. I had to cross the Elbe, come what may. But all of the bridges I was familiar with had been blown. After some time I saw before me a pontoon bridge which had been erected by the Tommies. A large English convoy was just crossing the broad river. Summoning my courage, I joined the convoy and crossed over to the other side unmolested. On the way I was checked repeatedly by the English, but my Swedish passport seemed to be in order and I got as far as just outside Merseburg. There the first Americans were sitting in the ditches; I came to a checkpoint!

"Stop!" Their first question was: "where are you coming from?"

I passed my papers through the window, but the Sergeant was suspicious. I appeared suspect to him, dressed as I was in my modern civilian clothes, pipe in mouth.

"Follow me," said the driver of a jeep.

We roared into Merseburg at high speed and then turned into a schoolyard. I had to park my BMW and we went up the stairs into an American military office. The sergeant pushed me through a doorway. Inside there was a throng of officers and secretaries. He closed the door behind me and waited outside. I had no idea what I was supposed to do there. Nobody seemed to be concerned about me. There was a constant flow of traffic from one office to another and so I decided to follow one of the secretaries. After following her through five rooms I saw my chance to make off and go down another set of stairs. My car was still in the courtyard waiting bravely for its master. And so I left lovely Merseburg unmolested, direction: the Soviet zone of occupation. I made good time as far as Rochlitz on the Mulde but that was it. There were Americans on the sole intact bridge and they stopped me.

"Do you have a permit to leave the American zone?" asked a young GI.

"No Sir," I answered brazenly, "where can I get one?"

"Go back to the Rathaus and ask for Lieutenant Fitzmaurice, he'll help you."

And so I got to know the unfamiliar small city better, whether I liked it or not. There really was a Lieutenant Fitzmaurice. After a brief dispute over my point of departure and destination we came to terms. He was visibly moved by my story that I was searching for my family in a concentration camp south of Dresden in order to take them home to Sweden. I got my permit. I'll never forget his final words:

"and don't forget to come back with your family via Rochlitz, you're my guests!"

(My conscience still bothers me for having lied so shamefully to this fair man. But war is war and other rules apply, especially when one's survival is at stake.)

A few minutes later I was back at the bridge. The guards greeted me like an old acquaintance and raised the bar. Seconds later I was on the other side. Mounted Russians met me. They greeted me cordially and took my permit. I was allowed to go on. I felt uneasy. What was going to happen to me now? But all went well at first. I soon got onto the autobahn leading to Dresden. Then there was a halt. At a blown bridge I had to go down into the valley, across a pontoon bridge, and up the other side. But there were Russian sentries there. They shouted for me to stop while I was still some distance away. There was a Swedish permit on my windshield requesting assistance in four languages, including Russian, so I suspected nothing untoward when they indicated to me that I was to drive to a nearby military camp accompanied by a guard for an inspection. The Russian soldier didn't get in, instead he stood on the right running board. He held onto the inside of the car door with his left hand, while with his right he waved a large revolver back and forth. He sang loudly to himself and obviously considered me his booty. He shouldn't have done that. We drove calmly along the autobahn toward Dresden for some time, then he gestured for me to turn onto a forest road. I had been waiting for this moment. Carefully I removed my 7.65 from the housing. The Russian wasn't watching me. I pointed the pistol at his left hand and pressed the trigger, at the same time turning the car sharply. He fell onto the roadway as if struck by a thunderbolt. I watched in the rear-view mirror as he slowly got to his feet, holding up his bloody left hand. (The beast in me had lashed out again. Perhaps the poor man is a cripple today. But it was him or me, that was the question then.) My pulse raced. Bathed in sweat I raced onwards, determined to defend my life at any price. The way to Dresden was clear, no more checks or blown bridges, only an occasional Russian panje wagon loaded with pigs, goats, and calves. When I turned off the autobahn I felt as if a great weight had been lifted from my shoulders. I was now only a half hour from Gohrisch. What might have taken place at home in the meantime? I was filled with worry. From Königstein I drove up into the Elbsandstein Mountains. I didn't go straight home, instead I drove through a small wood so as to approach unseen from the back side. One never knew! I waited until it was quite dark and then I saw them, my family, in the kitchen, healthy and cheerful, having supper. Maria from Kharkov was at the stove. She was the first to see me and at first thought I was a ghost when I came up the stairs. The whole family came out of the house. Father was back, he was alive!

". . . .He Who Casts the First Stone."

I have never spared myself. Often I ask myself: did I belong to a generation which became innocent murderers? One at whom men today point their fingers? Then I look far back into history. How many nations, peoples, and generations have raised and are raising men to be killers, right up to the present day?

"*Dulce et decorum est, pro patria mori?*"

Was it honourable to die for one's fatherland? It is a question to which only the hypocrites (and we have an endless supply of those) have an answer. In any case I have none. No, what I have described is not a story such as those taken from the Bible. It is the life story of a man who meant to give his best for the good of his nation. "Right or wrong, my country," where have I heard that before? Is this valid only for Great Britain in the Falklands or even in the Gulf? Have I told everything, described everything as I remember it? What have I forgotten? What have I changed? Where have I erred? Ought I to be ashamed of my past? Should I ask forgiveness? Am I guilty of having fought for something we would much rather forget about today, notions such as fatherland, home, and family, of having fought against criminal communism, bolshevism, stalinism? Do I even belong in the present where such values no longer seem to matter?

It almost seems to me as if our nation has been made responsible for every conflict on the globe. The nations of the world have long sought a beast of burden which they could strike at will, one ready to say thank you as it accepts each new burden, ready to pay for the guilt of others wherever it may be found.

Many might damn me, especially the "comrades" who sit about their tables after a few beers, still arguing about kills, and ex-Generals who still wish to be addressed as *Herr General* by their former subordinates. After a half century they've learned nothing and consider my conduct unworthy of a former officer. I, however, have no difficulty living with it.

In my opinion it is a case of a loss of a sense of reality, but especially of a consciousness of the past, true to Hegel's theory that all that one can learn from history is that one can't learn anything from history. But we who were in the front lines should know better than anyone that we must learn from the past. Is time really the enemy of truth?

In any case I can do nothing but ask the forgiveness of those upon whom I was once forced to inflict so much misery, especially the hospitable Russian people. Often I cannot sleep at night. They're always there before me: the heaps of bodies of those who starved to death in Kharkov, the hanged along the Sumskaya, the prisoners in the camp at Liubotin, the road labourers, the men slaughtered in Bucharest. I also think about the others with whom I had direct or indirect contact, those who were gassed, shot or tormented, Russians, Jews, and so on. God knows I have enough to answer for, but I can't undo what has been done. No one can. Forgive me sir, because I knew what I did? The workers' and farmers' paradise on earth, where is it, when is it coming? I have my doubts if it will ever come as long as there are men upon the earth. This account, my book, could only be a personal story, in which I have spared many of my former comrades in arms, avoiding things which might have been embarrassing to them. I have tried to wipe many from my memory because I am ashamed of them, otherwise they might yet be called to account for their actions. I do not consider out and out cowards to be worthy of mention. Dealing with the language of war and all its colloquialisms was somewhat more difficult. Yes, it was nothing more than a way of relieving our souls of their waste material. In doing so I have restrained myself somewhat, for after all this war was no eastern excursion by a mission school.

It is very strange, but today I receive letters from all over the world asking for autographs, and photos if possible. The letters come from the USA, Belgium, New Zealand and Australia, the CSSR, from Austria and Germany, of course, at least a dozen a month. What a strange world! We weren't actors, we were just soldiers with all their failings and weaknesses. I often ask myself: were there only "noble knights" on the other side. It's strange, but since the war I haven't met any, although I've seen a great deal of the world in the meantime.

The Epitome of Hypocrisy

There is a full measure of cynicism and impertinence attached to the recent dedication in London, by of all people the Queen Mother, of a monument honouring one of the greatest criminals of the war. The subject of this honour, the unscrupulous "Bomber Harris," was the man responsible for the deaths of more than one-million German women, children, and old people, killed in their homes, cellars, and in the streets of our cities by his policy of area bombing, burned alive, asphyxiated, or crushed beneath the rubble. Names such as Dresden, Cologne, Frankfurt, Wiesbaden, Hamburg, Bremen, Berlin, Pforzheim, Hannover, Lübeck, Freiburg, Darmstadt, Giessen, Trier, Mainz, Worms, Plauen, Würzburg, Potsdam, Bruchsal, and sixty other large, medium and small cities provide eloquent testimony to the vileness of the "Honourable" Sir Arthur Harris. As a colonial officer Harris is said to have played a macabre role in the war against the Kurds in the then British possession of Iraq, where the English used poison gas long before Saddam Hussein's mass murders of the same Kurds. Documents relating to Harris' "activities" were released recently from secret British archives, but were quickly withdrawn again in view of the dedication of his monument. The English Royal Family does not mention that 55,573 RAF personnel were killed carrying out Harris' policies.

I can't imagine a monument being erected today in Berlin to Rommel, the desert fox, who was killed on Hitler's order. And Rommel was an honourable man who destroyed no cities!

Seventy-two-year-old former bomber pilot Jeffrey Chapman recently wrote in "The Independent":
"During the pre-takeoff briefing prior to the raid against Dresden on February 13, 1945, Harris told us: 'Dresden is an old city with a great deal of wood. It will burn wonderfully and what is more we know that the city is packed with refugees from the East!' "
Harris was right, more than 150,000 people died agonizing deaths in Dresden, mostly women and children. Whole classes of school children were wiped out, thousands of charred corpses piled up on the sidewalks.

Chapman: "It is disgusting that this mass murderer is still respected for what he did."

When informed about Auschwitz by a Swiss informant and asked to bomb the rail lines and roads leading into the camp, Harris is supposed to have answered:

"The wiping out of German cities is my priority, not the fate of the Jews!"

The following anecdote is still told in RAF officers messes:

"A policeman stopped a speeding limousine in London. At the wheel was Harris. When told that he should slow down lest he kill someone, he said to the policeman with a smile: 'Man, I kill thousands of Germans every night.' "

The butcher died, unperturbed and incorrigible, at the age of 91, on April 5, 1984. One of his last quotes:

"No, I don't mourn for our enemies!"

I consider the notion that "fairness" was invented in England to be a rumour. But after a half century we intend to build a new Europe together, and there should be no more monuments for war heroes. However the portrait of "Butcher Harris" doesn't even belong in the British War Museum.

On February 14 I was in the mountains of Saxony, on my way home from Berlin to spend some time with my family. On the autobahn from Dresden I met thousands of women, children and elderly people, all going the other way. They were pushing the last of their belongings ahead of them in baby carriages, carts, and small wagons. I stopped, for I was surprised to encounter masses of pedestrians on the autobahn. Then I learned what had taken place in Dresden the night before. They described unbelievable events: Dresden was a pile of rubble, thousands had been burned alive in the streets and in their homes. I simply couldn't believe it, but the impression left by those bewildered people led me to suspect the worse. The scale of the terror bombing which been unleashed upon this former cultural centre the night before became more obvious as I neared Dresden. Whole blocks of houses were still blazing fiercely. The charred bodies in the streets and the painful cries for help from the cellars and collapsed houses caused the blood to freeze in my veins. I felt a rage, a feeling of hatred I had never felt before, rising in me as I steered my car through the smoking wreckage of houses. On my arrival at the railway station I was met by a scene which took my breath away. I thought I must be witnessing the apocalypse, the holocaust. Workmen were carrying in lifeless bodies and heaping them in huge piles. The first piles of bodies had already been set ablaze. I became ill at the sight. The sweet smell of decomposing flesh filled the entire city. Torn bodies of children hung in the trees in the English Gardens. Even Ghengis Khan in his day couldn't have murdered so terribly. A voice inside screamed at me to get away from this scene of horror. Tears choked my sadness. I'm not sure how I found my way out of the inferno which had once been called Dresden, I only knew that I had to get back to the front to extract a measure of revenge in my own way and that it would be merciless. An eye for an eye, a tooth for a tooth, so help me God!

"Do You Want To Kill Them?"

I was on my way back to Magdeburg with Ettinger, my driver. It was a beautiful March morning, so beautiful that one could easily have forgotten that we would soon have six years of war behind us. To the left and right of the autobahn, well-camouflaged in the forest, stood hundreds of Messerschmitt 109s and the new Me 262 jet fighters, ready to take off from the highway against the American and British bomber streams. I had just finished saying to Ettinger that I hoped they wouldn't come before we got off the autobahn, when we were stopped by military police and directed into a clearing.

"Bombers approaching Berlin," said one of the men, "It would be best if you drove your car deep into the forest, because on their way back from bombing Berlin the Ami escort fighters fly low over the autobahn and shoot up anything they find."

I felt rather silly, sneaking off into the forest in full uniform with all my decorations, but what wouldn't a man do to protect his own life, even if only for a few more days? So we rumbled down several forest roads and drove into a stand of juniper bushes. The Amis would never spot us here. Ettinger had just lit a cigarette when we heard a tremendous droning overhead. The first Messerschmitts lifted off from the autobahn and climbed toward the bomber formations. I was able to follow the events in the air very well through my binoculars. I estimated that the bombers, which streamed white contrails as they moved towards Berlin, were at about 4,000 metres and the fighters above at 5,000 metres. The Me 262s soon closed with the Flying Fortresss and opened fire. A B-17 caught fire and sheared out of formation. I counted eight parachutes emerging from the machine. Everything happened directly above us.

"If I'm not mistaken," I said to Ettinger, "They're going to come down right on top of us."

My suspicion proved correct. The round, white parachutes came down at a considerable speed and a few seconds later landed not far away in a clearing surrounded by pine trees. I shouted to them loudly:

"Come here, we'll help you!"

But they fled before us as if they had been stung by a spider. We couldn't follow so quickly and the Americans had soon disappeared from our view into the dense forest. I was sure of one thing: they wouldn't get far. The surrounding area was densely populated and I was sure the Volkssturm would round them up before long. So we walked back to the car and waited for what was to happen, for the bomber stream was still heading for Berlin. A good hour passed. I slowly grew tired of this standing about. We readied the car and drove slowly along a forest road in the direction of Löttgenziatz. When we emerged from the forest I couldn't believe my eyes. A few hundred metres in front of us there was a gathering of people. In the middle were two of the Americans whom we had seen bail out. Several people were in the process of tying them to a tree in order to shoot them. Shouting loudly, I jumped from my car and walked up to an *Unteroffizier* of the military police and two Volkssturm men, who were obviously intending to shoot the pair.

"Are you out of your mind!" I shouted at the fellow, "are you about to execute these two? They're prisoners of war and as of this moment are under my protection."

The mob pulled back a little. At first the *Unteroffizier* didn't know how to react and stared helplessly into the crowd. I ordered an older *Volkssturm* man to bring the two Americans to me. As I suspected, they were two of the eight we had seen come down earlier. Both were deathly pale and their blue flight suits hung in tatters. One of the pair introduced himself as William Woulters, the other's name was Mark McLean. They were obviously overjoyed that I had appeared on the scene at the last moment.

"Where are the other six?" I asked the taller of the two.

"I don't know," he replied, "We got separated in the woods."

The crowd around us grew larger by the minute. Several women heaped abuse on the Americans and were of the view that they ought to be hanged from the nearest tree. Then a party man, probably an *Ortsgruppenleiter* (local party branch leader), came up to us and said:

"There is a directive from the Ministry of the Interior which says that all captured enemy airmen are to be taken into custody and handed over to the nearest police station."

"You're right," I added, "But there's no mention of killing them."

We soon agreed that the local branch leader would now take charge of the Amis and that we would take them to Mäckern in my car. The two squatted behind me on the drive to the police station, watched over by the "golden pheasant." When we climbed out one of the Americans gave me a letter to his parents and asked that I inform them that he had been taken prisoner. Unfortunately I was unable to do him this small favour, for on my arrival in Berlin I found our house in flames. During my efforts to extinguish the blaze my uniform jacket, which I had removed, was burned up together with the envelope when the roof collapsed. Sorry! Perhaps Mr. Woulters or Mr. McLean is still living in the USA; God willing they might someday read my book. "All the best to you and a long, long life in the midst of your family."

What of the UN?

Since 1945 until the present day there have been more than 200 wars on this globe of ours, including those still being fought, some of them at our front door. These have cost more human lives than the First and Second World Wars combined and there is no end in sight in spite of the United Nations. Its 12,000 bureaucrats, who receive handsome salaries from our taxes, have been unable to prevent a single one of these conflicts. Efforts by the European Community have been equally ineffective. While the organisation's foreign minister hides behind empty threats, in the former Yugoslavia hundreds and thousands are being killed, millions are being put to flight, and centuries-old monuments are being destroyed forever. It's also a disgrace for this organisation. There's said to be more than 16,000 of them, helping themselves in Brussels, Luxembourg, and Strasbourg, paid with our money! Gone are the days of using force to maintain the status quo in the struggle of peoples for self-determination. Palestine? Israel? Azerbaidzhan? Armenia? South Africa? Cambodia? Yugoslavia? The blue helmets were supposed to clean up the conflict in Yugoslavia. Instead they fled under fire with their headquarters from the people's army, leaving the inhabitants of Sarajevo to their fate instead of seizing the reins and hitting the Serbs hard. The United Nations? It is what it has always been: a symbolic world organisation. The perversions we are witnessing today are only the beginning. We haven't seen anything yet.

. . . .No, I'm Not Going To Canossa

If there is a supreme judge, and after all I've lived through I might be forgiven for having my doubts, I will nevertheless bow to his judgement, bravely and calmly. What was it that a certain Martin Luther had said at the Diet of Worms?
:
"Here I stand, I can do nothing else, God help me! Amen"
My credo for these dreadful, unhappy, privation-filled years?
"Stranger, come to Germany, say that you have seen us fight and die as ordered by the law!"
"*De mortuis nihil nisi bene?*" Where have I read similar things in history?
It is curious that only among the victors do the brave enjoy fame and honour, among the defeated they are branded as criminals. There are countless examples of this, especially in our own land.

Sequel

The fate which I had tried so hard to avoid had caught up with me: captivity. I wanted to spare my wife and four small children the worst. They were in the middle of Soviet-occupied Saxony, not far from Königstein. Until now my family and our small house had been spared by the plundering hordes of the Red Army thanks to Maria from Kharkov, who defended us like a she-lion. But it was our dear neighbours, the ones we had helped in the difficult years of the shortages, who finally alerted the Soviet commandant to the presence of the "Nazi" up in Gohrisch. One night I was awakened by Maria.

"Sir, you must get away from here. In a few hours the Soviet commandant intends to search the house and take you away as a prisoner of war. Flee as quickly as you can, God be with you!"

It was a good thing that my wife had prepared for just such an eventuality . Not far from the house she had hidden a small car containing all the necessities, such as a Swedish passport, a Swedish letter of safe conduct (in five languages, including Russian), the necessary papers for the car, and so on.

I bade my wife a hurried farewell, the children were still sound asleep. Moments later I drove off into the night; many more were to pass before I saw my family again. At dawn, on the autobahn just outside Dresden, I became entangled in a column of Soviet tanks which I was unable to get free of until Leipzig. There was a T 34 in front of me and another behind me. Turning off the autobahn or passing was out of the question. The soldiers were friendly, tossing bread and sausage to me from the open hatches, what more could I want? Not until we had passed Leipzig was I free of this plague. My objective was to reach Elbingerode, where I hoped to find shelter with a family I knew while I surveyed the lay of the land, and to put the boundary between the British and Soviet zones of occupation behind me as quickly as possible. I hoped my Swedish passport would enable me to do that. I finally reached my destination at about noon, but the Schwarz family was no more. The father and mother and their two small girls had been killed by strafing American fighters a few days before the end of the war. They had been out in the open and the American fighters had shot them down as if for fun. I was dismayed. There was nothing that could keep me in this city and so I drove towards the demarcation line. Over and over I told myself:

"You can't let yourself be taken prisoner by the Soviets."

I was only a few metres from the narrow strip of land separating the two zones when I was stopped by Soviet soldiers. They checked my passport and the papers for the car, but I was soon forced to realise that they were illiterate and couldn't even read the information in Russian on the placard on my car. It was obvious that I wasn't getting through. Instead they impounded my car, sat down beside me, and directed me to drive to Wernigerode. In front of a school building they told me to get out and follow them. They shoved me into a first-floor classroom which had been converted into an office. A tall NKVD officer wearing a green cap gestured for me to sit down. All was quiet in the large room for some time. He studied my papers and then began to speak in fluent German:

"Wouldn't it be better if you just admitted that you're a Nazi criminal? That would spare both you and I a great deal of trouble."

I looked at him uncomprehendingly for some time, then shrugged my shoulders and shook my head. I answered first in Swedish, then in English. He was taken aback at first, but then he shouted something into the adjoining room. In walked a broad-hipped woman in Soviet uniform, presumably an interpreter. She spoke no Swedish but her English was quite good. Then there began a dialogue which I will never forget:

"Just how did you get into the Soviet-occupied zone? It's quite unlikely with your Swedish papers. How and when did you arrive here, and from where?" she droned at me loudly.

"I was officially handed over from the Americans to Russian troops near Rochlitz, on the Mulde. They allowed me to continue my journey after I convinced them that I was searching for my family," I replied firmly but amicably.

"How many children do you have?" she asked, having become curious. When I pulled a photo from out of my jacket pocket showing my family nestled about me, the ice was broken. Then the tall Soviet Lieutenant interrupted our conversation and began a long palaver with the woman in Russian. I couldn't understand what they were saying, but it soon became obvious that I wasn't going to escape the clutches of the NKVD for some time. The Lieutenant called in the two guards and without ceremony I was pushed down the stairs and locked up in a wash-room in the cellar. The guard in charge slammed the door behind me, a key turned twice in the lock and I was alone. I had hidden half a razor blade in the cuff of my pants, so that if everything went wrong I could slit an artery. But I was still a long way from that point!

I had been a "suspect guest" of the NKVD for more than two weeks now. The night seemed endless. I tossed and turned on the bare cement floor. My back was already sore. All my attempts to speak to the Lieutenant on the first floor were rejected by the guard in charge. Perhaps he didn't know what I wanted, although my neighbours in the next cell, all Russians, with whom I had made contact and one of whom spoke some English, tried to explain it to him. The tap in the cell next to me dripped incessantly, almost driving me mad. My next-door neighbour had been a forced-labourer in Germany. He had been beaten that morning and had not yet regained consciousness. It had been like this for days. The tall Lieutenant was trying to get him to admit that he had worked with the Germans as a collaborator. He had been employed near Nordhausen building Me 262 aircraft in the underground tunnel installations. Through a narrow crack in the boards of the wall I could see that his head was a blood-encrusted mass. His left arm appeared to be broken and hung motionless from the rusted bed frame onto which they had tossed the poor unfortunate. The beast with the green cap worked with his fists until he thought he wasn't getting anywhere, then he turned to his pistol. Only the day before I had watched from my basement window as four more Russian "collaborators" were shot in the schoolyard. Two of those shot were Polish Jews who had just been released from the Buchenwald concentration camp and who had been picked up trying to cross illegally into the British zone. (The names of the two have been burned into my memory: Lippschitz and Baruch.) The victim was first hung from a brick wall with chains, then the NKVD officer drew his pistol and shot him in the forehead from close range. The skullcap burst into a thousand small pieces and brains, mixed with blood, sprayed against the brick wall. I had counted 23 executions to this point. Still twitching, the body was tossed onto a truck and driven away to be buried in a mass grave, of which the "heroic Red Army" has left us so many.

It was then that I realised for the first time why I had risked my life in the fight against bolshevism. The recently-discovered mass graves in the former East Germany, which contain victims of the NKVD (later the KGB), hundreds of thousands of civilians, even children, give shocking evidence of the crimes committed against our fellow Germans in the name of the "farmers' and workers' paradise."

Names like Sachsenhausen, Buchenwald, Fünfeichen, Mühlberg, Jamlitz, Ketschendorf, Torgau, Weesow, and many others still speak a terrible language. In Sachsenhausen alone more than 45,000 out of 60,000 internees were brutally murdered by the NKVD in the period from 1945 to 1950. Similar crimes are believed to have occurred in the other camps. All of the mass graves haven't even been discovered yet!

I had lost track of what day it was when a guard fetched me from the washroom and prodded me upstairs at the point of a bayonet. The tall Lieutenant (whose name was Vassili Cribachov, by the way) greeted me with a wolfish grin. The female interpreter was at his side.

"You will now be taken to our central office where they will convince you that you are a nazi criminal."

He turned around. Two guards took me by the arms and led me to my own car, which I was allowed to drive into the centre of the city of Wenigerode. I was told to stop in front of a sumptuous villa, my hands were tied, and I was led inside. Several officers, all wearing green caps, were waiting for me in a large room, as well as a female interpreter who spoke perfect English. I was forced to sit and there now began a five-hour question and answer period always with the same theme, why, how, where, when, and so on and so on. At first I was worried that the NKVD criminals might wear me down, but after I realised that they had no evidence against me I gained ground hour by hour. When I kept demanding to be handed over to the Swedish Consulate-General in Leipzig they gave up. Their attitude changed abruptly. I was cordially invited to have a glass of tea, was given back all my personal things, even the cigarettes I had on me when I tried unsuccessfully to cross the border, and an hour later was released. My car, however, had been requisitioned and I had no other choice but to set out on foot for the train station carrying my few belongings. There I bought a third-class ticket to Oschersleben. I would have to be careful if I wasn't to fall into the hands of that criminal organisation again. Not far from that small city on the Bode there was supposed to be a pressed-coal factory on the Soviet side and on the English side the associated brown coal pit. It should be relatively easy to slip into the English pit under one of the cars. This information was provided to me by a friendly conductor whom I trusted. The name of engineer in the pit was Adler. Would luck be with me? But what did "relatively easy" mean?

"You may only approach the pressed-coal factory at midnight. The Russians will be sleeping then and Adler can stow his 'guest' in one of the empty cars for the trip to the English pit." In closing my guardian angel said, "You can't take any baggage with you. You'll be lying under the car on a narrow iron girder, and you'll have to hang on to it tightly. Engineer Adler takes nothing for his help, but he'll look after your things until you look him up some day. No one will pay you any mind when you reach the open pit mine on the English side. The Tommies pay it little mind. God be with you!"

FINAL NOTES

Half a century has passed in our land and once again I must search the contents of my consciousness and ask myself about my service at the front, especially during the Defence of the Reich. What did I really feel? Had I been conscious of the fate of those far below, facing the bombing war in their cities, houses and cellars? Did I consider that at 7,000 metres, did I draw from it the motivation for my own actions? What actually moved me in those days, squeezed into my tiny cockpit, high above the earth where details are invisible and where the usual scales of perception become irrelevant? Yes, in the beginning I felt my knees shaking, the pitiless fear of the unknown, fear of what was to come, fear that I might be killed. But then there arose in me that strange, almost perverse mixture of emotions, of which one can't deny a certain innocence, at least as it's perceived today. I was overwhelmed by a drive and desire to destroy the enemy, but especially to shoot down the bombers which I saw purely as objects and not consciously as the carriers of destruction. They were just containers of aluminum and plexiglass in which sat hostile, unhuman bodies, worthy only of destruction. It was as if it was an exceptionally demanding sport which made such great demands on one's intellect and concentration that it seemed as if nothing else existed. And yet at the same time there registered in a quite different level of my consciousness the optical phenomenon of atmospherics, as if from another star, without analysis, without regard to reality. The fires far below looked like the glowing coals in a blacksmith's fire, the rising tracer like glistening pearls which climbed into the sky in strings and which finally dimmed and were extinguished in the clouds like a breath slowly dying away. But the grim contents of this devilish, overpowering magic seemed hidden to rational consciousness. Was it the overfilling of reasoning by the aerial task at hand which left no room for anything else? Or was it the immaturity of my youthful understanding, which evaluated only the immediate, that which lay right before me, and that what it wanted to see or was forced to see? It wasn't until many years after the end of the war, when I learned of the thousands of people who had been killed in Dresden alone, that I began to comprehend fully the frightful, human dimension of this immense misery, collectively and as the fate of individuals. Only then was I struck by the horror of the event, but also by the fact that at the time I had shut it out of my mind as a matter of course, as if my responsibility, including that of my heart, was limited to altitudes between 3,000 and 9,000 metres. But then I gave the matter more thought: were not many calamities made possible only when men closed their consciousness to everything, to the possibilities? It became clear to me that the pressures were much more difficult to bear for those who were older at the time, those who knew what was happening and who had more to lose, than for we younger ones, who rarely thought any farther than that which touched us immediately. However the older ones, those who not only had the present with them but the past as well, and who knew what the future held, they hoped and worried. How must they have suffered, suffered for their fellow men as well whose distress they understood, unlike us. In contrast how small was my world then. As a pilot I rarely saw death, I only heard of it. The dying occurred somewhere else, whether in burning Berlin or Hamburg or Dresden, or on Red Cross ships carrying thousands of refugees which were sunk in the Baltic by Russian submarines. Ignorance can be more gracious, also more human, than the awareness of calamity. Oh God, where were you then? I could so have used you!